W9-BIQ-468

Reading and Growing

by Wilbert J. Levy

Chairman, English Department
Newtown High School, New York City

Dedicated to serving

AMSCO

our nation's youth

When ordering this book, please specify:
either N 392 P or READING AND GROWING

AMSCO SCHOOL PUBLICATIONS, INC.
315 Hudson Street   New York, N.Y. 10013

ISBN 0–87720–328–8

Printed in the United States of America

Preface

The central aim of READING AND GROWING is to foster language power growth.

The book is designed around relatively short, interesting reading passages as centers of learning. The passages are selected for their richness in content, theme, and language.

From these centers, the book reaches out to develop insight, understanding, and grasp in virtually every facet and level of language.

Broadly, the student is stimulated towards growth in reading comprehension, appreciation, and interpretation. He is guided towards extended personal response in thinking, discussing, and writing.

More concretely, the student is brought into meaningful confrontation with the whole gamut of language and literary skills. He is taught to understand elements of sentence composition and style and to improve his own. He is taught vocabulary functionally and introduced to many nuances of word meaning. He is taught such operations of language as humor, mood creation, imagery, simile, metaphor, symbolism, allusion, quotation, diction.

The method of the book emphasizes the humanistic, the functional, and the vital. To revive and revise an old but still meritorious precept, the book, through its exercises, emphasizes learning through guided doing.

W.J.L.

Contents

Begin here . . .

Read the following sentences and give their meaning.

Это кни́га? Да, э́то кни́га.

What! you cannot? Why, a seven year old can do it.

Yes, a seven year old can do it—provided, of course, that he is a seven year old who has grown up in Russia. Looking at the sentence, a Russian child would see the same meaning as you do when you look at the following sentences.

Is this a book? Yes, it is a book.

From this example, you can see that the first step in the all-important skill of reading is the basic recognition of letters and the familiar words into which they are shaped.

You can also see that this first step is an enormous step, almost a miracle. When you look at the Russian letters and words, all you see is black marks on the page. When you look at the familiar English letters and words, they speak to your mind! You see meaning!

The first step in the skill of reading is a big and marvelous step. However, there are many big additional steps to be taken beyond the first one. Reading ability runs way beyond the recognition of letters and a few familiar words.

At your age and stage of experience, you have already taken quite a few steps in reading growth beyond the first one. However, improvement in one's reading ability can and should continue without end. The purpose of this book is to help you take steps towards a sharply advanced level of reading ability. Suppose we compare a little toddler learning to take his first steps as a walker to a reader learning to take the first steps as a reader. Then, in your work with this book, we can compare you to a track-team member training to run a four-minute mile.

There are twenty lessons in READING AND GROWING. Each unit of five reading selections and lessons is followed by a section called GROWING. The GROWING exercises will review, enrich, and extend all you have learned in the preceding five lessons. Here is some helpful explanation of the main sections and exercises of each lesson and of GROWING.

Reading

READING SELECTION

Each lesson begins with a short reading selection. Although these selections vary in many ways, they all have one thing in common. They all deal with one of the most interesting and important periods of life—the growing years, the years of childhood and adolescence. Therefore, you and every reader will find personal meaning in them. You will be familiar with the particular pleasures and pains, the particular problems and satisfactions that go with the growing years. If you read the passages thoughtfully, you will learn something about yourself and the ways in which you are like other people and the ways in which you may be different from them. By being *personally involved* in this way in your reading of the passage, you will read with enjoyment. You will also read with profit, for there is no better way to become a better reader than by reading widely with enjoyment. You can and should go further by using these brief reading selections as a stepping-stone to additional reading. In some cases, you may want to read the rest of the story or book from which the selection comes. You may wish to read other works by the same author. You may wish to read other books of a similar type or on a similar theme. Remember that ever-widening reading with enjoyment is not only deeply satisfying in itself, but is also the surest path to reading growth and personal growth.

2

READING COMPREHENSION

Each reading selection is followed by a number of multiple-choice reading comprehension exercises. The purpose of these exercises is to train you in the use and application of important, specific reading techniques. As a result of the training, you will learn to put these techniques into operation automatically and habitually. Your total effectiveness as a reader will develop noticeably. It is important that you bear the following key suggestions in mind as you work with the reading comprehension exercises.

1. Think of the exercises as a means towards learning, *not as tests*. The way in which you thoughtfully decide on which choice is best and which are not so good is more important than whether or not you come up with the "right" answer. The person who calmly and carefully reexamines the reading selection as necessary and who deliberately tries to reason out the relative merit of each choice will learn far more from doing these exercises than the person who anxiously gropes for and worries about getting the most "right" answers. For instance, if you clearly recognize why one or two choices should be rejected, you are achieving important growth in reading even if your final choice is not the best one.

2. The exercises are designed to give you various kinds of training in reading comprehension. In some cases, the question is based on information or ideas that are stated directly, in so many words, in the reading selection. In some cases, the question is based on information or ideas that do not appear directly in the text, but that are indirectly suggested in some definite way. In some cases, the question calls for the best judgment or interpretation of material in the reading selection. All three of these types of exercise are important in effective reading.

3. In working with the exercises, be sure to read the opening statement of the question carefully so that you know exactly what it is that you are looking for. To take an obvious example, the opening statement may be: *Which of the following*

is NOT mentioned as a cause of conflict between the two brothers? The best answer that you are looking for will then be the choice that does *not* agree with the reading selection. In a question of this type, you can see it is especially important that you thoughtfully check all of the choices against the reading selection.

4. Remember, in arriving at a decision, that you are looking for the *best* choice of those given. This often requires a different kind of thinking and judgment from solving a problem to which there is only one absolutely right answer, such as how do you spell *cat* or how much is 2 X 2.

LITERARY AND LANGUAGE SKILLS

At the highest levels of reading comprehension and appreciation, one has an understanding of the many elements that go into the skillful use of language to express meaning. The exercises in this section vary in form and content but they all have the common purpose of teaching you something about such literary and language skills as humor, allusion, metaphor, writing style, and the art of sentence composition, and thus helping to bring you to the highest level of reading ability. You will find a great deal of enjoyment in these exercises as you see yourself easily acquiring from them new and fascinating understanding about the inner and important workings of written language. As an extra bonus, these exercises will also help you to become a better writer!

VOCABULARY IN CONTEXT

Words are the basic building blocks of reading, and the person whose vocabulary is rich will be a better reader. Most of the words that a person knows, he learns naturally and without effort. However, one cannot depend only on the vocabulary one acquires almost unconsciously from the normal listening and speaking activities of everyday living or even from the still broader vocabulary that almost automatically comes with wide reading. Everyone

4

should supplement his naturally acquired vocabulary by deliberately learning some of the new words he comes across daily. The
purpose of these exercises is to help you in this planned vocabulary
growth.

You will find exercises carefully designed to take you through
two steps in the learning of five vocabulary words occurring in the
reading selection. You will not be learning any of these words
"in a vacuum." You will be learning them in a natural setting
(context). You will not only be learning the words, you will at
the same time be learning how to learn words. Here are some
explanations and suggestions to help you work profitably with
these exercises.

Exercise A

We often get a fair idea of the meaning of a word from the way
it is used in the context of a sentence or paragraph. This is the
first level of knowing the meaning of a word. This exercise asks
you, as a beginning, to examine the context in which the word
occurs and try to arrive at the first level of knowing the meaning
of the word—having a fair idea of its meaning from experiencing it
in use.

The *second level* of knowing the meaning of a word is being
able to give a specific definition of its meaning. This exercise helps
you to move on to the second level of the meaning of a word by
offering you four definitions as possible choices, from which you
are asked to select the best definition. By using your *first level*
knowledge of the meaning of the word, you will easily be able to
select the best definition from the four offered and thus arrive at
the *second level* of vocabulary knowledge.

Exercise B

The *third level* of knowing the meaning of a word is being able
to use it easily and comfortably yourself. The purpose of this

exercise is to move you towards the third level of knowing the meaning of the vocabulary words of the lesson. You are given new sentence contexts from which one word is omitted in each. You are asked to decide which one of the vocabulary words fits into each sentence. This simple exercise will review and reinforce your first and second level knowledge and will give you initial practice in handling the word yourself.

Growing

This book is called READING AND GROWING. The word GROWING in the title applies in three ways. First, the reading selections that form the core of the book are all about the "growing" years. Second, the book aims to help your own growing towards higher levels of reading ability. Third, the book aims to help your growing as a human being, to your becoming a "bigger" person, with greater understanding of yourself and others. The four sections called GROWING will especially help you to reach the latter two aims. Here is a helpful word of explanation about each part of GROWING.

VOCABULARY IN CONTEXT

Every word has a rich variety of possible uses in building a meaning, just as a brick can be used in a variety of ways as part of a structure, or a given dab of pigment as part of a painting. (For example, you will be amazed at what you will learn in one of the lessons about the many uses and meanings the simple word *and* can have.) Awareness of the variety of possibilities in the meaning of a word is the *fourth* level of vocabulary knowledge. The GROWING sections will develop your knowledge of the words you have learned at the fourth level, through a variety of interesting exercises.

Of these, verbal analogies are one kind of problem you will be asked to work with. Analogies can be challenging, but once you get the hang of them, you will find them fun to tackle. Here is a little help to begin with.

Suppose, for example, that you learn that the word *amenities* means "polite practices." Here is an analogy problem.

amenities : gentleman

> *a.* coordination : acrobat
> *b.* thank you : please
> *c.* makeup : lady
> *d.* uniform : costume

First, you decide what the relationship between the given pair of words is. If *amenities* means "polite practices," then amenities are a kind of behavior, or a characteristic that is very important to being a gentleman. The relationship, then, is a characteristic important to being a certain kind of person. The only pair of words among the choices that has a similar relationship is *coordination : acrobat*, for coordination is a characteristic of an acrobat.

In solving analogy problems, you must remember to think of the *relationship* between the given words, not just their separate meanings. Among the important kinds of relationship (and an example of each) are—

thing : characteristic	(amenities : gentleman)
whole thing : part	(horse : mane)
thing : use	(pencil : writing)
cause : effect	(overwork : fatigue)
oppositeness	(hot : cold)
sameness	(ancient : old)
difference of degree	(warm : hot)

LITERARY AND LANGUAGE SKILLS

These exercises will review and extend what you have learned in the lessons. You will gain very specific know-how that will enable you to understand and appreciate sentences (and the literary and language skills that go into them) such as the following:

7

It was as if everything were looking at me with such matter-of-factness and such untroubled conscience, the town and the church tower, the fields and the path, the flowering grass and the butterflies, and as if everything pretty and pleasurable, everything that usually gave me delight, were now alien and under an evil spell.

—Hermann Hesse

The Montana sunset lay between two mountains like a gigantic bruise from which dark arteries spread themselves over a poisoned sky.

—F. Scott Fitzgerald

THEMES FOR GROWING

Which is the best part of life—childhood, youth, maturity? What are some of the "games people play"? Why do they do so? Who has a better start in life, a very rich child or a poor child? Or does it matter? These are examples of some of the important life problems and questions that come up in the reading selections, questions that almost every person faces at one stage or another as he attempts to deal with himself, with others, and with society in the course of growing.

In this final part of each GROWING section you are asked to "get it all together" by giving your own reactions, opinions, and judgments concerning these life questions. You are asked to express yourself at three levels: thinking privately, discussing, writing.

UNIT ONE

(Reading 1-5)

READING 1

*In legendary Greece, there lived a cruel robber named Pro-
crustes. He kept a wayside inn, where the unwary traveler
was put up for the night in an iron bed. One bed did not
exactly fit all the travelers; so Procrustes made them fit the*
5   *bed. If they were too tall, he cut off their feet; if they were
too short, he stretched them. Procrustes insisted upon
conformity.*

    Sometimes a teen-ager feels that everyone—her parents, her
school, her community—is trying to squeeze her into a Pro-
10   crustean bed. Sometimes she is her own Procrustes, so caught
up in thinking and doing what is expected of her that she
fails to consider her own wants and needs. Individualism
versus conformity is not just a teen-age problem, but it is a
problem particularly troublesome to teen-agers. When to—
15   and when not to—go along with the crowd, when to protest
an order that seems unjust, follow tradition or buck the system are important decisions. The balance you strike between
conformity and individualism is crucial to the way you grow
up and the kind of adult you will become.
20   In a number of situations, conformity is useful and necessary. Obeying rules is our payment for the convenience of
living among other people in relative safety and comfort.

Traffic regulations are necessary for efficient travel, rules of grammar permit effective communication, laws of property allow us to live in harmony with our neighbors. 25

Following custom often simplifies daily living. Etiquette, for example, facilitates social life. If you decided to be completely individualistic about your table manners, you would be faced with a half-dozen decisions every time you sat down to dinner. When you've spent a weekend with relatives, you 30 know that a bread-and-butter note will fulfill your obligation to everyone's satisfaction. The customary amenities make for smooth social situations.

Observing convention makes us feel secure. Conventional morality, which grows out of general sociological needs, is 35 aimed at achieving the greatest good for the greatest number of people. Conventional behavior is the way things are done by most of the people most of the time. Obviously, conventions change as "the old order changeth, yielding place to new." But following familiar patterns not only frees us from 40 constant decision-making, it also provides us with a feeling of well-being.

Conformity, therefore, is useful in its place. What is diminishing to a personality and dangerous to a society is *thoughtless* conformity: squeezing into a slot that is not your size; 45 blindly obeying foolish rules; mechanically following customs when the situation calls for a sincere expression of feeling; accepting conventions that are no longer relevant; sticking to habits that are no longer satisfying.

Do you know an overconformist? She's the girl whose 50 mind is made up as soon as she knows what others are thinking. Her principal reason for doing things is that "that's the way things are done."

Eventually, she loses contact with her own thoughts and feelings. It becomes impossible for her to act spontaneously. 55 Unless there are people to tell her what to think or feel, she feels empty, indecisive and dissatisfied with life.

The underconformist *seems* to be her opposite. To her,

the majority is always wrong. If bell-bottoms are the word,
60 she'll parade herself in a party dress. If all the girls are Sean
Connery fans, she can't bear him. She is the standout in any
group, the hold-out in any project. Yet, in latching onto
unpopular people and unpopular causes (regardless of their
merit), the underconformist is no more spontaneous or ra-
65 tional than the overconformist. She, too, is overly influenced
by her surroundings; only her reaction is reversed.

The girl who conforms rationally knows who she is and
what she really wants. She can enjoy trying out new fads and
fashions but can also stop short at those that she *knows* are
70 unbecoming to her. She can go along with group attitudes in
matters where her sense of integrity is not challenged, but
she also feels free to express dissent either by arguing or going her own way. She chooses her friends, her clothes, her
clubs, her hobbies, her opinions *on their merits* rather than
75 blindly following or rebelling against other people's choices.

The self-image of a girl in her teens is likely to be tenta-
tive, experimental, transient. In trying on attitudes, interests
and even personalities for size, she can hardly avoid following
others. She tends to be attracted—or repelled—by many out-
80 side influences, some of them so different from one another
that she may occasionally feel like a chameleon—taking on
the color of whatever environment she happens to be in at
the moment.

During the teen years the weight of parental authority usu-
85 ally diminishes, and the influence of friends and schoolmates
increases. When this shift in loyalty occurs, some girls react
by rejecting wholesale the attitudes and values of their parents. If Mother says it's good, it's got to be bad. If the
crowd says it's right, right it is. Wholesale rebellion against
90 parents may seem to be the height of individuality, but it's
often the opposite. The mature individual sees her parents—
and her friends—as neither heroes nor villains, but as real
people. How much they influence her is based on her choice,
not compulsive conformity or compulsive rebellion.

12

You'd probably be surprised at an objective assessment of 95
how much your behavior is affected by a desire to fit in with
your group of friends. If your group is one that maintains a
sound balance between independence and conformity, you're
lucky. Some teen groups, however, specialize in rebellion
against anything that has the approval of the adult world. 100
Caught up in such a crowd, you're likely to become a conforming nonconformist and to miss out on the questioning
and thinking-through that is an important part of discovering
yourself.

Reading Comprehension

The exercises that follow are based on the passage you have just
read. Each exercise consists of an incomplete statement or a question followed by four choices. Select the choice that best completes the statement or best answers the question. Go back to the
passage for rereading to whatever extent is necessary to help you
choose your answer.

1. The entire passage deals with the basic teen-age problem of
    a. individualism versus conformity.
    b. the generation gap.
    c. rebellion for the sake of rebellion.
    d. loneliness.

2. Which statement about Procrustes is NOT made?
    a. He was a robber.
    b. Outwardly, he was gentle and kind.
    c. He is a character from Greek legend.
    d. He was an innkeeper.

3. The authors mention "rules of grammar" as an example of
    a. a difficult teen-age problem.
    b. hampering individualism.
    c. mature behavior.
    d. useful conformity.

4. The general attitude of the authors towards etiquette is one of
   a. approval.
   b. disapproval.
   c. neutrality.
   d. approval in some instances, disapproval in others.

5. Which statement about conventional morality is NOT made?
   a. Conventional morality is based on a set of artificial but helpful rules.
   b. Conventional morality undergoes change.
   c. Conventional morality is intended to serve the greatest good for the greatest number of people.
   d. Following conventional morality provides people with a feeling of well-being.

6. An overconformist may tend to
   a. act too spontaneously.
   b. make up her mind without consulting others.
   c. be successful and popular.
   d. feel empty and unhappy if left on her own.

7. The underconformist generally is
   a. too easily influenced by her surroundings.
   b. characterized by a preference for party dresses.
   c. an unpopular person.
   d. spontaneous and rational.

8. The word *seems* (line 58) is printed in italics because the authors wish to
   a. emphasize the difference between the overconformist and the underconformist.
   b. show that there may be exceptions to every rule.
   c. make it plain that they are expressing an opinion, not a fact.
   d. suggest that appearances, in this instance, are deceptive.

9. The best description of the phrase "conforming nonconformist" (lines 101–102) is that it

a. sums up the well-balanced personality.

b. doesn't make sense.

c. refers to the person who rebels automatically against the adult world just for the sake of rebellion.

d. brings out the inner conflict of the insecure teen-ager.

10. The best statement of the most important recommendation made in the passage is

a. the opinions of parents merit respect.

b. choices and decisions should be based on the merits of each case.

c. don't do as the group does.

d. it is better to change than to be consistent.

Literary and Language Skills

ALLUSIONS

A writer may express himself by using the name of a person, place, or event taken from well-known or important stories. The use of such a name is called *allusion*. In this passage, the author's reference to the "bed of Procrustes" is an allusion. Through allusions, writers can express thought or feeling briefly and colorfully. Of course, a reader must be familiar with the name used in order to understand an allusion. The authors of this passage have helped their readers by explaining "Procrustean bed" in an introductory note, but usually the reader is expected to understand the allusion without such help.

Below are ten names often used as allusions. Study the names and the accompanying explanations.

Achilles' heel

Achilles was the Greek warrior-hero of Homer's *Iliad*. As an infant he was dipped into the river Styx by his mother. The waters would make him invulnerable, safe from wounds or hurts. The waters washed every part of

Achilles' body except the heel by which his mother held him. Eventually, it was on this one weak spot that Achilles was wounded fatally.

Amazon

The Amazons were a mythical race of strong, athletic female warriors.

Argus-eyed

Argus was a monster with 100 eyes, some of which were always open. He served the gods as a watchman.

Babbit

Babbit is the main character in a book by the American novelist, Sinclair Lewis. All his interests and beliefs are shaped by the business world of which he is a part. His life is hollow and pointless, though he tries to believe otherwise.

Cassandra

The god Apollo gave to Cassandra the gift of foreseeing the future. She prophesied doom and calamity, but no one believed her.

Damon and Pythias

Damon and Pythias were devoted, inseparable friends. Each was ready to give up his life for the other.

Pandora's box

Pandora, in Greek mythology, was the first woman. Every god gave her a gift. Zeus, who was angry with mankind, gave her a box which she was warned not to open. Unable to curb her curiosity, she did, and let loose all the evils and troubles that plague mankind.

Scylla and Charybdis

Scylla and Charybdis were monsters that preyed upon ships and their crews attempting to pass through a narrow strait between them. If the sailors attempted to avoid the one, they were almost sure to come too close to the other.

Shangri-la

In the novel *Lost Horizon* by James Hilton, Shangri-la is a kind of earthly paradise, where there is no illness, aging, war, or poverty.

Sherlock Holmes

Sherlock Holmes, created by Arthur Conan Doyle, is the greatest detective of fiction. He was masterful at observing and interpreting clues that would escape anyone else. He solved many difficult and puzzling crimes.

Exercise A

Can you apply your knowledge of these allusions? Select the one allusion that is most appropriate to each of the following five cases.

1. A famous ecologist warns that pollution will destroy life on earth unless preventive measures are taken. No one listens to her.

2. The curiosity of scientists about the structure of the atom has given man the atomic bomb.

3. A white football star, Brian Piccolo, and a black football star, Gayle Sayres, were roommates and inseparable friends. After Brian died of a serious illness, Gayle wrote a book telling of the depth of their friendship.

4. In an otherwise prosperous and booming economy, inflation remains a threatening weakness.

5. A storeowner has installed a photoelectric burglar alarm system. When the system is on, light-sensitive cells will detect a trespasser at any point on the premises.

QUOTATIONS

In this passage the authors quote a line from *Idylls of the King* by the poet, Alfred Tennyson,

"the old order changeth, yielding place to new."

Great writers have expressed many thoughts and feelings so aptly and so well that others will quote their words to make a point, just as the authors of this passage have done (lines 39–40). As a reader, you will find it helpful to recognize the way a writer uses a well-known or suitable quotation. You may enjoy becoming familiar with and using some well-known quotations yourself.

Exercise B

Shakespeare has written more quotable lines than any other writer. Below are ten famous quotations from Shakespeare. Following the quotations are ten statements. Match each quotation with the statement that best expresses its meaning.

1. What's in a name? That which we call a rose
   By any other name would smell as sweet.
   —*Romeo and Juliet*

2. Cowards die many times before their deaths;
   The valiant never taste of death but once.
   —*Julius Caesar*

3. When sorrows come, they come not single spies
   But in battalions.
   —*Hamlet*

4. There are more things in heaven and earth, Horatio,
   Than are dreamt of in your philosophy.
   —*Hamlet*

5. There's no art to find the mind's construction in the face.
   —*Macbeth*

6. Lord, what fools these mortals be!
   —*Midsummer Night's Dream*

7. How far that little candle throws its beams!
   So shines a good deed in a naughty world.
   —*Merchant of Venice*

8. By heaven, methinks it were an easy leap
   To pluck bright honour from the pale-faced moon.
   —*Henry IV, Part 1*

9. For there was never yet philosopher
   That could endure the toothache patiently.
   —*Much Ado About Nothing*

10. . . . love is not love
    Which alters when it alteration finds.
    —*Sonnet 116*

a. Keen suffering or pain cannot be relieved by reason or logic.

b. Life is full of puzzles and mysteries that no one can explain.

c. It's the person himself that counts, not his position or title or his family background.

d. People behave in a silly way.

e. Fear of danger is far worse than danger itself.

f. Goodness is so rare that it is easily noticeable when it does occur.

g. Do not try to judge inner character by outward appearances.

h. True love is not changed by changes in the loved one.

i. No effort is too great in behalf of a just or good cause.

j. Troubles come in bunches.

19

Vocabulary in Context

A. Carefully examine each word in its context; then decide which definition is most appropriate.

1. **crucial** (line 18)
   a. dependent on
   b. equal
   c. secure
   d. very important

2. **facilitates** (line 27)
   a. makes easier
   b. contradicts
   c. occupies
   d. offers conveniences

3. **amenities** (line 32)
   a. polite practices
   b. satisfactions
   c. food lists
   d. prayers

4. **spontaneous** (line 64)
   a. logical
   b. at fault
   c. self-acting
   d. happy

5. **integrity** (line 71)
   a. rebellion
   b. friendliness
   c. knowledge
   d. honesty

B. Match meanings and sentence context by writing the word which most suitably fills the blank in each sentence.

1. **crucial**
2. **facilitates**
3. **amenities**
4. **spontaneous**
5. **integrity**

a. It is an unusual child who always observes the ___ ? ___, saying "please" and "thank you" when he should.

b. The game was ___ ? ___, for the winning team would be recognized as number one in the nation.

20

c. Tom's generosity was ——?——, always coming from his natural instincts rather than the desire to make a favorable impression on others.

d. If judges in the courts do not have ——?—— then the whole system of justice will fail.

e. The new automatic guidance system ——?—— the landings and takeoffs of planes when ground visibility is poor.

READING 2

In the philosophy of Herbie Bookbinder there was a division
in the concept, Girls.

5

10

15

20

As a species of the genus Mankind he regarded girls as low
in the scale, a botched job. They played silly games; they
had unpleasant shrill voices, they giggled; they pretended to
be holy; they were in an everlasting conspiracy against normal human being (boys of eleven); they wore queer clothes;
and they were sly. He regarded most of these squeaky beings
with plain scorn.

It was nevertheless part of the mystery of life that from
time to time there came to Herbie's view a sublime creation
which could only be classified as a girl, since she would have
the outside features such as long hair, a dress, and a high
voice. But she would be as different from girls as the sun is
from a penny candle. One of these angels appeared every
year or so. There had been Rosalind Sarnoff, of the black
hair and bright smile, in the second grade. Sadie Benz, always
dressed in billowy white, in the fourth. Blond Madeline Costigan, who could throw a ball like a boy, in the fifth. And
two girls who had lived in his neighborhood, known only as
Mildred and Frances respectively, who had reduced his life to
ashes twice by moving to other parts of the Bronx.

The radiance of such a divinity could come to surround
an ordinary girl. Madeline Costigan had sat beside him in

Miss O'Grady's class for two months, undistinguished from the rest of the chirruping females. Then one afternoon they had both been kept after school for tardiness. And while they were beating out erasers together, a grand chord had sounded in Herbert's breast, he had seen the glory envelop Madeline like the dawn, and lo, he was her slave. Equally strangely the spell could die away, as it had in the case of Sadie Benz, leaving a commonplace girl whom Herbie despised. But this was not the rule. Most of these super-beings had been removed from Herbie by the forces of time and change. Diana Vernon had succeeded Madeline Costigan, the first adult in the golden procession.

The little stranger on the other side of the auditorium door who sat on the stairs facing away from him, placidly munching a sandwich, had hair of the same hue as Mrs. Gorkin's, and this may have been the reason Herbert's heart bounded when he first saw her. But a prolonged look persuaded him that, on her own merits, she was a candidate for the vacant office. Her starched, ruffled blue frock, her new, shiny, patent-leather shoes, her red cloth coat with its gray furry collar, her very clean knees and hands, and the carefully arranged ringlets of her hair all suggested non-squeaky loveliness. At the moment of his so deciding, it chanced that she turned her head and met his look. Her large hazel eyes widened in surprise, and at once there was no further question of candidacy. She was elected.

It now became obligatory upon Herbert to pretend that she did not exist. He looked out of the window and began to make believe that an extremely exciting and unusual event was taking place in the girls' playground below—just what, he was not sure, but it called for him to clap his palm to the side of his face, shake his head from side to side, and exclaim very loudly, "Gee whiz! Gosh! Never saw anything like *that!*" (By this time the imaginary sight had started to take shape as a teacher lying in a pool of blood, her head split open, after a jump from the roof.) He was compelled to run,

first down the side aisle of the auditorium to look out of the other windows, and then up the aisle again and through the leather door at the rear, feigning amazement at the discovery of the girl on the stairs. She was seated busily reading a
65 geography book upside down, having snatched it after watching all his pantomime up to the point when she saw he intended to come through the door.

After enacting an intensity of surprise at the sight of the girl that would have sufficed had he come upon a unicorn,
70 Herbert recovered himself and said sternly, "What are you doing here?"

"Who wants to know?" said the girl, putting aside the book.

"Me, that's who."

75 "Who's me?"

"Me is me," said Herbert, pointing to his three-starred yellow armband.

"Huh! Garbage gang," said the girl. Turning her back on him, she drew an apple out of a gleaming new tin lunch box
80 and began to eat it with exaggerated nonchalance, her eyebrows raised and her gaze directed out at the smiling day.

"Maybe you'd like to come down to Mr. Gauss's office with me," said Herbie fiercely.

Mr. Julius Gauss was the principal, a heavy, round-headed
85 gentleman seen by the children only at special assemblies, where he read psalms in a gloomy singsong and gave endless speeches which nobody understood, but which seemed in favor of George Washington, America, and certain disgusting behavior found only in molly-coddles. He was regarded
90 by the children as the most frightful thing outside the storybooks, a view which the teachers encouraged and which several of them seemed to share.

"And stop eating," added Herbie, "when you're talking to a head monitor."

95 Red Locks quailed and put down the apple, but she tried to brave it out. "You can't make me go down there," she

said. (It was always "down" to Mr. Gauss's office, possibly because of the general analogy to infernal regions.)

"Can't I?" said Herbert. "Can't I? It so happens that as *captain* of the Social Service Squad I have to see Mr. Gauss every Thursday, which is today, and make my report to him. And anyone who I tell to come with me has to come. But you can *try* not coming—oh, sure, you can *try*. I don't think you would try it more than *once*, but you can *try*."

The contents of this speech, excepting Herbert's rank, were a lie. But Herbert had not learned yet to draw the line between the facts devised by his powerful imagination and the less vivid facts existing in nature, and while he spoke he fully believed what he was saying.

"Anyway," said the girl, "he wouldn't do anything to me even if you did bring me down there, because I'm going to his camp this summer."

"His camp?" Herbie made the mistake of lapsing from his positive tone.

"Yes, his camp, smartie," sneered the girl. "I thought you knew everything. Camp Manitou, in the Berkshires. You just try bringing one of his campers down to him. He'll just demote you off your old garbage gang."

"He will not."

"He will so."

"He will not," said Herbie, "because I'm going to his old camp myself."

This was somewhat too newly minted a fact, even for the credulity of a small girl. "You're a liar," said she promptly.

"You mean you are," said Herbert, with no great logic, but with a natural grasp of the art of controversy.

"I'll bet you a dime I'm going to his camp," said the girl, falling into the trap and taking the defensive.

"I'll bet you a dollar I am," said Herbert.

"I'll bet you ten dollars you're not."

"I'll bet you a thousand dollars *you're* not."

"I'll bet you a million dollars."

"I'll bet you a *billion* dollars."

The girl, unable to think quickly of the next order of magnitude, said with scorn, "Where are you gonna get a billion dollars?"

"Same place you'll get a million," retorted Herbie.

"I can get a million dollars from my father if I want to," said Red Locks, vexed at being continually on the defensive, though sensing she was in the right. "He's the biggest lawyer in Bronx County."

"That's nothing," said Herbert. "My father owns the biggest ice plant in America." (He was manager of a small ice plant in the Bronx.)

"My father is richer than your father."

"My father could buy your father like an ice-cream cone."

"He could not," said the girl hotly.

"My father even has a way bigger lawyer for his ice plant than your father." Herbie speedily searched his memory, reviewing conversations of his parents. "My father's lawyer is Louis Glass."

The girl uttered a triumphant little shriek. "Ha, ha, smartie!" she cried, jumping up and dancing a step or two. "My father *is* Louis Glass."

This astounding stroke left Herbie with no available fact, real or improvised, for a counterblow. He was reduced to a weak, "He is not, either."

"Is too!" shouted the girl, her eyes sparkling. "Here, if you're so clever, here's my name on my books—Lucille Glass."

Herbert deigned to inspect the notebook offered for his view, with the large childish inscription, "Lucille Marjorie Glass, 6B-3."

"You should of told me so right away," he said magnanimously. "You can stay here, as long as your father is Louis Glass. 6B-3, huh? I'm in 7B-1. First on the honor roll."

"I'm third on the honor roll," said Lucille, yielding at last the deference due an upperclassman, a head monitor, and a mental giant.

With this advance in their relationship they fell silent, and 170 became aware of being alone together on the small landing. The gay voices of the girls playing in the yard came faintly to them through the closed window. Herbie and Lucille self-consciously turned and watched the darting, frisking little figures for a while. 175

"What were you doing up here, anyway?" said the boy at last, feeling that ease of speech was deserting him.

"I'm on the girls' Police Squad," said Lucille Glass, "and I'm supposed to watch this staircase during lunch."

She pulled a red band from her pocket and commenced 180 pinning it around her arm. Encountering difficulty, she was gallantly aided by Herbie, who received the reward of a bashful smile. All this while Herbie was struggling with the question, whether it was not inconsistent for a Radiant One to be practically a member of his family, as Lucille's tie to 185 his father's lawyer made her. His sister and his cousins were so empty of grace that he classed all family females in the low rank of girlhood. The aura of Red Locks seemed to waver and dim. However, as they grew silent once more, gazing out at the yard, Herbie felt himself quite tongue-tied, 190 and the glory brightened and shone as strongly as at first, and he realized that charms sufficiently powerful could over-come even the handicap of belonging to the family.

"Well, gotta make my rounds," he said abruptly. "So long." 195

"Good-by," said the little girl, wrinkling her snub nose and red, firm cheeks at him in a friendly grin. As Herbie walked off the landing into the corridor, she called after him, "Are you really going to Camp Manitou this summer?"

The boy turned and looked down his nose at her in the 200 crushing way teachers reacted to silly questions. He was no taller than the girl, so the effect was rather hard to get, but he managed a good approximation by tilting his head far back, and sighting along the edge of his nose.

205 "You'll find out," he enunciated after a dignified pause, and stalked off down the hall.

Mrs. Mortimer Gorkin had a weary afternoon of it with Herbie. Shortly after the children came back to class, she was summoned out of the room for a few minutes and returned
210 to find her trusted monitor standing on top of her desk, reciting a parody of "The Village Blacksmith" with an idiotic preciseness that she recognized as a burlesque of herself. "The muss-uls on his ba-rawny arrrms," he was saying, "are sta-rrong as rrrrrubba bands-sah." She punished this mal-
215 feasance of office by ordering Herbie to sit in the last seat of the last girls' row and forbidding him to speak for the rest of the day. He broke the injunction twice by shouting spectacularly accurate answers to questions that had reduced the rest of the class to silence. This put the teacher in the bad
220 predicament of having to reproach brilliance. The second time she tried sarcasm, saying heavily, "And pray, what makes you so very, very clever this afternoon, Master Bookbinder?"

It was a mistake. Herbert was inspired to jump to his feet
225 and rejoin, "Just celebrating your wedding, Mrs. Gorkin," touching off a demonstration of screaming hilarity which the reddened, angry teacher could not control until she stood, pounded her desk and shrieked, "Silence! Silence!" She effectively snuffed out Herbert by offering to conduct him
230 down to Mr. Gauss's office the next time he uttered a word. But this came too late. By his repartee, and by forcing her to a display of temper, he had clearly won the day.

When the class marched into the school yard at the end of the afternoon and broke ranks, he was at once surrounded,
235 the girls giggling and shouting at him, the boys pounding his back, shaking his hand, and assuring him with various curses that "he was a regular guy, after all." It was admitted by everyone that he had been under the spell of a "crush," an

28

ailment which all the children understood. The great Lennie Krieger himself condescended to lounge up to Herbert and 240 say, "Nice work, Fatso," which set the seal on his acclaim. He was received back into society. He was even permitted to pitch the first inning of the softball game as a mark of his redemption, and no criticism was heard of his mediocre efforts. 245

Reading Comprehension

The exercises that follow are based on the passage you have just read. Each exercise consists of an incomplete statement followed by four choices. Select the choice that best completes the statement. Go back to the passage for rereading to whatever extent is necessary to help you choose your answer.

1. The best description of Herbie Bookbinder's feelings and attitude towards girls is
   a. he secretly likes them but outwardly pretends to despise them.
   b. his general "principles" about girls as a class are the opposite of his actual feelings towards specific girls.
   c. like all boys his age, he neither likes nor understands girls.
   d. he likes girls but is put off by their antagonistic behavior.

2. Apparently, Herbie's definition of "normal" human beings would include
   a. males only.
   b. boys of eleven only.
   c. boys.
   d. everybody but girls, with the exception of a few specific girls.

3. Among the angels that had appeared in Herbie's life, the one adult was
   a. Rosalind Sarnoff.

b. Miss O'Grady.

c. Diana Vernon.

d. Madeline Costigan.

4. Herbie's reaction when he first sees the "little stranger" (Lucille Glass) suggests that Mrs. Gorkin

a. is Herbie's teacher.

b. usually wears dresses of blue.

c. frightens Herbie.

d. has been one of Herbie's angels.

5. "She was elected." (line 50) The meaning of this statement is the same as

a. "he regarded girls as low in the scale, a botched job." (lines 3–4)

b. "two girls . . . had reduced his life to ashes." (lines 20–22)

c. "lo, he was her slave." (line 30)

d. "she did not exist." (line 52)

6. Herbie's vision of a teacher lying in a pool of blood is

a. part of a pretense paralleled by Lucille's reading the geography book.

b. an excuse he gives himself to try to run away unnoticed.

c. a device used to arouse a sense of suspense in the reader.

d. probably an incident that Herbie is reliving out of his past.

7. The probable reason for the teachers' encouraging the children's view of Mr. Gauss is that

a. they use Mr. Gauss as a threat, to help keep discipline.

b. they share Mr. Gauss's favoring of George Washington, America, and certain behavior.

c. they have to do so because Mr. Gauss is the head of the school.

d. they, too, are frightened of him.

8. Lucille's statement that she is going to Camp Manitou is

a. a lie she has made up on the spur of the moment.

b. an attempt to establish a better relationship with Herbie as a future fellow-camper.

c. a real weapon in her "power struggle" with Herbie.

d. what Herbie would regard as typically female, having nothing to do with what they are talking about.

9. The meaning of "the art of controversy" (line 126) is

a. arguing logically.

b. arguing illogically.

c. putting the other person on the defensive, no matter how.

d. making bets of bigger and bigger sums of money.

10. Herbie makes his biggest mistake in his contest with Lucille when he says

a. "And stop eating when you're talking to a head monitor." (lines 93–94)

b. ". . . I'm going to his old camp myself." (lines 121–122)

c. "Same place you'll get a million." (line 137)

d. "My father's lawyer is Louis Glass." (lines 150–151)

11. "Are you really going to Camp Manitou this summer?" (line 199) In asking this question, Lucille is expressing

a. final triumph.

b. defeat.

c. mockery.

d. friendliness.

12. "It was admitted by everyone that he had been under the spell of a 'crush' . . ." (lines 237–238) From all the evidence, the best guess as to the meaning of this statement is that

a. the children realize that Herbie has a crush on Lucille and that is why he misbehaved in the classroom.

b. until her recent marriage, Herbie has had a crush on Mrs. Gorkin, the teacher.

c. because of his crush on Madeline Costigan, who was a good softball player herself, Herbie had not played softball with the boys.

d. Herbie had alienated himself from the other boys in the class because of his interest in girls.

31

13. Each of the following is probably an accurate description of Herbie EXCEPT
    a. he is tall.
    b. he is chubby.
    c. he is a bright student.
    d. he is a mediocre ballplayer.

Literary and Language Skills

ENJOYING HUMOR

MY PARENTS

At Six: My parents—they are the smartest people in the world; they know everything.

At Twelve: My parents don't know as much as I thought they did.

At Seventeen: My parents don't know anything—they just don't understand the younger generation.

At Thirty-five: My parents knew much more than I thought they did. They were really quite worldly-wise.

At Fifty: My parents were always right. Everything they did was for my benefit.

Most people who read this set of opinions about parents will smile. They will find humor in it.

Humor is one of the most popular and enjoyable kinds of reading matter. But, just what is humor anyhow? Let us see if we can begin to learn a little bit about humor. *Why* are these opinions about parents funny?

At seventeen a person sees his parents as not understanding him at all. When he reaches fifty, the same person views his parents as being perfect. This can't be. Something doesn't fit. Something clashes; or, to use exactly the right word, there is *incongruity* in the opinions. Incongruity is an important element in many forms of humor in writing.

However, notice also that there is *truth* in this set of *incongruous* opinions. People really do tend to have differing views about their parents at different stages in life. Therefore, the humor in this case lies in the way people really are. The writer has helped us to see the humor in the way people really are by setting down these opinions about parents in just the way he did.

Actually, human behavior is humorous in many different ways. One important kind of humorous writing helps us to smile at our own human incongruities. Much of the humor in Herman Wouk's narrative about Herbie Bookbinder is of this type. Try an exercise that will help you to understand the humor of Herbie's behavior a little more exactly.

Exercise

Below you will find ten descriptions, with brief explanations, of ten types of behavior that can be humorous (*a–j*).

a. Wild prejudice

Everyone has a tendency to think highly of himself. The more inexperienced and ignorant a person is, the more likely he is to build himself up through wild prejudices. Such a person is *for* whatever is most like himself and *against* whatever is different.

b. Inconsistency

When a person believes, says, or does what is most convenient at a given time, his behavior is going to be very inconsistent and even self-contradictory.

c. Exaggerated emotions

Some people enjoy dramatizing their emotions. Everything is a crisis, an extreme of feeling. (But, each crisis is soon forgotten.)

d. Illogical behavior

People sometimes deliberately behave in a way that is likely to produce a result opposite of what they are after, as when a child has a temper tantrum in order to attract affectionate attention.

e. Fantasies of hostility

Millions of schoolchildren have dreamed of schools burning down with all records, particularly when they have expected a poor grade on a test. Fortunately for the welfare of the human race, we confine this kind of "protection" from "enemies" to daydreams and fantasies.

f. Noncommunication

"What you think you heard me say is not what I said. Anyhow, it doesn't matter because what I said is not what I meant." These remarks sum up the difficulties that all people have in communicating with each other through words. There is probably no situation in which "noncommunication" occurs more often than between mature adults and young adolescents.

g. Face-saving

When a person is more concerned with the impression he is making on others than anything else, regard for truth and honesty will shrink to almost nothing. If it seems that telling a lie will improve his appearances, he will tell a lie.

h. Exaggerated language

Sometimes we get carried away in our enthusiasms and make statements so extreme as to be ridiculous.

i. Boasting

Sometimes exaggerated language takes the form of boasting about supreme achievements or status.

j. Rebellion against authority

Every once in a while something happens that makes a person feel very satisfied with himself, very important, and overstimulated. He gets carried away and asserts himself against authority in a silly way, which he almost certainly comes to feel very ashamed about when he is calmed down.

Write the letter of the type of humor that best matches each excerpt below, taken from the selection.

1. "I'll bet you a *billion* dollars." (line 133)
2. "He will not . . . because I'm going to his old camp myself." (lines 121–122)
3. "they were in an everlasting conspiracy against normal human beings (boys of eleven) . . ." (lines 6–7)
4. "Mr. Julius Gauss was the principal, a heavy, round-headed gentleman seen by the children only at special assemblies, where he . . . gave endless speeches which nobody understood . . ." (lines 84–87)
5. "It now became obligatory upon Herbert to pretend that she did not exist." (lines 51–52)
6. ". . . Mildred and Frances . . . had reduced his life to ashes twice by moving to other parts of the Bronx." (lines 21–22)
7. "By this time the imaginary sight had started to take shape as a teacher lying in a pool of blood, her head split open, after a jump from the roof." (lines 58–60)
8. "She . . . returned to find her trusted monitor standing on top of her desk, reciting a parody of 'The Village Blacksmith' with an idiotic preciseness that she recognized as a burlesque of herself." (lines 208–212)
9. "My father owns the biggest ice plant in America." (lines 142–143)
10. "It was nevertheless part of the mystery of life that from time to time there came to Herbie's view a sublime creation which could only be classified as a girl . . ." (lines 10–12)

Vocabulary in Context

A. Carefully examine each word in its context; then decide which definition is most appropriate.

1. **concept** (line 2)
   - *a.* error
   - *b.* example
   - *c.* idea
   - *d.* difference

2. **sublime** (line 11)
   - *a.* feminine
   - *b.* opposing
   - *c.* exalted
   - *d.* chosen

3. **nonchalance** (line 80)
   - *a.* hunger
   - *b.* hatred
   - *c.* foolishness
   - *d.* coolness

4. **credulity** (line 124)
   - *a.* belief
   - *b.* honor
   - *c.* interest
   - *d.* cruelty

5. **injunction** (line 217)
   - *a.* contract
   - *b.* command
   - *c.* judgment
   - *d.* silence

B. Match meaning and sentence context by writing the word which most suitably fills the blank in each sentence. (Note that two words, 6 and 7, from the previous lesson are included for review.)

1. concept
2. sublime
3. nonchalance
4. credulity
5. injunction

6. facilitates
7. integrity

a. Despite the fact that this was his first public performance, the young musician appeared on stage with the __?__ of an experienced professional.

b. The new bridge makes possible direct access to the beach and thus greatly __?__ our car trip.

c. The late afternoon sun shone through the stained glass windows and brought a __?__ quality to the interior of the building.

d. The man was practically a saint, whose honesty, idealism, and __?__ were infallible.

e. The court issued the __?__ requiring the company to cease the operations that were polluting the river.

f. The __?__ that primitive people had of the earth and the heavens was very different from the reality.

g. The television shots of man walking on the moon were so astonishing as to be almost beyond __?__.

READING 3

The sun blazed, fledglings flew, roses bloomed. But there was still, for Southern California, an indication of a lingering spring: green grass. There had been late rains and the yellow look had not yet come to the foothills and the grass in the Delahanty back yard was still February fresh. Now in late afternoon each bent blade carried on its hump a drop of water left over from the midday shower. The low sun, slanting through these drops, gave them jewel colors and Crescent, walking toward the house, put her feet down carefully. She was now fourteen years old and oppressed by the brevity of life, the fugaciousness of blossoms, and the evanescence of raindrops. Even words like evanescent and fugacious could set up, with their suggestive syllables, delicious tremors of sorrow in her heart. Ending, ending, everything is ending, she thought. In spite of her care, raindrops like emeralds and diamonds went flying down to nothing as she walked. She was even sorrowful about the box of tin cans she had just taken to the stack behind the barn. She had put them down with benedictory thoughts: finished and done with! Gone from the orderly kitchen shelves and the bright lights of the house into the cold earth.

There were tears in her eyes as she walked through the grass. She had more feelings than she knew what to do with, more emotions than her tranquil life permitted her to discharge. She had to invent sorrows and concoct dramas. She would stoop down to rejoice with a daffodil that had pushed a stone aside in its upward thrust, or would loosen a butterfly from a spider web with wailings that brought her no sympathy from any listener. As if she cared for sympathy! She was capable emotionally of a woman's tragedies and, up to now, she had been unable to overtake any of these. Now, however, she loved and was not loved in return. No one, not even Calvin Dean, knew anything of this; though she could not believe it would matter if he did. That was a part of his appeal: his indifference. He didn't know Crescent Delahanty existed. Why should he?

With rubies and emeralds and diamonds transformed by her feet into simple raindrops and the raindrops themselves shattered into the shapelessness of moisture she thought, I'm King Midas in reverse. I change jewels to water. I can touch gold and make it into a base metal, lead or tin. She stood ankle deep in the diamonds and rubies she had yet to ruin and figured what her name was. Midas in reverse was Sadim. I am King Sadim, she told herself, and the jewels I touch are water and the gold I touch is dust and the people I love hate me.

With these thoughts, she went into the kitchen, which was warm and fragrant with the tamale pie her mother was making. Her mother was at the sink shaking olives from a bottle. Cress watched her for a second or two, then said, "I am King Sadim."

Her mother, who did not turn around, asked in a cheerful voice, "Who's King Sadim, dear?"

"King Midas had a brother and Sadim was his name," Cress said, the relationship coming to her as she spoke.

"I never heard of him," Mrs. Delahanty replied. "I didn't know King Midas had a brother."

"This brother was not popular. He was King Midas in reverse. Everything he touched turned into dust. It may be bad to have everything you touch turn to gold—but it's a lot better than having everything you touch turn to dust. Nobody liked King Sadim and everybody tried to forget him. I may be the only person in the world who remembers him."

Her mother, who had the olives out of the bottle, now began to stir them into her pie. She looked up from her stirring
with amused interest, as Cress related this bit of unknown
mythology. Cress regarded her mother dispassionately. The
rain and the steam in the kitchen had made her new permanent too frizzy. There was a big splash of cornmeal mush
across her apron. Her lipstick formed a dot at each corner of
her mouth. She was smiling quite happily. Happy, Cress
thought, on a spring evening of unutterable beauty, with
nothing better to do than make a tamale pie. A pie that will
be eaten tonight and forgotten tomorrow.

"Oh, Mother," she cried. "Poor, poor Mother." She dug
an olive out of the pie and put it into her mouth. Under her
closed lids she felt the happy smart of tears saying, You are
alive and suffering. She took the olive seed from her mouth
and pushed it deep into the well-watered soil about one of
the African violet plants which her mother kept in pots along
the window sill over the sink.

"What are you doing, Cress?" her mother asked.

"Giving it one more chance," Cress whispered, patting the
soil in tenderly over the buried seed.

"Giving what one more chance?"

"The olive seed. It had given up. Into the bottle, into the
pie, into my mouth. Like Jonah. Then when it thought all
was over I spat it up. Rescue. Escape. It will be a tree
again."

"It never was a tree, Cress. Any more than an egg ever was
a chicken."

"It is an embryonic tree, Mother. It has leaves and limbs
locked in its heart." All those surprising l's. *They* brought
tears to her eyes, too.

"Leave them locked," Mrs. Delahanty said unfeelingly. "I
don't want leaves and limbs in my kitchen. I want African
violets."

"O.K.," Cress said, "if that's the way you feel about it."
She began disinterring the seed. "The choice is yours, Life or

Death. You choose Death." She opened the window over 100
the sink and flung the olive pit out into the April twilight.
"Die," she bade it in a tragic voice. "Cease to be. It is my
mother's wish."

Her mother slid the tamale pie into the oven. "How much
death do you think there is in that tamale pie, Mother?" 105
Cress asked.

Her mother looked startled and Cress said, "One cow at
the very least. Two maybe."

"Cress," her mother said, "you have a bad case of spring
fever. You need some vitamins or minerals or something." 110

Death in the world, spring passing, love never coming, and
vitamins were recommended.

"Do you know it's spring?" Cress asked. "That this is a
day that will never again be upon this earth? Never, never,
never? And that it's the last day on earth a lot of people will 115
ever see? There," she said, pointing to the fragment of pale
sun still visible through the darkening leaves of the eucalyptus
tree, "that sun is going down forever for someone at this
very minute."

Something came into her mother's face, agreement, she 120
was afraid. And she couldn't bear agreement or understanding just now. What she longed for was sorrow and contention,
lasting disorder and sudden death. She ran out of the kitchen
slamming the door behind her. In her own room she flung
herself onto the chair in front of her bamboo desk, put her 125
arms on the open lid of the desk and her face on her arms.
"Oh, Calvin," she whispered. Then, very daringly, "My darling." The word made a pulse beat on her cheekbone.

Reading Comprehension

The exercises that follow are based on the passage you have just
read. Each exercise consists of an incomplete statement followed
by four choices. Select the choice that best completes the state-

ment. Go back to the passage for rereading to whatever extent is necessary to help you choose your answer.

1. "The sun blazed, fledglings flew, roses bloomed." (line 1) Apparently, for this part of Southern California, these signs go with
   a. a lingering spring.
   b. the beginning of summer.
   c. February.
   d. late rains.

2. "Even words like evanescent and fugacious could set up, with their suggestive syllables, delicious tremors of sorrow in her heart." (lines 12-14) Concerning the "sorrow in her heart," this sentence suggests that Crescent is
   a. insincere.
   b. mature.
   c. enjoying the "sorrow."
   d. in the habit of using big words whose meaning she does not know.

3. As she walks toward the house, Crescent puts her feet down carefully because
   a. she is deep in thought.
   b. she doesn't want to get her feet wet.
   c. she doesn't want to get back to the house too soon.
   d. she doesn't want to disturb the drops of water on the grass.

4. The "benedictory thoughts" with which Crescent puts down the box of tin cans are comparable to
   a. a prayer at a burial.
   b. a farewell to an old friend.
   c. a blessing for a loved one.
   d. thanksgiving for good things to eat.

5. The "tears," "feelings," and "emotions" referred to in the second paragraph are probably mainly a result of the fact that Crescent is

a. fourteen years old.
b. leading an unhappy life.
c. a lover of all living things, even insects.
d. a woman in love.

6. The conversation between Cress and her mother about King Sadim shows that
   a. Mrs. Delahanty does not understand Cress.
   b. Mrs. Delahanty pretends to know less than she really does.
   c. Cress knows more about mythology than Mrs. Delahanty.
   d. Cress has a lively imagination.

7. The thought or statement that is out of keeping with Cress's underlying pessimistic mood is
   a. "Ending, ending, everything is ending . . ." (line 14)
   b. "She was even sorrowful about the box of tin cans . . ." (lines 16–17)
   c. "A pie that will be eaten tonight and forgotten tomorrow." (lines 73–74)
   d. "It has leaves and limbs locked in its heart." (lines 92–93)

8. Mrs. Delahanty thinks that Cress
   a. has spring fever.
   b. has a secret "crush" on a boy.
   c. is really making a lot of sense.
   d. loves nature.

9. "And she couldn't bear agreement or understanding just now." (lines 121–122) The best explanation for this reaction of Cress is that
   a. she despises her mother.
   b. she doesn't want anything to interfere with the self-pity she is enjoying.
   c. she knows that her mother couldn't possibly really understand.
   d. she is too proud to accept sympathy.

10. In all likelihood, Calvin Dean is
    a. imaginary.

    b. a movie star.

    c. a schoolmate of Cress.

    d. a character in a book Cress has read.

Literary and Language Skills

VERBAL IMAGERY

Crescent Delahanty is a little bit like Herbie Bookbinder. There is humor in her behavior. Can you, for example, give one illustration of *exaggerated emotions* and one illustration of *illogical behavior* from the story of Cress?

However, there is a difference in the humor of the two stories. This difference can be summed up by saying that we may laugh aloud at the antics of Herbie, but we will only smile gently with Cress. There are several reasons for this difference; the most important lies in the style of writing of the novel, *Cress Delahanty*.

As the passage you have read well illustrates, the writing style of Miss West, the author, is characterized by delicate and touching beauty. Much of this beauty is achieved by *verbal imagery*, word-pictures that appeal to or stimulate one or more of our five senses— seeing, hearing, feeling, smelling, tasting.

Exercise A

To understand verbal imagery better, try this little exercise. Each of the five sentences below is a verbal image, appealing to one of the five senses. Name the sense (seeing, hearing, feeling, smelling, or tasting) appealed to in each case.

1. The delicate fragrance of the roses perfumed the air.
2. The black python writhed among the branches.
3. The peppery sauce burned my mouth.
4. The icy grip of the water numbed the swimmer's body.
5. The dog's sharp bark echoed through the silent house.

Exercise B

Now see if you can recognize and appreciate better some examples of verbal imagery taken from the passage about Cress Delahanty. Section I below lists ten excerpts from the passage. Section II names one or more senses to which each excerpt may appeal, or states that the excerpt contains no verbal imagery. Match the choices in Section II with those in Section I so that each excerpt is correctly described as to its verbal imagery.

SECTION I

1. The low sun, slanting through these drops, gave them jewel colors.
2. Ending, ending, everything is ending, she thought.
3. With these thoughts, she went into the kitchen, which was warm and fragrant with the tamale pie her mother was making.
4. Her mother was at the sink shaking olives from a bottle.
5. Cress watched for a second or two . . .
6. Her lipstick formed a dot at each corner of her mouth.
7. She dug an olive out of the pie and put it into her mouth.
8. . . . patting the soil in tenderly over the buried seed.
9. . . . the fragment of pale sun still visible through the darkening leaves of the eucalyptus tree.
10. The word made a pulse beat on her cheekbone.

SECTION II

NOTE: Choice *a* correctly matches *four* of the excerpts.
Choice *b* correctly matches *two* of the excerpts.
Each of the remaining choices matches *one* of the excerpts.

a. seeing
b. no verbal imagery
c. feeling

d. feeling and tasting
e. seeing and feeling
f. feeling and smelling

Vocabulary in Context

A. Carefully examine each word in its context; then decide which definition is most appropriate.

1. **evanescence** (line 11)
   - *a.* shine
   - *b.* hope
   - *c.* beauty
   - *d.* brevity

2. **tranquil** (line 24)
   - *a.* peaceful
   - *b.* crowded
   - *c.* uncertain
   - *d.* emotional

3. **concoct** (line 25)
   - *a.* create
   - *b.* dream
   - *c.* speak
   - *d.* avoid

4. **indifference** (line 35)
   - *a.* unusualness
   - *b.* love
   - *c.* lack of interest
   - *d.* patience

5. **disinterring** (line 99)
   - *a.* examining
   - *b.* unburying
   - *c.* eating
   - *d.* ignoring

B. Match meaning and sentence context by writing the word which most suitably fills the blank in each sentence. (Note that two words, 6 and 7, from the previous lesson are included for review.)

1. evanescence
2. tranquil
3. concoct
4. indifference
5. disinterring
6. concept
7. sublime

a. The lake was so ___?___ that its surface was almost as smooth as a sheet of glass.

b. The dog went to his favorite hiding place and began ___?___ the bone that he had buried there the day before.

c. The spectators showed their growing ___?___ to the dull game by beginning to leave well before the end.

d. The old ___?___ that oil supplies are inexhaustible has given way to the idea that we must find new energy sources.

e. The Italian painters produced many ___?___ works of art, whose glory and beauty have been admired for centuries.

f. The young boy liked to ___?___ plans for running away to a life of wild adventure, but his schemes never went beyond his imagination.

g. The violent storm lasted only a few moments, and the sailors were thankful that its fury was matched by its ___?___.

READING 4

Until he was almost ten the name stuck to him. He had literally to fight his way free of it. From So Big (of fond and infantile derivation) it had been condensed into Sobig. And Sobig DeJong, in all its consonantal disharmony, he had re-
5   mained until he was a ten-year-old schoolboy in that incredibly Dutch district southwest of Chicago known first as New Holland and later as High Prairie. At ten, by dint of fists, teeth, copper-toed boots, and temper, he earned the right to be called by his real name, Dirk DeJong. Now and
10   then, of course, the nickname bobbed up and had to be subdued in a brief and bitter skirmish. His mother, with whom the name had originated, was the worst offender. When she lapsed he did not, naturally, use schoolyard tactics on her. But he sulked and glowered portentously and refused
15   to answer, though her tone, when she called him So Big, would have melted the heart of any but that natural savage, a boy of ten.

The nickname had sprung from the early and idiotic question invariably put to babies and answered by them, with
20   infinite patience, through the years of their infancy.

Selina DeJong, darting expertly about her kitchen, from washtub to baking board, from stove to table, or, if at work in the fields of the truck farm, straightening the numbed

---

back for a moment's respite from the close-set rows of
carrots, turnips, spinach, or beets over which she was labour- 25
ing, would wipe the sweat beads from nose and forehead
with a quick duck of her head in the crook of her bent arm.
Those great fine dark eyes of hers would regard the child
perched impermanently on a little heap of empty potato sacks,
one of which comprised his costume. He was constantly 30
detaching himself from the parent sack heap to dig and
burrow in the rich warm black loam of the truck garden.
Selina DeJong had little time for the expression of affection.
The work was always hot at her heels. You saw a young
woman in a blue calico dress, faded and earth-grimed. Be- 35
tween her eyes was a driven look as of one who walks always
a little ahead of herself in her haste. Her dark abundant
hair was skewered into a utilitarian knob from which soft
loops and strands were constantly escaping, to be pushed
back by that same harried ducking gesture of head and bent 40
arm. Her hands, for such use, were usually too crusted and
inground with the soil into which she was delving. You saw
a child of perhaps two years, dirt-streaked, sunburned, and
generally otherwise defaced by those bumps, bites, scratches,
and contusions that are the common lot of the farm child of 45
a mother harried by work. Yet, in that moment, as the
woman looked at the child there in the warm moist spring of
the Illinois prairie land, or in the cluttered kitchen of the
farmhouse, there quivered and vibrated between them and all
about them an aura, a glow, that imparted to them and their 50
surroundings a mystery, a beauty, a radiance.

"How big is baby?" Selina would demand, senselessly.
"How big is my man?"

The child would momentarily cease to poke plump fingers
into the rich black loam. He would smile a gummy though 55
slightly weary smile and stretch wide his arms. She, too,
would open her tired arms wide, wide. Then they would say
in a duet, his mouth a puckered pink petal, hers quivering
with tenderness and a certain amusement, "*So-o-o-o* big!"

49

60   with the voice soaring on the prolonged vowel and dropping
suddenly with the second word. Part of the game. The child
became so habituated to this question that sometimes, if
Selina happened to glance round at him suddenly in the
midst of her task, he would take his cue without the familiar
65   question being put and would squeal his "So-o-o-o big!"
rather absently, in dutiful solo. Then he would throw back
his head and laugh a triumphant laugh, his open mouth a
coral orifice. She would run to him, and swoop down upon
him, and bury her flushed face in the warm moist creases of
70   his neck, and make as though to devour him. "So big!"
    But of course he wasn't. He wasn't as big as that. In fact,
he never became as big as the wide-stretched arms of her
love and imagination would have had him. You would have
thought she should have been satisfied when, in later years,
75   he was the Dirk DeJong whose name you saw (engraved) at
the top of heavy cream linen paper, so rich and thick and
stiff as to have the effect of being starched and ironed by
some costly American business process; whose clothes were
made by Peter Peel, the English tailor; whose roadster ran on
80   a French chassis; whose cabinet held mellow Italian vermouth
and Spanish sherry; whose wants were served by a Japanese
houseman; whose life, in short, was that of the successful
citizen of the Republic. But she wasn't. Not only was she
dissatisfied: she was at once remorseful and indignant, as
85   though she, Selina DeJong, the vegetable peddler, had been
partly to blame for this success of his, and partly cheated
by it.

Reading Comprehension

The exercises that follow are based on the passage you have
just read. Each exercise consists of an incomplete statement followed by four choices. Select the choice that best completes the
statement. Go back to the passage for rereading to whatever

extent is necessary to help you choose your answer.

1. The "early and idiotic question" (lines 18–19) is
   a. How old are you?
   b. How big is baby?
   c. What do you want to be when you grow up?
   d. What's a turnip?

2. Sobig's real name is
   a. Dirk.
   b. Selina.
   c. Peter.
   d. not given.

3. This passage tells about the central character's life from
   a. infancy to mature manhood.
   b. infancy to age ten.
   c. age ten to mature manhood.
   d. boyhood to young manhood.

4. The ten-year-old boy got into fights chiefly because of his
   a. mother.
   b. temper.
   c. nickname.
   d. copper-toed boots.

5. The entire passage suggests that a central trait of Dirk DeJong's character is
   a. savagery.
   b. determination.
   c. sullenness.
   d. greed.

6. Dirk's father is
   a. a farmer.
   b. a salesman.
   c. dead.
   d. not mentioned.

7. As a two year old in the fields while his mother worked, Sobig
   a. was a nuisance to the hardworking woman.
   b. wore a potato sack.
   c. helped his mother dig up the vegetables.
   d. sat patiently on a heap of potato sacks while his mother worked.

8. Selina's existence appears to be dominated by
   a. hopelessness and despair.
   b. ambition for material success.
   c. bitterness at her hard lot.
   d. devotion to her son.

9. When her son is a grown man, Selina feels
   a. happy and fulfilled because he is so successful.
   b. unhappy because he is a vegetable peddler.
   c. dissatisfied for reasons not given, even though he is successful.
   d. remorseful that she could not have given him a better start in life.

Literary and Language Skills

THE POWER OF SUGGESTION

Look at each of the following words. What is the meaning of each word for you as a reader?

> **murder**
> **dictatorship**
> **summer**
> **frankfurter**
> **football**

Each word has a direct or "dictionary" meaning. *Murder* means the act of deliberately and without justification killing another human being. *Dictatorship* means a system of government under which the ruler or rulers have absolute and unquestionable power. *Summer* is the warmest season of the year. A *frankfurter* is a type of smoked beef or pork sausage. *Football* is a field sport played between two teams of eleven members each.

These words also have additional, suggested meanings that are at least as important as the dictionary meanings. The words *murder* and *dictatorship* will arouse strongly negative emotions in most readers. They will suggest feelings of horror and distaste. For the individual reader, depending on his background of experience and interest, they may have more specific associated meanings. The person who has suffered under and then escaped from life in a dictatorship will recall specific incidents and experiences when he sees the word. What emotional meanings and specific associations do the words *summer, frankfurter,* and *football* suggest to you?

Now look at the following words:

    iceberg
    skyscraper
    earthquake
    alligator
    surfboard

Each of these words, too, has "the power of suggestion." That is, each of these words will express, for many readers, important meanings that are broader than the direct or dictionary meaning. The word *iceberg* may suggest desolate scenes of Arctic seas and Arctic wastes, of polar fields and polar bears, of howling blizzards. *Skyscraper* may create in the reader's mind familiar pictures of big cities, such as Manhattan's famed skyline. What settings and scenes are suggested to you by the words *earthquake, alligator,* and *surfboard?*

To review, here are two simple exercises on the "power of suggestion" of individual words.

Exercise A

What strong emotional meanings does each of the following words suggest to you? Write a plus sign (+) for each word that has a positive emotional meaning. Write a minus sign (−) for each word that has a negative emotional meaning. Write a zero (0) if the word has no particular emotional meaning. (Everyone will not necessarily have the same answers!) Be ready to explain to and discuss with the class the reasons for your answers.

1. brother
2. winter
3. journey
4. exercise
5. industry

6. money
7. graduation
8. milk
9. automobile
10. baby

Exercise B

From the following list of ten words, select the three that most powerfully suggest specific pictures of associated scenes and settings. Use words and phrases to jot down the highlights of these pictures.

1. seagull
2. bridge
3. desk
4. red
5. departure

6. conversation
7. leaves
8. book
9. sky
10. cellar

Individual words may have suggested meanings for the reader beyond the directly stated dictionary meaning. Whole sentences also have the "power of suggestion." Whole sentences may have important meanings beyond the meaning directly stated in the words. As an example, look at this sentence.

> Seeing the last patient come out into the waiting room, Mr. Jones picked up his case of samples and went into the office.

Notice that nowhere does this sentence directly tell us the exact location where the incident takes place. Is it a factory? a railroad station? a park? a doctor's office? Through suggestion, you know it is a doctor's office! This location is suggested strongly though indirectly by the words *patient, waiting room, office*. Notice also that nowhere does this sentence tell us directly what Mr. Jones is. Is Mr. Jones a patient? a bill collector? a repairman? a salesman? Through suggestion you know that Mr. Jones is a salesman! Mr. Jones's occupation is suggested strongly by the words *last patient comes out* and *case of samples*.

Now you know that written language has a strange and important power that we have called "the power of suggestion." Words can express important meanings beyond what they actually and directly state. Since the author has not directly expressed these meanings, it is the reader who must see them. The reader is just as important as the author, therefore, in creating the final meaning of any piece of writing, whether it be prose or poetry, fiction or nonfiction; book, magazine, or newspaper.

In answering a number of the READING COMPREHENSION questions on the passages you have read so far, you have already made important use of the "power of suggestion," perhaps unconsciously, as the following little exercises will show you.

Exercise C

Refer to Lesson 2 (from *The City Boy*) and reexamine READING COMPREHENSION questions 4, 12, 13. In each case, how did you have to use suggested meanings to arrive at your answer?

Exercise D

Refer to Lesson 3 (from *Cress Delahanty*) and reexamine READING COMPREHENSION questions 2, 5, 6, 9. In each case, how did you have to use suggested meanings to arrive at your answer?

Exercise E

Suggested meanings are especially important in this lesson since it is characteristic of the style of the author of *So Big* to suggest meanings rather than state them directly. Give the number of at least four of the READING COMPREHENSION questions in which you had to arrive at the answer through suggested rather than directly stated meanings. Explain how this is so in each case.

Vocabulary in Context

A. Carefully examine each word in its context; then decide which definition is most appropriate.

1. **condensed** (line 3)
    a. spelled
    b. combined
    c. moved
    d. repeated

2. **subdued** (line 11)
    a. supported
    b. crushed
    c. pronounced
    d. carried

3. **portentously** (line 14)
    a. with importance
    b. cleverly
    c. protectively
    d. threateningly

4. **utilitarian** (line 38)
    a. practical
    b. complicated
    c. annoying
    d. unusual

5. **orifice** (line 68)
   - *a.* picture
   - *b.* flower
   - *c.* opening
   - *d.* noise

B. Match meaning and sentence context by writing the word which most suitably fills the blank in each sentence. (Note that two words, 6 and 7, from the previous lesson are included for review.)

1. condensed	6. tranquil
2. subdued	7. concoct
3. portentously	
4. utilitarian	
5. orifice	

a. Trapped and harassed in the rat-race, he longed for the ___?___, carefree days of his youth.

b. The function and organization of many separate agencies were ___?___ into a single agency through the creation of the Department of Health, Education, and Welfare.

c. Modern furniture designers place more emphasis on the ___?___ purposes of their pieces than on the beauty of their appearance.

d. After the heavy rains, the river began to rise ___?___, and people evacuated their homes in fear of floods.

e. The paramecium has a tiny ___?___ through which it takes in food.

f. The fans left the stadium silent and ___?___ after the stunning upset of their team.

g. Many a cook faces the problem of trying to ___?___ a dinner that is delicious without being fattening.

57

READING 5

Here the high wooded promontory sheltered an arm of the bay that reached for almost half a mile into the woods. It was no more than a hundred yards wide and so was called the Narrow Arm. For Lisbeth it was an enchanted spot, a
5   place where she could watch the otter and the mink, the seal and the eagle. Up the creek at the end of the Narrow Arm she had seen beaver and marten. Ravens circled over the forest and the red-breasted sapsuckers flashed in the trees. In May small birds came to nest in the brush at the forest's
10   edge. On one side of the Arm there were grassy flats with sandspits reaching out into the clear salt water. On the other side the forest grew down steeply to the very limits of the tide. Here seaweed, carried on the big tides, still clung to the lower branches of the cedar trees, and goosetongue and beach
15   grass grew in the seams of the rocks. The tide ran free in the deep tapering channel until it spread itself over a white pebble beach where the creek came in.

Lisbeth loved this place with a deep and incommunicable love. She knew each moss-covered windfall along the edge
20   of the forest, each stump where she could sit and wait for the birds to come near, the big rock where she could hide and watch the otter fishing and eating their fish. Best of all was the beaver dam up the stream in the alders. Sometimes in midsummer she would lie on her back on the sandspit

where the paintbrush grew, eating wild strawberries and dreaming. She had built a little fireplace on the sandspit where she could make tea, and she always had a waterproof grub box in her skiff. She spent hours and hours in the Narrow Arm.

On this day in April, she rowed past the sandspit so close in that her oars touched bottom and stirred the sand into little whirls like whirls of smoke in the clear water. On the opposite side where the channel was deep, a seal, swimming with his head up, looked at her curiously and sank down again with hardly a ripple of water. When an otter dove you could see his back as he curved to go down, but a seal's head simply sank out of sight. In a moment her seal was there again, sliding easily through the water, disappearing and reappearing but keeping even with her boat all the time. Any other day Lisbeth would have spoken to him, or she might have crossed the Narrow Arm and stood on the high rocks on the other side where she could see him swimming under the water. But today her face was grave and preoccupied and every now and then she stopped rowing and sat drifting in the eddy, lost in thought.

Paul's remark that most girls knew nothing about oars and boats had awakened unbearable doubts. At a girls' school there would be no room for the sort of thing in which she excelled: tracking wild animals in the woods, where she could distinguish the tracks of the marten from the mink, the otter from the beaver as easily as reading her A B C's; making tea in the pouring rain; scenting a bear in the dense forest. She sniffed, thinking of it, because the mother bears were out of hibernation now with their tiny cubs. A breeze drifted offshore and for a moment she thought she detected the musky smell, sharper than skunk but not as unpleasant as mink or raven. Dad said bears smelled something like pigs but not quite. Lisbeth had never smelled pigs.

She watched the edge of the timber but nothing moved, and her doleful thoughts continued. At school none of these things would matter. There would be tennis and golf and horseback riding because there was nothing better to do. She would never kneel down to drink from a cold spring or lie in the deep moss dreaming.

65   With aching heart, she vowed to try to face things squarely. She had known few people. From her one trip to the States she remembered not individuals but crowds. Toward people in the mass she felt a vague hostility and an indefinable fear. When tourists flocked off the ships that came in to load
70   salmon at the Craig cannery, only Lisbeth's eagerness to see the captain kept her from taking to the woods to avoid the curious eyes and the ever-present cameras. It was like an invasion from the outside world, this rush of well-dressed strangers with questions about ordinary things that every-
75   body knew. Were the bears really dangerous? Were the "pines" so dense all over the coast? Every evergreen tree was a pine to them. Actually there were no pines at all in the forest of Hermit Bay. It was forest of cedar, hemlock, and spruce, but city people couldn't tell them apart. Someone
80   always asked, "Don't you get lonely, little girl?"

Why, the hours of the day were never long enough. You never had quite enough of each season before it changed into the next. The long days of summer would change all too soon to the short days of winter, when you would hear the
85   wolf chorus and know that never, never could such exciting and eerily beautiful sounds come from anywhere except nature herself. These tourists called it howling without ever having heard it. Lisbeth's revulsion contained an element of fear because, to her, outsiders seemed to be all alike and all
90   alien. As she tried to picture in her mind just what her arrival at school would be like, she thought of the commencement crowd at Robert's school.

"I'll never be able to get through it," she said desperately, as tears suddenly gushed out of her eyes.
95   She dropped her oars and impatiently blew her nose. Then she rowed on slowly toward the white beach at the end of

the Arm. Ahead of her swam two small ducks, trailing perfect V's on the smooth water. Gradually she felt the quiet seeping into her, the April quiet that was waiting for the songbirds to return and the first flowers to open their 100 petals. She loved the firsts—Johnny-jump-ups for spring, the first wild strawberries for summer, and the snowflakes for winter. All of nature's announcements of her changing seasons she awaited with a sort of mystical attentiveness, as though they were religious rites. She was filled with wonder 105 at the detailed and varied beauty of a wilderness where new discoveries never ended.

It did not occur to her that if she were one of the wild animals, as she sometimes imagined herself to be, she would not be aware of this beauty nor of the mysticism apparent in 110 it. Lisbeth felt the wonder of nature as she herself was part of it, but thinking about it made her doubtful and frightened lest she lose her wonderful world.

Because her life was taken up with the natural world around her, she read very little, for the most part only those 115 books that were required in the courses of her correspondence school. But she studied faithfully and always managed to get her lessons in the mail in time for the boat that came from Juneau every Saturday. Those lessons were the price she had gladly paid for being permitted to stay at home. 120

As she approached the white pebble beach, the evening song of a wood thrush poured joyously out of the trees just beyond the ruins of the old hermit's cabin. She stopped rowing and listened. The first songbird had arrived! April's first thrush! 125

Reading Comprehension

The exercises that follow are based on the passage you have just read. Each exercise consists of an incomplete statement followed by four choices. Select the choice that best completes the statement. Go back to the passage for rereading to whatever extent is necessary to help you choose your answer.

1. On the basis of all the evidence in this passage, it is most likely that the locale of this story is a coastal region of
   a. Alaska.
   c. Maine.
   b. California.
   d. Mexico.

2. The fact that all sorts of wild animals could be seen on the Narrow Arm causes Lisbeth to feel
   a. sadness.
   c. enchantment.
   b. fear.
   d. adventurousness.

3. The reach of the high tides on the forest side of the Narrow Arm is
   a. well above the base of the trees.
   b. just to the foot of the trees at the edge of the forest.
   c. well up the beach but short of the edge of the forest.
   d. almost a half mile into the woods.

4. Of all the places she loved, Lisbeth loved best of all
   a. the big rock where she could hide and watch the otter.
   b. the beaver dam up the stream.
   c. the sandspit where the paintbrush grew.
   d. the fireplace she had built on the sandspit.

5. Lisbeth did not, on this day, speak to the seal that was accompanying her boat because
   a. she could never do such a thing.
   b. the seal kept disappearing.
   c. she was more interested in the otter.
   d. a serious problem occupied her attention.

6. Lisbeth feels that going away to a girls' school will be entering
   a. a new and exciting world.
   b. a world not very different from her own land of tourists.
   c. an alien and hateful world.
   d. a necessary new and important phase of her life.

7. Lisbeth's preference is for a life of
   a. crowds and excitement in a big city.
   b. freedom to travel and seek adventure on the seas.
   c. isolation amidst the beauties of wild nature.
   d. active sports such as boys usually enjoy.

8. According to this passage, one can judge that
   a. evergreens are pines.
   b. pines are not evergreens.
   c. only cedar, hemlock, and spruce are evergreens.
   d. cedars are evergreens.

9. "It did not occur to her that if she were one of the wild animals, as she sometimes imagined herself to be, she would not be aware of this beauty nor of the mysticism apparent in it." (lines 108–111) In this sentence, the author seems to be suggesting that
   a. Lisbeth's way of life is wrong and needs to be changed.
   b. Lisbeth is the kind of person who should lead a life close to nature and therefore should not go away to school.
   c. Lisbeth needs to balance her appreciation of wild nature with appreciation of herself as being human and therefore distinct from the wild.
   d. Lisbeth is rather irresponsible about her obligations.

Literary and Language Skills

APPRECIATING THE SETTING

Television has made it possible for a person to sit in his home and have brought before his eyes scenes and settings from every corner of the earth as well as from purely imaginary realms. One can see in vivid and exact detail the beautiful cities of Europe and the frigid wastes of the Antarctic; farmers at work in China and surfers at play in Hawaii; astronauts at work in their modules in outer space; and science-fiction travelers on far-off planets.

A fine author can also make an unfamiliar setting come to life through the skill of his writing. He fills his story with vivid and specific details that are part of the setting, details that make the setting very real for the reader, as though he were there. As a matter of fact, the reader uses his imagination and his senses to help create the setting. He is more actively involved than the television viewer, who is just an onlooker. Therefore, many readers will experience a setting created in words far more richly than a picture they see on television.

The passage you have read from *Ride Out the Storm* is a very good example of how an author can make an unfamiliar setting come to life for the reader. The following exercise will help you to appreciate the creation of this setting in the wilderness.

Exercise A

An important part of the creation of the northern wilderness setting is the naming of various members of the animal kingdom of land, sea, and air that populate the region. Examples are: *otter, ravens.* Look through the passage and list at least ten more members of the animal kingdom that are mentioned.

Exercise B

Members of the plant kingdom that are native to this wilderness are also named. Examples are: *seaweed, cedar.* List at least ten more members of the plant kingdom that are mentioned.

Exercise C

Exact observations of behavior of some of the animal populace are made. An example is: *Ravens circled over the forest and the red-breasted sapsuckers flashed in the trees.* List at least three more observations of behavior of the animal populace.

Exercise D

Sentences give concise yet picturesque descriptions of the landscape and seascape which contribute to the creation of the setting. An example is: *The tide ran free in the deep tapering channel until it spread itself over a white pebble beach where the creek came in.* Find and list at least two more examples of concise, picturesque descriptions of the landscape and seascape.

Exercise E

Sentences narrate Lisbeth's own inner feelings and outer acts as she interacts with the wilderness setting. An example is: *Sometimes in midsummer she would lie on her back on the sandspit where the paintbrush grew, eating wild strawberries and dreaming.* Find and list at least three more examples of narration of Lisbeth's interaction with the wilderness setting.

Vocabulary in Context

A. Carefully examine each word in its context; then decide which definition is most appropriate.

1. **promontory** (line 1)
   a. an easily visible object
   b. an evergreen forest
   c. a high point of land projecting into the sea
   d. an arm of the sea

2. **preoccupied** (line 43)
   a. having a prior task
   b. wasting time
   c. lost in thought
   d. too busy

3. **doleful** (line 60)
   a. sorrowful

    b. charitable

    c. wandering

    d. important

4. **revulsion** (line 88)

    a. decision

    b. determination

    c. fear

    d. disgust

5. **rites** (line 105)

    a. roles

    b. ceremonies

    c. announcements

    d. mysteries

B. Match meaning and sentence context by writing the word which most suitably fills the blank in each sentence. (Note that two words, 6 and 7, from the previous lesson are included for review.)

1. **promontory**	6. **condensed**
2. **preoccupied**	7. **utilitarian**
3. **doleful**	
4. **revulsion**	
5. **rites**	

a. The ___?___ reached out into the sea as though the land were extending a giant arm testing its own strength against the might of the oceans.

b. The girl stepped back in involuntary ___?___ at the sight of the garden snake, although she knew it to be harmless.

c. The lengthy book was ___?___ into a much shorter version for publication in the magazine.

d. The driver was so ___?___ that he didn't notice that the light had turned green until he heard the impatient honking of horns from the cars behind him.

e. The prospect of having to take three exams in one day plunged Harold into a —— ? —— state of mind.

f. The newly married couple found to their disappointment that their wedding gifts were of no —— ? —— value and would merely take up space without giving any practical benefit.

g. The three witches performed strange —— ? —— including the murmuring of unpleasant chants over unpleasant parts of unpleasant animals.

GROWING
(Unit One)

Vocabulary in Context

WORD LIST

1. amenities	14. nonchalance
2. concept	15. orifice
3. concoct	16. portentously
4. condensed	17. preoccupied
5. credulity	18. promontory
6. crucial	19. revulsion
7. disinterring	20. rites
8. doleful	21. spontaneous
9. evanescence	22. subdued
10. facilitates	23. sublime
11. indifference	24. tranquil
12. injunction	25. utilitarian
13. integrity	

Exercise A—FORMS

1. The word *amenities* is a plural noun. What is the singular form?

2. Which other word on the list is a plural noun? What is its singular form?

3. What is the plural form of *credulity*? of *promontory*?

4. The word *portentously* is an adverb. It is formed by adding the suffix *ly* to the adjective *portentous*. Select two adjectives from the list from which adverbs can be formed by adding the suffix *ly*. What are the two adverbs?

5. The words *condensed*, *preoccupied*, and *subdued* are formed from verbs. What are the three verbs of which they are forms?

6. Name two different ways in which the verb forms *condensed*,

preoccupied, *subdued*, and similar forms of any verb could be used in a sentence.

7. Which other word in the list illustrates a form of a verb?

8. The words *evanescence*, *indifference*, and *nonchalance* are nouns. What are two suffixes, then, that signal the noun form of a word?

9. What one change in form will turn the nouns *evanescence*, *indifference*, and *nonchalance* into adjectives?

10. The suffix *ion* is one signal that a word is a noun, as in *injunction* and *revulsion*. What nouns ending in *ion* can be formed from the verbs *concoct*, *condense*, *preoccupy?*

Exercise B—SYNONYMS

Each list word below is followed by a group of words. All of the words in each group EXCEPT ONE have been taken from *Roget's International Thesaurus of English Words and Phrases* as a synonym of or as having a meaning similar to the list word. In each group, which word DOES NOT belong?

1. **amenities**
   manners, politeness, courtesies, chivalries, competitions

2. **concoct**
   design, create, scatter, devise, invent

3. **doleful**
   studious, depressed, mournful, downcast, sorrowful

4. **injunction**
   command, order, retirement, ultimatum, edict

5. **integrity**
   uprightness, honor, purity, size, incorruptibility

6. **orifice**
   idol, opening, mouth, aperture, inlet

7. **preoccupied**

   inattentive, absent-minded, dreaming, thoughtful, active

8. **promontory**

   height, laboratory, headland, summit, cliff

9. **sublime**

   illustrious, glorious, unknown, noble, lordly

10. **tranquil**

    plain, pacific, calm, peaceful, untroubled

Exercise C—CONTEXTS

facilitates, credulity, promontory, doleful, crucial

Below are five summaries of front page news articles. Which one of the above words is most likely to appear in each article? Justify your choices carefully.

1. A tunnel is built under the English Channel to make possible ordinary automobile travel between England and France.

2. More and more evidence is reported contradicting statements that have been made by high government officials.

3. The whole world mourns the unexpected death of a great and respected leader at the height of his career.

4. A new lighthouse, the brightest in the world, is built on an especially suitable location.

5. A summit meeting is held to establish permanent world peace.

Exercise D—MORE CONTEXTS

In the right-hand columns are list words. In the left-hand columns are occupations. In each group of columns, write the list word with which the occupation is most closely associated. Justify your choices carefully.

GROUP I

OCCUPATIONS	LIST WORDS
philosopher	**concept**
judge	**concoct**
ship's navigator	**injunction**
minister	**promontory**
inventor	**rites**

GROUP II

mortician	**credulity**
performer	**facilitates**
advertising writer	**interring**
artist	**nonchalance**
engineer	**sublime**

Exercise E—ANALOGIES

Decide what the relationship is between the pair of words given first. From the four choices, select the pair of words that comes closest to expressing the same relationship as the given pair.

1. amenities : rude
   a. man : boy
   b. rules : behavior
   c. act : active
   d. charities : selfish

2. doleful : tears
   a. joyous : smiles
   b. water : river
   c. silence : sound
   d. real : pretending

3. tranquil : summer
   a. vacation : rest
   b. stormy : winter

    c. boredom : interest

    d. spring : rain

4. facilitates : effort

    a. lifts : exertion

    b. directs : traffic

    c. falls : down

    d. economizes : waste

5. subdued : enemy

    a. assisted : ally

    b. knowledge : ignorance

    c. mind : matter

    d. cause : effect

Literary and Language Skills

Exercise F—ALLUSIONS

Here are the ten allusions you have studied.

Achilles' heel	**Damon and Pythias**
Amazon	**Pandora's box**
Argus-eyed	**Scylla and Charybdis**
Babbit	**Shangri-la**
Cassandra	**Sherlock Holmes**

Select the allusion that best answers each question below.

1. What is the name of a place in which living has a *sublime* quality?

2. What was the source of lots of trouble because an *injunction* of Zeus was disobeyed?

3. Who spoke *portentously* of doom and calamity?

4. What was the weak spot through which a great warrior was finally *subdued?*

73

5. Who was often *preoccupied* with the meaning of clues that might lead to the solution of a crime?

6. Who were the monsters that sailors might escape from to safety only through the narrowest *orifice?*

7. Who represent the *concept* of perfect friendship?

8. What is the name of a race of women who showed *indifference* to living a *tranquil* life?

9. What character learned of the *evanescence* of the rewards of material success?

10. How might a person with unusually *utilitarian* visual abilities be described?

Exercise G—QUOTATIONS

Here are five quotations. Restate each quotation in your own words so as to express simply and clearly the meaning you see. Try to write three sentences for each quotation and try to make use of the list word in parentheses, or a form of it, in your restatement.

1. This above all: to thine own self be true,
   And it must follow, as the night the day,
   Thou canst not then be false to any man.

   (integrity)   —Shakespeare

2. The mind is its own place, and in itself
   Can make a heaven of hell, a hell of heaven.

   (concoct)   —Milton

3. Hope springs eternal in the human breast:
   Man never is, but always to be blest.

   (sublime)   —Pope

4. Oh what a tangled web we weave,
   When first we practise to deceive!

   (doleful)   —Scott

5. There is a pleasure in the pathless woods;
   There is a rapture on the lonely shore;
   There is society where none intrudes,
   By the deep sea, and music in its roar.

   (tranquil)   —Byron

Exercises H, I, and J, which follow, are all based on the passage below from *Lord Jim* by Joseph Conrad, with permission of the publisher, Doubleday & Company, Inc.

> A marvellous stillness pervaded the world, and the stars, together with the serenity of their rays, seemed to shed upon the earth the assurance of everlasting security. The young moon recurved, and shining low in the west, was like a slender shaving thrown up from a bar of gold, and the Arabian Sea, smooth and cool to the eye like a sheet of ice, extended its perfect level to the perfect circle of a dark horizon. The propeller turned without a check, as though its beat had been part of the scheme of a safe universe; and on each side of the *Patna* two deep folds of water, permanent and sombre on the unwrinkled shimmer, enclosed within their straight and diverging ridges a few white swirls of foam bursting in a low hiss, a few wavelets, a few ripples, a few undulations that, left behind, agitated the surface of the sea for an instant after the passage of the ship, subsided splashing gently, calmed down at last into the circular stillness of water and sky with the black speck of the moving hull remaining everlastingly in its centre.

Exercise H—VERBAL IMAGERY

From the passage, choose and list at least one example of each of the following types of verbal imagery.

seeing   hearing   feeling

Exercise I—POWER OF SUGGESTION

The information required to answer each question below is not given directly anywhere in the passage, but is suggested indirectly. Justify your answer in each case.

1. What time of day is it?
2. What is the *Patna?*
3. What change is likely to occur?

Exercise J—APPRECIATING THE SETTING

1. What is the setting that is brought to life in this passage?

2. Give three examples of exact observations that help make the setting come to life for the reader.

Themes for Growing

FOR THINKING

All of the passages in this book deal with the years that many people think are the most important and difficult in life—the growing years, the years of later childhood and adolescence. Among the important problems that come up in the passages of this unit are:

Choice making

How will you choose your friends? How will you dress? What will be your work habits, your ambitions and goals? How will you relax and enjoy yourself? Who will be your idols, the persons you admire most and would most want to be like? Who will have the most influence in making these choices—yourself? your parents? others?

The opposite sex

What is a "crush" and what does it mean? Are crushes good or bad? Is it better, during the growing years, to have one deep relationship with a person of the opposite sex or better to keep yourself relatively free and independent?

Dealing with parents

How much influence do parents have in shaping their children? What is the best kind of relationship between parents and children? the worst? Why are many parents (like Selina DeJong) disappointed in the way their child grows up, although they have worked hard and made many sacrifices for the child?

Crucial changes

Beginning with the first day of school, the growing years present crucial changes. What are some of the crucial changes that young people may be faced with? Why are they upsetting (as in the case of Lisbeth)? Are such changes good or bad?

FOR DISCUSSION

Consider the following periods of life: infancy, early childhood, later childhood, adolescence, youth, maturity, middle-age, the "golden" years, old age. Which is the worst period? Which is the best? Why?

FOR WRITING

Decide what you have found to be the greatest single problem of the growing years. Write a composition in which you explain clearly what the problem is, why you have found it to be the most serious problem, and what advice you could give to others as to the best way of handling the problem.

UNIT TWO

(Reading 6-10)

READING 6

A born vagabond, Leonardo! So thought Ser Antonio, and in a sense he was right.

Today, for instance, was not the first time that Leonardo had stolen away and wandered to the nearby hill. But then, when wasn't he adrift? And why did he wander? He had his reasons, and they were three. He was restless and lonely; insatiable curiosity compelled him to investigate everything from the building of a bird's nest to the building of a villa; and when he was roaming around he was out of his grandfather's way.

So he climbed the hills. Or he would go to a meadow where Ser Antonio's mules and horses grazed, and where grasshoppers had him patiently searching the grasses in order to find the insects and learn how they made that crackly noise, as of thorn twigs burning. Often, soon after daybreak, Leonardo would scale a slopeside to watch larks soar singingly into the morning's blue. Often, at day's end, he would again be on a slope, his pensive eyes following the flight of dark-winged hawks, as they wheeled high, then dived, seemingly, into the flaming crater of the setting sun.

Oh, to have wings! To rise up and up and up, past flying fluffs of cloud! Rise and dip, then rise and glide to the farthest edges of the open sky! Limitless space and limitless freedom! What must it be to feel that, to fly?

Then again, Leonardo would go to the swift and narrow river. The willows so dense around him that he was hidden,

Reprinted by permission of Dodd, Mead & Company, Inc. from LEONARDO DA VINCI, PRINCE OF PAINTERS by Covelle Newcomb. Copyright © 1965 by Covelle Newcomb.

he pondered for hours the riddle of the unseen current that made the water swirl and twist like a glittery tress of loosened hair, lifted and blown by invisible wind.

Other times, he plunged into rustly ravines, choked with osiers. For ages they had grown thick as thistles in this whole area. The village took their name, and also Leonardo's father's family, *Vinci* being the plural of *vinco*, the Tuscan word for willow. Leonardo wove the reeds into wicker baskets for the kitchen maids to carry eggs and fruits in; he plaited rush mats and rush for chair seats. And almost always on his walks he amused himself by interlacing the reeds in chain and knot-work designs. But not ever would he make of them a cage for a bird or a tiny one for a cricket. Encage a living thing? Deny it freedom? No, never!

Frequently, Leonardo kept the shepherds company, and sometimes at sundown he played the Panpipes which he had made of a row of tubular reeds of uneven lengths. Blowing across the top open ends, the boy, the shepherds said, coaxed magic from the pipe, for cows, goats, sheep, and lambs would gather closer in a slow quiet way and stand looking at him and listening as if bewitched.

However, more than piping in a pasture, with a crowd of cattle come to listen, set upon Leonardo the mark of an enchanter. Witnesses made oath on it that, with his hands and voice alone he could enchant wild stallions into meekness. Unafraid, with a running jump, he would mount on the bare back of a savage horse. Clutching its mane with one hand, he repeatedly drew the other gently over the horse's neck, and spoke to it. Quite suddenly, the beast would slacken its mad pace and cease to scream and quiver.

Without time, practice, halter, and saddle, nobody else could do this. How, then, was Leonardo able to bring a wild horse to submission?

Opinions varied. The stable grooms shared that of Leonardo's uncle. An experienced horseman, Ser Francesco believed, reasonably enough, that Leonardo had a way with horses, simply that. He loved them, he'd been around them since he was four years old. The more powerful and nervous the beast, the more Leonardo loved and understood it.

Superstitious folk, among them Ser Antonio, explained it differently. Leonardo, they claimed, was born with the dubiously happy power to cast spells and enchant. There was white magic and black. Which kind was Leonardo's? *Chi lo sa!*—Who knows!—is what they said, with a certain shrug of the shoulder. The gesture implied that Leonardo's magic was wickedly black.

His strength, even that, became suspect.

Unaware of his vigor, and thinking him a sissy, some village boys decided one day to test him.

"Where is he?"

"Up at the old fortress."

"Doing what?"

"Leaning against a tree and staring."

"At what?"

"Who can say! He just stands and dreams with his eyes open. Queer."

"Something else is queer. We go barefooted, yet everybody hears us coming. He wears shoes and nobody hears him."

"And something else: the sun blackens us, but him it seems not to touch."

"Watch! He'll have color before we finish with him. Let's go."

"What will he think when he sees us?"

"Think? He won't! He'll run."

Leonardo did not run. Openmouthed with wonder, he went toward them, smiling, believing he had friends. Then bewilderment held him rigid, while one roughneck poked fun at his golden hair and tried to caress it, and another ran a dirty finger down his flawless profile. In a flash he understood. They had come only to ridicule and taunt him. And in a flash he shook them off as easily as one waves off flies.

82

They dealt blows; he dealt stiffer ones. Away they ran, like bloodied bantam cocks sprinting to the safety of a roost. 100

Judge him by his looks? Not again! So delicate he was, they'd thought. Delicate, nothing! Leonardo had the muscles of a lion! For all they knew, he might even have the power to summon power from some unnatural source!

Retaliate! How? There must be a way. There was. 105

Scoffingly, these and other village bullies dubbed Leonardo *il mago*, the enchanter, the sorcerer. If they so much as glimpsed him from afar, they would half shout, half sing, their own version of an old wives' tale:

> "Leonardo is a witch-boy. 110
> Leonardo is a *mago*.
> His wet-nurse was a sorceress.
> Of goat-skin was her dress.
> Her bones clacked like a skeleton's.
> Her lullabies were funeral chants. 115
> *Dies irae, dies illa.*
> "Hey, witch-boy! *Mago!*
> *Non è vero?*"

Of course it was not true, yet a few ignorant Vincians held it to be as true as that Italy existed. 120

The fun it gave the boys to torment him in this fashion! What devilish satisfaction on their faces and in their voices!

Leonardo was too proud to let them see the misery they caused him. He covered his hurt with an air of calm aloofness. Even so, this false, unholy lore goosefleshed his skin 125 and filled him with a nameless little fear that never left him. At noonday or midnight, at any hour at all, suddenly it was there, to touch him like an icy whisper.

Sooner than suffer mockery and sarcasm, he became tight-lipped and secretive and stayed out of the way of everyone, 130 except the few persons in his life whom he knew he could trust. Long before he was thirteen, Leonardo had learned how to be alone and not mind it—not too much.

He was alone now, and taking his time, and despite his

135 knowing this trail as well as he knew his name, he observed
this, that, and the other thing with avid interest. He paused
before a shrub abloom with white and lemon butterflies. He
peered at the unblinking eyes of a lizard whose lean length
banded with vivid green the side of a tawny rock. Farther
140 along, he marveled at the crinkled tissue of poppies that
shone amid stones like spurts of flame. Again and again he
scanned the sky for a kite lifting itself on long pointed
wings to a lofty crag far away. But the hawklike birds that
he loved had flown to shade.

145 Halfway to the crest, a sound brought him to a halt. He
turned and looked toward Vinci through the shimmery haze
that seemed to wave in the heat like a gigantic cobweb
suspended in space. Throb of the mill wheel, rumble of the
milldam. Was that what he heard? At this distance? At this
150 height? He knitted his brow, and a lot of thinking was going
on inside his head.

How strange! He stared harder at the haze, as if to find
the answer in it. Now it came to him that on misty and
rainy days the song of Santa Croce's bell rose clear and high,
155 higher than his grandfather's house, near the top of Vinci.
Yet when there was no mist or rain, the church bell's tone
was dimmer.

At his belt hung a string with scraps of paper strung on it
and a pencil tied to one end. He stood thinking; he reasoned;
160 he nodded his head. Haze *was* the answer! Quickly, he jotted
down his conclusion. In time to come, Leonardo da Vinci
was to solve many mysteries of the atmosphere. Today, on a
hillside, he rightly attributed to haze the principles of a
sounding board, realizing that fog, rain, and haze reflect and
165 intensify sound.

Lost in his discovery, Leonardo straggled ahead. On
reaching the last turn in the trail, the threshing of the mill
wheel, the roaring of the weir, were forgotten. Noises of a
different kind absorbed him now: the crunch of gravelly
170 earth under the tread of laborers' feet; pound of mallets and

hammers; ring of spade, pickax, and shovel; metallic clink
of trowels bonding stones with mortar; a drone of talk. For
Leonardo, these were joyous sounds.

His eyes shone. His heart drummed with anticipation. In
this little skytop world of peasants he felt secure and wel- 175
come. Here, nobody made him feel unwanted; nobody
scolded if he merely looked on, without talking. If he asked
questions, he was not told to keep still. Not once would he
hear an echo of his grandfather's irritable orders:

"Don't be a bother! Be quiet! Go away! Make yourself 180
useful!"

Only minutes later, Leonardo was perched on the boulder
where he always sat, and he thrilled, as he always did, to the
spontaneous shout of greetings. Right off, he looked for
Vittore. Then he saw something he had not expected. Vittore 185
was standing at the wobbly table, his curly black head bent
over the ground plan. Beside him stood a gentleman in
water-green silk.

"Are you thirsty, Leonardo?" Dino called out, as he came
toward Leonardo, shovel in one hand, a carved gourd water 190
flask in the other.

"Hello, Dino."

"Here, drink."

"Beautiful! Pale green as the Etruscan sea, that silk!"

"Oh, him," said Dino, understanding. 195

"Who is the gentleman, Dino?"

"Messer Biagio da Ravenna."

"And who is Messer Biagio da Ravenna?"

"He is who I said he is," replied Dino, and shoved the
gourd at Leonardo. "Does it matter who he is?" 200

"No, I guess it doesn't."

Had Leonardo been told how much it was to matter to
him, he would not have believed it. Still less would he have
believed that this Italian architect of some renown would
befriend him. Any such thing was as far from his thoughts 205
as is the falcon from the wrist that has freed it.

85

Reading Comprehension

The exercises that follow are based on the passage you have just read. Each exercise consists of an incomplete statement or a question followed by four choices. Select the choice that best completes the statement or best answers the question. Go back to the passage for rereading to whatever extent is necessary to help you choose your answer.

1. Which statement about Ser Antonio (lines 1–10) is NOT true?
   a. He is Leonardo's grandfather.
   b. He expects Leonardo to change his ways.
   c. He thinks Leonardo is an aimless vagabond.
   d. He has caused Leonardo to want to stay out of his way.

2. Leonardo's behavior can best be explained by saying that he is deeply curious about
   a. nature.
   b. art.
   c. science.
   d. everything.

3. The chief effect of the fourth paragraph (lines 21–24) is to
   a. show that Leonardo has a strong sense of poetic but unrealistic imagination.
   b. suggest that Leonardo will soon try to escape the imprisonment of his village.
   c. show that Leonardo loves nature more than people.
   d. suggest that some day the adult Leonardo will try to invent a "flying machine."

4. Leonardo's study of "the swift and narrow river" (lines 25–26) shows that the chief difference between him and most observers is that he
   a. looks beneath the obvious to the hidden and unseen because he is seeking explanations of what he sees.
   b. has lots of time to spare.
   c. appreciates the beauties of nature more than others.

d. prefers being a "lover" to being in the company of others.

5. Apparently, *osiers* (line 31) are a kind of
   a. willow.
   b. vine.
   c. thistle.
   d. dust or smoke.

6. Ser Antonio believed that the explanation for Leonardo's handling of horses lay in
   a. his simply having a way with horses.
   b. good magic.
   c. evil magic.
   d. his strength.

7. "... the sun blackens us, but him it seems not to touch." (lines 86–87) This statement is best explained by saying that
   a. Leonardo stayed out of the sun as much as he could because he was wise in the ways of nature.
   b. the statement simply reflects the prejudiced imagination of the village boys.
   c. unlike the others in the village, Leonardo had golden hair and the fair complexion that goes with it.
   d. the boys really mean that they are going to beat Leonardo black and blue.

8. The passage clearly suggests that the boys' tormenting of Leonardo had the effect of
   a. damaging him forever.
   b. making him realize all the more his own superiority.
   c. simply strengthening his own preference for being alone.
   d. making him give up most of his former habits.

9. The incident of the church bell especially reveals Leonardo's talent for
   a. appreciating musical sound.
   b. keen hearing.
   c. sincere religious feeling.
   d. scientific reasoning.

10. The "Italian architect of some renown" (line 204) is
    a. Dino.
    b. Michelangelo.
    c. Messer Biagio.
    d. unnamed.

Literary and Language Skills

SIMILES

Look at these two sentences:

1. Her unhappiness lay deep and destructively inside her.
2. Her unhappiness ate away at her like a worm inside a bud.

Both of these sentences are about the same thing, a girl's great and harmful unhappiness. But the same thought is expressed in two sharply different ways. The first sentence tells us directly, or *literally*, that the unhappiness was deep and destructive. The second sentence tells imaginatively, or *figuratively*, that the unhappiness can be compared to a worm eating away at the inside of a bud. The imaginative comparison used in the second sentence makes it a more forceful, interesting form of expression. This kind of imaginative comparison is a *simile*.

A simile consists of two parts. The first part is the actual situation or experience the writer is telling about. The second part is an imaginative picture to which the real situation is being compared. The words *like* or *as* (sometimes *as if* and *as though*) are usually used to express the comparison.

In this sentence the two parts are

> *real situation*—her unhappiness
> *imaginative picture*—a worm inside a bud ate away
> *comparing word*—like

The passage you have read from *Leonardo da Vinci* is sprinkled with similes which add to the interest of the aware reader. The following exercises will help you to recognize, understand, and appreciate similes as they occur in your reading in general as well as in this particular piece of writing.

Exercise A

Here are five sentences taken from earlier passages. All the sentences do include use of the words *like* or *as*. However, they do not necessarily include the imaginative (figurative) comparison which forms a simile. First decide which sentences are similes, then analyze each simile-containing sentence as in the following example:

> The exhausted fireman was as soggy, as crumpled, and as dirty as a wet towel flung into the corner of a room.
>
> *real situation*—fireman was soggy, crumpled, dirty
> *imaginative picture*—a wet towel flung into the corner of a room
> *comparing word*—as

1. . . . he had seen the glory envelop Madeline like the dawn . . .

2. Even words like evanescent and fugacious could set up, with their suggestive syllables, delicious tremors of sorrow in her heart.

3. In spite of her care, raindrops like emeralds and diamonds went flying down to nothing as she walked.

4. On this day in April, she rowed past the sandspit so close in that her oars touched bottom and stirred the sand into little whirls like whirls of smoke in the clear water.

5. All of nature's announcements of her changing seasons she awaited with a sort of mystical attentiveness, as though they were religious rites.

Exercise B

All of the following sentences from *Leonardo da Vinci* contain similes. Analyze each as in Exercise A.

1. Or he would go to a meadow where Ser Antonio's mules and horses grazed, and where grasshoppers had him patiently searching the grasses in order to find the insects and learn how they made that crackly noise, as of thorn twigs burning.

2. The willows so dense around him that he was hidden, he pondered for hours the riddle of the unseen current that made the water swirl and twist like a glittery tress of loosened hair, lifted and blown by invisible wind.

3. And in a flash he shook them off as easily as one waves off flies.

4. Away they ran, like bloodied bantam cocks sprinting to the safety of a roost.

5. At noonday or midnight, at any hour at all, suddenly it was there, to touch him like an icy whisper.

6. Farther along, he marveled at the crinkled tissue of poppies that shone amid stones like spurts of flame.

Exercise C

This exercise will test your skill with similes at a more advanced level. Decide which of the three choices best completes each sentence to form a good simile. What is your reason for each choice?

> *Example:* Sometimes misfortune springs suddenly on its victims like
> *a.* a fog creeping out of the hills.
> *b.* any other expected event.
> *c.* an assailant springing out of the night.
> (*Answer: c*)

Explanation:

 a. This picture is not a good imaginative comparison because the imaginative picture a "creeping fog" doesn't fit "springs suddenly."

 b. There is no picture here and nothing imaginative. No simile is formed.

 c. This is a strong imaginative picture that matches the meaning "springs suddenly" and "victims" in the real situation. This is the best answer.

1. Bright yellow butterflies flickered along through the shade like
   a. dark shadows.
   b. flecks of sunlight in a forest.
   c. spotlights.

2. The fly buzzed desperately, and the vibrations of his tiny wings sounded in the morning like
   a. a roar of thunder.
   b. a noise I had heard before.
   c. a far-off string orchestra.

3. My own men were deserting me as
   a. they showed themselves to be cowards.
   b. rats do a sinking ship.
   c. water pours out of a faucet.

4. A complete silence took possession of the land; a silence, cold, mournful, profound; more like
   a. morning than evening.
   b. death than peace.
   c. the ocean than the desert.

5. He stood unyielding under the strain, as solid and motionless as
   a. a football star scoring a touchdown.
   b. a jet plane with engines roaring.
   c. one of the big trees of the surrounding forest.

Vocabulary in Context

A. Carefully examine each word in its context; then decide which definition is most appropriate.

1. **insatiable** (line 7)
   - *a.* capable of great achievement
   - *b.* curious
   - *c.* not able to be satisfied
   - *d.* ordinary

2. **submission** (line 59)
   - *a.* obedience
   - *b.* difficult task or assignment
   - *c.* secret task or assignment
   - *d.* pasture

3. **vigor** (line 74)
   - *a.* energy
   - *b.* character
   - *c.* determination
   - *d.* poise

4. **retaliate** (line 105)
   - *a.* strike back
   - *b.* do evil
   - *c.* perform
   - *d.* compete

5. **avid** (line 136)
   - *a.* altogether unjustified
   - *b.* half-hearted
   - *c.* eager
   - *d.* thoughtful

B. Match meaning and sentence context by writing the word which most suitably fills the blank in each sentence. (Note that two words, 6 and 7, from the previous lesson are included for review.)

1. insatiable
2. submission
3. vigor
4. retaliate
5. avid

6. doleful
7. rites

a. When the price of beef was raised, some consumers tried to ___?___ by advocating a boycott against the butcher shops.

b. The country was stunned by the ___?___ news that a great leader had died at the height of his career.

c. The rioters and looters were finally brought to ___?___ by the firm actions of the majority of citizens.

d. The government was ___?___ in its quest for the designing of a non-polluting automobile engine.

e. The small cult practiced strange ceremonies and ___?___ that involved worship of snakes and curious idols.

f. Growing boys sometimes have what seems to be an ___?___ appetite, the only pause in their eating coming when they are asleep.

g. The health and ___?___ of the young track star were such that he competed in and won three events in a single afternoon.

93

READING 7

"The very man we've been looking for," he said. "Yessir. Old Bottles Rubbernose Barton. He can win the jumping events for us."

"Come on, Bottles," they said. "Save the day for us. Be a good old Rubbernose."

Anna Louise was one who laughed the most and it was the third time I'd wanted to pop her on the nose.

I went away from there and didn't turn back when they laughed and called and whistled at me.

"She'd be surprised if I did," I said.

I kept thinking this over and pretty soon I said, "Well, maybe you could."

Then when I was sweeping the drugstore floor I all of a sudden said, "I can!"

"You can what?" Mrs. Patch asked me.

"Nothing," I said.

"You can hurry about sweeping the floor, that's what you can do," she said.

There was a big crowd out for the track meet and we were tied when I went up to our coach. It was just time for the jumping to start.

"What are you doing in a track suit?" he asked me.

"I'm going to save the day for Brinkley," I said. "I'm going to jump."

"No, you aren't," he said. "You run along and start a marble game with some other kid."

I looked him in the eye and I spoke in a cold, level tone of voice.

"Mr. Smith," I said, "the track meet depends on the high jump and the pole vault and unless I am entered we will lose those two events and the meet. I can win and I am willing to do it for Brinkley. Do you want to win the meet?"

He looked amazed.

"Where have you been all the time?" he asked. "You talk like you've got something on the ball."

I didn't say anything, I just smiled.

The crowd all rushed over to the jumping pits and I took my time going over. When everybody had jumped but me the coach turned and said, "Come on now, Barton, let's see what you can do."

"Not yet," I said.

"What do you mean?" he asked.

"I'll wait until the last man has been eliminated," I said. "Then I'll jump."

The crowd laughed but I just stared coldly at them. The coach tried to persuade me to jump but I wouldn't change my mind.

"I stake everything on one jump," I said. "Have faith in me."

He looked at me and shook his head and said, "Have it your own way."

They started the bar a little over four feet and pretty soon it was creeping up toward five feet and a half. That's always been a pretty good distance for high school jumpers. When the bar reached five feet seven inches all our men except one was eliminated. Two from Fairfield were still in the event. They put the bar at five feet nine inches and one man from Fairfield made it. Our man tried hard but he scraped the bar and knocked it off.

60   The crowd started yelling, thinking Fairfield had won the event.

"Wait a minute," I yelled. "I haven't jumped yet."

The judges looked at their lists and saw it was so. Maybe you think it was against the rules for them to allow me to
65 skip my turn but anyway that's the way it was.

"You can't make that mark," one of the judges said. "Why try? You're not warmed up."

"Never mind," I said.

I walked up close to the jumping standard and stood there.
70   "Go ahead and jump," one of the judges said.

"I will," I said.

"Well, don't stand there," he said. "Come on back here so's you can get a run at it."

"I don't want any run at the bar," I said. "I'll jump from
75 here."

The judge yelled at the coach and told him to take me out on account of I was crazy.

I swung my arms in back of me and sprung up and down a second and then I jumped over the bar with inches to spare.
80 When I came down it was so silent I could hear my footsteps as I walked across the sawdust pit. The judge that'd crabbed at me just stood and looked. His eyes were bugged out and his mouth hung open.

"Good Lord!" he said. "Almighty most loving Lord!"
85   Our coach came up and he stood beside the judge and they both looked the same, bug-eyed.

"Did you see that?" the coach asked. "Tell me you didn't. Please do. I'd rather lose this track meet than my mind."

The judge turned slowly and looked at him.
90   "Good Lord!" he said, "there's two of us."

All of a sudden everybody started yelling and the fellows near me pounded me on the back and tried to shake my hand. I smiled and brushed them aside and walked over to the judge.
95   "What's the high school record for this state?" I asked.

"Five feet, eleven inches," he said.

96

"Put her at six," I said.

They put the bar at six and I gathered myself together and gave a heave and went over the bar like I was floating. It was easy. Well, that just knocked the wind out of everybody. They'd thought I couldn't do anything and there I'd broken the state record for the high jump without a running start.

The crowd surrounded me and tried to shake my hand and the coach and judge got off to one side and reached out and pinched each other's cheek and looked at the bar and shook their heads. Frank Shay grabbed my hand and wrung it and said, "Gosh, Bottles, I was just kidding the other day. I didn't know you were such a ring-tailed wonder. Say, Bottles, we're having a frat dance tonight. Will you come?"

"You know what you can do with your frat," I said. "I don't approve of them. They're undemocratic."

A lot of the fellows that'd made fun of me before crowded around and acted as if I'd been their friend all along.

When Anna Louise crowded through the gang and said, "Oh, you're marvelous!" I just smiled at her and said, "Do you think so?" and walked away. She tagged around after me but I talked mostly with two other girls.

They didn't usually have a public address system at our track meets but they started using one then.

"Ladies and gentlemen," the announcer said, "you have just witnessed a record-breaking performance by Bottles Barton——."

He went on like that telling them what an astonishing thing I'd done and it came to me I didn't mind being called Bottles any more. In fact, I kind of liked it.

Mr. and Mrs. Patch came up and Mrs. Patch tried to kiss me but I wouldn't let her. Old man Patch shook my hand.

"You've made our drugstore famous," he said. "From now on you're a clerk. No more bottle washing."

"We'll make him a partner," old lady Patch said.

"No, you won't," I said. "I think I'll go over to the McManus Pharmacy."

Then they called the pole vault and I did like I'd done before. I wouldn't jump until our men'd been eliminated. The
135 bar was at eleven feet.

"It's your turn," our coach told me. "Ever use a pole before?"

"Oh, sure," I told him.

He gave me a pole and the crowd cleared away and grew
140 silent. Everyone was watching me.

I threw the pole down and smiled at the crowd. The coach yelled for me to pick up the pole and jump. I picked it up and threw it ten feet away from me. Everybody gasped. Then I took a short run and went over the bar at eleven feet.
145 It was simple.

This time the coach and the judge took pins and poked them in one another's cheeks. The coach grabbed me and said, "When I wake up I'm going to be so mad at you I'm going to give you the beating of your life."
150 Anna Louise came up and held my arm and said, "Oh, Bottles, you're so wonderful! I've always thought so. Please forgive me for calling you Rubbernose. I want you to come to our party tonight."

"All right," I said. "I'll forgive you but don't you call me
155 Rubbernose again."

They moved the bar up again and the fellow from Fairfield couldn't make it. I took a short run and went over. I did it so easy it came to me I could fly if I wanted to but I decided not to try it on account of people wouldn't think it
160 so wonderful if a fellow that could fly jumped eleven feet without a pole. I'd won the track meet for Brinkley High and the students all came down out of the stand and put me on their shoulders and paraded me around and around the track. A lot of fellows were waving papers at me asking me to sign
165 them and get $1000 a week as a professional jumper. I signed one which threw in an automobile.

That's what I did once and nobody knows about it, so I am writing about it so people will know.

Reading Comprehension

The exercises that follow are based on the passage you have just read. Each exercise consists of an incomplete statement followed by four choices. Select the choice that best completes the statement. Go back to the passage for rereading to whatever extent is necessary to help you choose your answer.

1. It is most likely that young Barton has been given the nickname "Bottles" because
   a. of the shape of his nose.
   b. he works in a drugstore.
   c. he is an alcoholic.
   d. of his general appearance.

2. The narrative shifts without warning from reality to Barton's fantasies or daydreams. The first shift to fantasy from reality occurs at line
   a. 8   c. 19
   b. 16   d. 37

3. A possible characteristic of young adolescents in their behavior towards each other that is suggested by the opening lines of the passage is
   a. understanding of each other.
   b. school spirit.
   c. a sense of humor.
   d. unthinking cruelty.

4. "No, you aren't ... You run along and start a marble game with some other kid." (lines 25–26) The best explanation of this remark by the coach to Barton is
   a. the coach, like everybody else, fails to recognize Barton's real abilities.
   b. this note of realism in the fantasy will make Barton's imaginary triumph all the sweeter.

c. the coach wants deliberately to stimulate Barton to a supreme effort.

d. Barton is known for his skill in playing marbles.

5. "The crowd laughed but I just stared coldly at them." (line 45) A somewhat humorous aspect of this statement is that
   a. in reality, the crowd couldn't possibly have heard Barton's remark to the coach.
   b. the crowd was in for a big surprise.
   c. Barton has infected the crowd with hopeful gaiety.
   d. a crowd doesn't laugh.

6. "... I'd broken the state record for the high jump without a running start." (lines 101–102) The basis for Barton's statement is
   a. he has a thin, light build.
   b. he has invented a new jumping technique.
   c. he has been keenly motivated by his frustrations.
   d. he has a rather wild imagination.

7. It seems clear that Barton's real feeling towards Anna Louise is that he
   a. dislikes her.
   b. has a "crush" on her.
   c. thinks she doesn't treat him as a sister should.
   d. admires her as a person but has no personal interest in her.

8. From his fantasies, it can be seen that the main feeling towards other people that Barton's experiences have created in him is
   a. understanding.
   b. hostility.
   c. forgiveness.
   d. superiority.

9. The author probably intended, through this story, to leave his reader with a feeling of
   a. disgust.   c. pity.
   b. excitement.   d. gaiety.

100

10. "nobody knows about it" (line 167) The reason is that
    a. it never happened.
    b. Barton has not told his real name.
    c. a high school track meet gets little newspaper publicity.
    d. Barton never jumped again.

Literary and Language Skills

APPRECIATING CHARACTERIZATION

Good stories create characters for the reader. A well-created character seems like a real person. The reader can talk or think or argue about the character as though he were a real person. Through a well-created character, the reader will see and understand better something of himself, or of other people he knows, or of all human beings generally. How is such characterization accomplished?

The author can tell us something about a character *directly:* "George Brown was a mean old man." This is not a very good method of creating a character because we simply take the author's word for it. We don't come to see it for ourselves.

The better kind of characterization permits us to draw our own conclusions *indirectly* (we use the "power of suggestion"!) from various kinds of behavior given in the story. Six types of behavior on which character creation is based are most important and occur most frequently. Study and understand the list below. (Note that no one story will necessarily include all of these.)

Types of behavior

1. The actions of the character
2. The spoken words of the character
3. The thoughts of the character
4. The actions of others towards the character
5. The words spoken by others to the character
6. The thoughts of others about the character

Exercise A

Each of the six types of character-creating behavior is illustrated by an excerpt from a story. Which choice best expresses the character trait suggested by the excerpt? Be ready to explain the reasons for your choice.

1. *The actions of the character*

   Paul entered the gym crowded with couples dancing or talking and laughing together. He quickly edged towards a darkened corner where he stood sweating and trembling with near panic.

   insecurity   anger   snobbishness

2. *The spoken words of the character*

   Let me tell you, my dear, the only way to handle these natives is to be firm.

   prejudice   firmness   friendliness

3. *The thoughts of the character*

   I'll do it tomorrow, she thought, and when tomorrow came, she thought again, as always, I'll do it tomorrow.

   determination   foresight   irresponsibility

4. *The actions of others towards the character*

   As the stranger approached, Rover abruptly stopped his cheerful frolicking and instead held his body tense and motionless, eyes fixed on the newcomer, teeth bared with a threatening snarl.

   courage   foolhardiness   untrustworthiness

5. *The words spoken by others to the character*

   For the past ten years, there were only two words that Jones ever used to respond to his wife's remarks—"Yes, dear."

   worthy of respect   domineering   frightened

6. *The thoughts of others about the character*

He was regarded by the children as the most frightful thing outside the story books.

worthy of respect   fearsome   imaginary

Exercise B

Character creation—specifically that of Bottles Barton—is the highlight of *That's What Happened to Me.* This exercise will help you to appreciate the characterization better.

Below are ten excerpts from the passage. For each excerpt (*a*) tell which of the six types of behavior is illustrated (note that in the case of this story you have to be careful in making your decision), and (*b*) be ready to explain at length what the excerpt tells you about the main character.

1. "Yessir. Old Bottles Rubbernose Barton. He can win the jumping events for us." (lines 1–3)

2. "Anna Louise was one who laughed the most . . ." (line 6)

3. "She'd be surprised if I did" . . . (line 10)

4. "I can!" (line 14)

5. "You can hurry about sweeping the floor, that's what you can do" . . . (lines 17–18)

6. "They didn't usually have a public address system at our track meets but they started using one then." (lines 118–119)

7. "I think I'll go over to the McManus Pharmacy." (lines 131–132)

8. "Oh, Bottles, you're so wonderful!" (lines 150–151)

9. ". . . I could fly if I wanted to but I decided not to try it on account of people wouldn't think it so wonderful if a fellow that could fly jumped eleven feet without a pole." (lines 158–161)

10. "That's what I did once and nobody knows about it, so I am writing about it so people will know." (lines 167–168)

Vocabulary in Context

A. Carefully examine each word in its context; then decide which definition is most appropriate.

1. **level** (line 27)
    a. loud
    b. emotional
    c. angry
    d. unchanging

2. **amazed** (line 33)
    a. surprised
    b. frightened
    c. disappointed
    d. satisfied

3. **eliminated** (line 43)
    a. removed
    b. repeated
    c. numbered
    d. moved

4. **persuade** (line 46)
    a. argue
    b. convince
    c. coax
    d. encourage

5. **heave** (line 99)
    a. act of throwing straight
    b. act of taking a deep breath
    c. act of lifting with effort
    d. a shout

B. Match meaning and sentence context by writing the word which most suitably fills the blank in each sentence. (Note that two words, 6 and 7, from the previous lesson are included for review.)

1. level   6. vigor
2. amazed   7. avid
3. eliminated
4. persuade
5. heave

a. It was difficult to ___?___ Mary to run for president of the student council, but we were finally able to convince her that the job would not seriously interfere with her other obligations.

b. The audience was ___?___ by the remarkable tricks of the trained seal.

c. The poll showed that all the candidates but two could be ___?___ from any serious consideration as possible victors in the election.

d. He was a remarkable old man, whose strength and ___?___ might be envied by any youth.

e. The four men put all their strength into one mighty ___?___, but they could not budge the car out of the soft mud.

f. It has been a long time since food prices have followed a ___?___ course, the trend having been up, up, up.

g. The speaker's eager concern for a clean environment implanted an equally ___?___ resolve in his audience to fight pollution.

READING 8

It was the Christmas after my aunt had left the house, and since it was she who always supplied the tree and the presents for my brother and myself, this first Christmas without her was a bleak and empty one. I remember that I was more or 5 less reconciled to it, because my father had worked only spasmodically throughout the year. Two of our rooms were vacant of boarders and my mother was doing her marketing farther and farther away from our neighborhood. This was always a sign that we were dangerously close to rock bottom, 10 and each time it occurred I came to dread it more. It was one of the vicious landmarks of poverty that I had come to know well and the one I hated the most. As the bills at our regular grocer and butcher went unpaid, and my mother dared not even be seen at the stores lest they come to the 15 doorways and yell after her publicly, she would trudge ten or twelve blocks to a whole new neighborhood, tell the new grocer or butcher that we have just moved in to some fictitious address around the corner, and establish credit for as long as she could. Thus we were able to exist until my father found 20 work again, or all the rooms were rented, and she could pay our own grocer and butcher, and gradually the others. This time, however, they had all of them gone unpaid and my mother was walking twenty blocks or more for a bottle of milk.

25 Obviously Christmas was out of the question—we were barely staying alive. On Christmas Eve my father was very

From ACT ONE, by Moss Hart. Copyright © 1959 by Catherine Carlisle Hart and Joseph M. Hyman, Trustees. Reprinted by permission of Random House, Inc.

silent during the evening meal. Then he surprised and startled me by turning to me and saying, "Let's take a walk." He had never suggested such a thing before, and moreover it was a very cold winter's night. I was even more surprised when he said as we left the house, "Let's go down to a Hundred Forty-ninth Street and Westchester Avenue." My heart leapt within me. That was the section where all the big stores were, where at Christmastime open pushcarts full of toys stood packed end-to-end for blocks at a stretch. On other Christmas Eves I had often gone there with my aunt, and from our tour of the carts she had gathered what I wanted the most. My father had known of this, of course, and I joyously concluded that this walk could mean only one thing—he was going to buy me a Christmas present.

On the walk down I was beside myself with delight and an inner relief. It had been a bad year for me, that year of my aunt's going, and I wanted a Christmas present terribly—not a present merely, but a symbol, a token of some sort. I needed some sign from my father or mother that they knew what I was going through and cared for me as much as my aunt and my grandfather did. I am sure they were giving me what mute signs they could, but I did not see them. The idea that my father had managed a Christmas present for me in spite of everything filled me with a sudden peace and lightness of heart I had not known in months.

We hurried on, our heads bent against the wind, to the cluster of lights ahead that was 149th Street and Westchester Avenue, and those lights seemed to me the brightest lights I had ever seen. Tugging at my father's coat, I started down the line of pushcarts. There were all kinds of things that I wanted, but since nothing had been said by my father about buying a present, I would merely pause before a pushcart to say, with as much control as I could muster, "Look at that chemistry set!" or, "There's a stamp album!" or, "Look at the printing press!" Each time my father would pause and ask the pushcart man the price. Then without a word we

would move on to the next pushcart. Once or twice he would pick up a toy of some kind and look at it and then at
65 me, as if to suggest this might be something I might like, but I was ten years old and a good deal beyond just a toy; my heart was set on a chemistry set or a printing press. There they were on every pushcart we stopped at, but the price was always the same and soon I looked up and saw we were
70 nearing the end of the line. Only two or three more pushcarts remained. My father looked up, too, and I heard him jingle some coins in his pocket. In a flash I knew it all. He'd gotten together about seventy-five cents to buy me a Christmas present, and he hadn't dared say so in case there was
75 nothing to be had for so small a sum.

As I looked up at him I saw a look of despair and disappointment in his eyes that brought me closer to him than I had ever been in my life. I wanted to throw my arms around him and say, "It doesn't matter . . . I understand . . . this is
80 better than a chemistry set or a printing press . . . I love you." But instead we stood shivering beside each other for a moment—then turned away from the last two pushcarts and started silently back home. I don't know why the words remained choked up within me. I didn't even take his hand
85 on the way home nor did he take mine. We were not on that basis. Nor did I ever tell him how close to him I felt that night—that for a little while the concrete wall between father and son had crumbled away and I knew that we were two lonely people struggling to reach each other.

Reading Comprehension

The exercises that follow are based on the passage you have just read. Each exercise consists of an incomplete statement followed by four choices. Select the choice that best completes the statement. Go back to the passage for rereading to whatever extent is necessary to help you choose your answer.

1. Moss Hart especially missed his aunt when she left because
   a. she had supported the family.
   b. she was the only one who loved him and his brother.
   c. she had bought the Christmas tree and presents.
   d. she had helped his mother with the marketing.

2. "Two of our rooms were vacant of boarders . . ." (lines 6–7)
   This statement suggests that
   a. another relative besides the aunt had been living with the family.
   b. the family rented rooms in their home to outside boarders as a source of income.
   c. the father did not live at home at this time.
   d. the family had once been wealthy.

3. Moss Hart tells about his mother's shopping for food farther and farther from home to show that she was
   a. dishonest.   c. a victim of poverty.
   b. a good manager.   d. a careful shopper.

4. Moss Hart's reaction to his father's suggestion that they take a walk to Westchester Avenue was one of
   a. pleasant surprise because he then expected a Christmas present.
   b. pleasure because his father had never shown an interest in him before.
   c. displeasure because it was a bitterly cold night.
   d. puzzlement because he couldn't figure out what his father had in mind.

5. As a child at the time, Moss Hart had felt that
   a. his parents showed little sympathy with his suffering.
   b. his parents showed in whatever way they could that they cared about his suffering.
   c. only his aunt cared about him.
   d. only his grandfather cared about him.

6. As he began to walk with his father among the pushcarts, the young Moss Hart felt that
   a. he would be satisfied only with a chemistry set or a printing press.
   b. he would be happy with any toy.
   c. his father had brought him there just to look, not to buy.
   d. he didn't want a present because he knew his father couldn't afford it.

7. The end result of the shopping expedition was that
   a. father and son were finally able to communicate with each other openly.
   b. the "concrete" wall between them remained thicker than ever.
   c. the boy lost all respect for his father.
   d. for a little while there was unexpressed closeness between father and son.

8. If this were one chapter in the autobiography of Moss Hart, the best title would be
   a. The Generation Gap.   c. The Richest Gift.
   b. My Aunt.   d. The Curse of Poverty.

Literary and Language Skills

AND

The seemingly simple and common word *and* is one of the most important words in the English language. The word *and* is a basic tool for writing clear, mature, and interesting sentences.

Exercise A

Look at these sentences.

The word *and* is a basic tool for writing clear sentences. The word *and* is a basic tool for writing mature sentences. The word *and* is a basic tool for writing interesting sentences.

1. Use the word *and* as a tool to rewrite the above sentences in a better form.
2. What is one important way, then, in which the word *and* can help you to write better sentences?
3. As you surely know, *and* is used to connect. In the sentence you wrote in answer to (1) above, what sentence parts has *and* been used to connect?

Exercise B

The word *and* can be used to connect many sentence elements. The word *and* can be used to connect—

> single-word nouns
> single-word verbs
> single-word adjectives
> single-word adverbs
> whole subjects
> whole predicates
> phrases
> subordinate clauses
> independent clauses (to form a compound sentence)

Look at each of the five sentences below. From the above list, give the name of the sentence elements that *and* has been used to connect.

1. Abraham Lincoln believed in government of the people, by the people, *and* for the people.

2. Because it was raining heavily *and* because we were all tired, we canceled the trip.

3. Government officials of New York *and* government officials of New Jersey met to discuss common problems.

4. The cat finished her milk *and* stretched out lazily on the rug.

5. The fans cheered wildly *and* the band played the school victory song.

Exercise C

As a skillful writer, Moss Hart has used the word *and* to keep his story flowing smoothly and interestingly. Below are ten examples from the passage. In six of these, Hart has used the word *and* to connect independent clauses. Identify those six examples. Then, name the sentence elements connected by *and* in the other four examples. (Base your answers only on the italicized *and* in each example.)

1. Two of our rooms were vacant of boarders *and* my mother was doing her marketing farther and farther away from our neighborhood.

2. This was always a sign that we were dangerously close to rock bottom, *and* each time it occurred I came to dread it more.

3. ... she would trudge ten or twelve blocks to a whole new neighborhood, tell the new grocer or butcher that we had just moved in to some fictitious address around the corner, *and* establish credit for as long as she could.

4. Then he surprised *and* startled me by turning to me and saying, "Let's take a walk."

5. He had never suggested such a thing before, *and* moreover it was a very cold winter's night.

6. On other Christmas Eves I had often gone there with my aunt, *and* from our tour of the carts she had gathered what I wanted the most.

7. My father had known of this, of course, *and* I joyously concluded that this walk could mean only one thing—he was going to buy me a Christmas present.

8. I needed some sign from my father or mother that they knew what I was going through *and* cared for me as much as my aunt and grandfather did.

9. Each time my father would pause *and* ask the pushcart man the price.

10. My father looked up, too, *and* I heard him jingle some coins in his pocket.

Exercise D

The simple three-letter word *and* is amazingly complex in its possibilities for use and meaning as the entry for *and* from an unabridged dictionary will show you. Look through the entry on the next page, then answer the questions below.

1. What is the abbreviation used to tell you the *part of speech* of *and?*

2. What example is given of *and* used to express a *difference?*

3. What example is given of *and* used to introduce a contrary or unexpected outcome?

4. In what technical language is *and* used to mean *or?*

5. What example is given of *and* used to mean a junction or point of intersection?

and (ănd; *unstressed*, ănd, ăn, *etc.*, 71), *conj.* [AS. *and,* *end ;* akin to OS. *endi,* OHG. *anti, enti, inti, unti,* G. *und,* D. *en,* MD. *ende,* and perh. Skr. *atha* then, also. Cf. AN if.] **1.** Expressing the general relation of connection or addition, esp. accompaniment, participation, combination, contiguity, continuance, simultaneity, sequence; thus: along or together with; added to or linked to; as well as; as without ceasing; as at the same time; then; in addition to being; not less truly; — used to conjoin word with word, phrase with phrase, clause with clause. Also, having an implication of: **a** Repetition; as, they rode two *and* two; hundreds *and* hundreds. **b** Variation or difference; as, there are women *and* women, that is, women of different sorts. **c** Logical or semantic modification of one of the connected ideas by the other: (1) In figurative expression, joining elements, one of which logically qualifies the other; as, your fair *and* outward character, that is, outwardly fair character; in poverty *and* distress, that is, in a distressful state of poverty. (2) Now colloquially, after certain adjectives which when followed by another adjective become equivalent to adverbs; as, nice *and* warm, that is, agreeably warm; good *and* ready, that is, quite ready. (3) Now colloquially, between finite verbs the first of which is *go, come, try, send, mind, learn, stay, stop, write,* the second logically equivalent to an infinitive of purpose.

> At least to try *and* teach the erring soul. **_Milton._**

(4) Colloquially, between verbs the first of which represents a position or state, the second an attendant action more accurately expressed by a participle; as, he sat *and* smoked; to sit *and* wait. **d** A consequence or sequel; as, I said go, *and* he went; one step farther *and* he had been a dead man. **e** Contrary action or incongruous outcome; antithesis; as, he promised to come *and* didn't; he sailed for Venice *and* landed in Africa. **f** Reference to either or both of two alternatives. "Which he would not like you *and* me to peep into." **_Thackeray._** In legal language *and* is interpreted as if it were *or,* and vice versa, whenever this construction is plainly required to give effect to the intention of the person using it; thus, in a bequest to "a person *and* her bodily issue," or in a law providing that certain cities may tax property "taxable for State *and* county purposes," *and* may be read as *or.* Sometimes in legal papers *and/or* is used to represent *and* as interchangeable with *or.* **g** Supplementary explanation or restriction, often with climactic emphasis, in an appended phrase; as, he, *and* he alone, could control it; *and* that room a cellar. **h** At the point of junction or intersection; as, State Street *and* Fifth Avenue. **2.** If; though; as if. *Obs.* See AN, *conj.*

> As they will set an house on fire, *and* it were but to roast their eggs. **_Bacon._**

— **and all. a** *Colloq.* And so forth; and the rest; and everything else, esp. everything suggested by the previous context or a part of it; as, here comes Jack, pipe *and all.* **b** *Dial., Chiefly Brit.* (1) Besides; in addition. (2) Used to emphasize the previous context, as in the Irishism *and all, and all.* (3) Truly; with a vengeance. — **and so forth.** And others or more of the same or of similar kind; further in the same or similar manner; and the rest; and other things or ingredients. The abbreviation, *etc.* (*et cetera*), or *&c.,* is usually read *and so forth.* — **and so on.** = AND SO FORTH.

and. Used as a mere expletive, as in Biblical style, initially, and in old songs.

> When that I was *and* a little tiny boy. **_Shak._**

and, *n.* The conjunction *and ;* also, *Colloq.,* an added particular; as, I want to hear no ifs or *ands* about it.

Exercise E

Five of the different shades of meaning *and* may have, as suggested by the dictionary, are illustrated in the uses of *and* by Moss Hart. In the two lists below, which shade of meaning for *and* applies to each excerpt from the passage?

I

1. along with and equal
2. in addition to and making more emphatic
3. following as a result
4. following in time sequence
5. expressing a contrary relationship (having the meaning of *but*)

II

a. Two of our rooms were vacant of boarders *and* my mother was doing her marketing farther and farther away from our neighborhood.

b. He'd gotten together about seventy-five cents to buy me a Christmas present, *and* he hadn't dared say so in case there was nothing to be had for so small a sum.

c. The idea that my father had managed a Christmas present for me in spite of everything filled me with a sudden peace *and* lightness of heart I had not known in months.

d. Each time my father would pause *and* ask the pushcart man the price.

e. He had never suggested such a thing before, *and* moreover it was a very cold winter's night.

Vocabulary in Context

A. Carefully examine each word in its context; then decide which definition is most appropriate.

1. **reconciled** (line 5)
   - *a.* looking forward
   - *b.* accustomed
   - *c.* adjusted
   - *d.* opposed

2. **vicious** (line 11)
   - *a.* evil
   - *b.* important
   - *c.* interesting
   - *d.* rare

3. **fictitious** (line 17)
   - *a.* unreal
   - *b.* named
   - *c.* acceptable
   - *d.* new

4. **token** (line 44)
   - *a.* present
   - *b.* money
   - *c.* sign
   - *d.* surprise

5. **mute** (line 48)
   - *a.* understood
   - *b.* loving
   - *c.* silent
   - *d.* unclear

B. Match meaning and sentence context by writing the word which most suitably fills the blank in each sentence. (Note that two words, 6 and 7, from the previous lesson are included for review.)

1. reconciled
2. vicious
3. fictitious
4. token
5. mute
6. persuade
7. heave

a. Only by hinting at the use of force was the United Nations able to ___?___ the combatants to sign a cease-fire.

b. We have discovered how ___?___ has been our unthinking waste of our natural resources.

c. The two nations ___?___ their differences through compromises reached in a series of meetings.

d. The boy remained stubbornly ___?___ despite all his parents' efforts to get him to explain how his clothes had been torn.

e. The anchor was stuck in the bottom, and the crew was finally able to lift it only by joining together in one great ___?___ on the rope.

f. We think of certain ___?___ places, such as Shangri-la and Atlantis, as though they were real.

g. Every Friday, the husband brought home to his wife a bunch of flowers as a ___?___ of his affection.

READING 9

Omar knelt at the bottom of the small dugout canoe and let his hand drift in the balmy water of the Red Sea. He loved this hour of the day, heading homeward with the keel of the canoe deep in the water, heavy with a day's catch of
5   fish. It usually made him feel peaceful to watch the sun sink slowly behind the jagged mountains that lined the dry, hot desert.

Today, however, there was no peace in Omar for he had failed again. As if in answer to his shame came his father's
10   soothing voice, "Do not worry too much, my Son. Tomorrow you will be able to hold your breath underwater longer than you did today."

Omar's father was known to be the best spearfisherman from Suez all the way down to Port Sudan. He was a big
15   man with strong muscles rippling underneath his tanned skin. Clad only in a loincloth, he squatted in the canoe and paddled homeward with even, powerful strokes.

Omar's brother Gomez, who knelt in the stern of the canoe, cleaning and drying his underwater goggles with the
20   tail of his galabia shirt, started to laugh. "Tomorrow Omar will be bobbing up for air every few seconds just like he did today," Gomez mocked. "How can he ever be a spearfisherman if he is afraid he might drown as soon as he is underwater for more than a few seconds?"

25   "Tomorrow I shall stay underwater for hours, you will

A SPEAR FOR OMAR by Heddy Rado, reprinted by permission of the author.

see!" cried Omar. Deep inside he was thoroughly ashamed of his fear of drowning.

With an angry motion Omar's father jarred the paddle against the canoe. "There will be no more fighting between you two," he said. "And as for you," he added, turning around to Gomez, "it would not harm you to exercise some more caution. It is not well to show fear, but also it is not wise to disregard danger altogether as you so often do. The sea is full of danger for the reckless spearfisherman." After that he took up his paddle, and no one spoke again.

Omar sighed and looked with deep longing at the spears at the bottom of the canoe. His father had promised him a spear of his own as soon as he had conquered his fear. The spears were slender, long shafts of smooth wood with metal points that gleamed dark red in the last rays of the sinking sun. To Omar the spears looked beautiful and well worth the effort he silently promised to make.

The next morning Omar's father announced that he would stay behind. "I want you two to go to sea alone today," he said. "Gomez is well able to do some spearfishing alone, providing he will be careful. And as for you, Omar," he continued, "I expect you to keep your promise and do some real diving today."

Omar respected his father too much to argue, although he did not want to go without him. Silently he nodded, and then the two boys went on their way.

Gomez smirked at Omar and said, "Let's go. I'll race you to the beach."

The minute the two brothers jumped into the crystal-clear water Omar forgot his disappointment that his brother had won the race over the burning sand. As much as Omar resented his brother's teasing, he felt great admiration for him. Now he admired the way Gomez gripped the heavy spear and shot downward with the ease and grace of a dolphin. It took only a few seconds until he bobbed up

119

again with his first catch. He threw the fish into the canoe and grinned at Omar.

"How about coming down yourself?" he asked.

Omar held onto the canoe. "I will, I will," he said hastily. "But, Gomez, please don't take any chances and stay down too long. You know that father warned you yesterday."

"You worry about yourself," Gomez called. Then he flipped back his hair, took a few deep breaths, and down he went again.

Now came the big moment for Omar to dive himself, and he was determined to dive well today. He let go of the canoe and submerged quickly.

A few feet below the surface the very water seemed to be alive with fish. The trembling rays of the sun penetrated the clear water and illuminated the colorful fish in a soft, mysterious light. Yet the whole scene seemed almost unreal because no sound broke the deep silence.

By now Omar's breath began to give out and he felt like darting to the surface. However, he forced himself to overcome his panic and swam deeper toward the pink coral reef. It was covered with flaming red sponges and the curiously nodding heads of purple worms. Scattered over the coral like precious diamonds were thousands and thousands of sparkling sea gems.

But the sight of numerous clams half hidden in the reef dampened Omar's enthusiasm a little. With their wide-open jaws they seemed to be just waiting for Omar. If he swam too near they would close their shells as quick as a flash over a finger or an arm. Omar kept well away from the gaping jaws of the clams, swimming with smooth, careful strokes.

When he finally came to the surface he was very happy. His father would be proud of him when he heard how well Omar had dived today.

Gomez emerged a few feet away with another catch. He was panting for air but nevertheless didn't linger long.

After treading water for a few moments he took a deep breath and went down again.

A slight breeze had come up and sent gusts of hot air from across the desert. The water, however, was still as cool and smooth as flowing silk. 100

Omar turned on his back and paddled slowly to the canoe. He held onto the crudely carved wood which gave him a funny, tickling feeling in his palms. Then as he hung onto the canoe he suddenly went limp all over. The water around him became cold as ice. 105

Before Omar even saw the motionless shadow he knew that a shark must be near. With a quick glance he scanned the water below him and saw that most of the fish had disappeared into the countless alcoves of the reef. That was all he needed to know. In one smooth motion he slipped 110 into the canoe.

The shark slowly emerged from the deep water and started circling the boat. He had a huge, silvery, streamlined body, small, murderous eyes, and a set of teeth that made Omar shudder. The boy leaned over the side of the canoe and 115 looked frantically about for his brother. The water was almost deserted. Only a few herring fish darted about.

There was no sign of Gomez.

Omar scanned the water from the other side of the boat. About fifteen feet below, half hidden by the protruding ridge 120 of a deep alcove in the reef, he saw his brother.

Omar's hand went to his mouth to stifle a cry. He saw that his brother's hand had been caught in one of the many lams and he was trying desperately to free himself. But he was already weakened by lack of air and seemed unable to 125 pry his hand loose.

"Oh, how could he have been so careless," moaned Omar. He knew that he had only a few precious seconds in which to save his brother.

There was a slim chance that the shark might not attack if 130 Omar could disregard him completely. He felt his mouth go dry as he lowered himself into the water. He did not turn his head when the shark moved in closer. Without any outward sign of his deadly fear he went straight down.

135   Never before had Omar dived as deep as that, and he felt as if his lungs would burst. For a second everything went black before his eyes.

But then he saw his brother in front of him. His body was swaying, helpless from the terrible lack of air. His hand was

140   caught in the closed jaws of the clam. If he had not stayed underwater until there was hardly any breath left in him, he might have been able to free himself somehow. The cocky expression Gomez usually wore was gone. He looked at Omar with horror in his eyes.

145   Omar acted quickly. With deft fingers he pried the clam loose from the coral. He left it attached to Gomez's hand because he didn't want to waste precious time. He could attend to the clam when they were safe in the canoe, if they ever reached it.

150   The shark, whose giant shadow had been hovering above their heads, swam toward them. Omar tried to ignore the shark as he grabbed Gomez by his armpits and started upward. Suddenly the shark seemed to look directly at Omar with his murderous, yellow eyes. He came in closer, almost

155   brushing against him with his powerful, fanlike fins. Omar's fingers began to loosen their grip on his brother, and they started to sink. The water around them had grown murky with waves churned by the shark.

If it was true that a shark might not attack if his victim

160   showed no sign of fear, then Omar knew what he had to do. He tightened his fingers around his brother's arm until he could feel his nails sinking into the soft flesh. Then he turned his back on the shark and began to swim upward in calm, slow motions.

165   The effect took all Omar's strength and courage. Only a few feet more and they would be safe. A few feet more was all they needed.

When their heads broke the surface the shark came in for attack. He made a sharp turn and shot directly at Omar through the boiling waves. For a split second they were face 170 to face, the shark a dreadful sight with his huge set of razor-sharp teeth.

In desperation Omar took the last measure his father had taught him in an emergency like this. He let go of Gomez, raised his right arm and slapped the shark across its pointed 175 nose. Then he struck again and again and again.

For a long moment the shark seemed stunned and motionless. Then he churned about, brushing against Omar's face with his rough fins as he turned toward the deep water.

Omar grabbed Gomez and pulled him into the canoe. 180 Gomez sank to the floor, too exhausted to move, while Omar fell forward on his knees. His breath came in painful gasps and his eyes felt as if they would burst from their sockets. For a moment he gave way to the wave of faintness that washed over him, and supported his head against his 185 arms on the seat in the boat's stern.

But only for a moment. Then he felt for his brother's arm. He took a knife and with its strong handle chipped away part of the shell. Although Gomez winced with pain, Omar worked fast until he could press the knife in and pry 190 the clam open.

"It's only a flesh wound and will heal fast," Omar said after he had examined the wrist. He wrapped his dry shirt around it to stop the bleeding.

His brother opened his eyes weakly. He smiled at Omar 195 and his smile was full of love and admiration. "Thank you, my brother," he said, "thank you."

Omar gave the makeshift bandage a last tug. "Shhh," he said, "do not speak now. You must rest."

Suddenly he felt very weary. His whole body ached and 200 his right hand was bruised from fighting off the shark. However, it was not time for him to rest yet. Slowly he took the paddle and brought the boat in safely to the dock.

The next morning when Omar awoke he found a spear
205 next to his sleeping mat. His father stood looking down at
him, warm approval in his eyes. Omar jumped to his feet,
gripping the spear tightly in his hand.

"You will be a fine spearfisherman, my Son," his father
said and Omar lowered his head, a great surge of happiness
210 rushing through him.

Reading Comprehension

The exercises that follow are based on the passage you have
just read. Each exercise consists of an incomplete statement followed by four choices. Select the choice that best completes the
statement. Go back to the passage for rereading to whatever
extent is necessary to help you choose your answer.

1. The time of day at which the story opens is
   a. sunrise.
   b. early afternoon.
   c. sunset.
   d. late evening.

2. In the opening incident of the story, each of the following
   conflicts is established EXCEPT
   a. Omar is torn between his desire to be a spearfisherman
   and his fear of drowning.
   b. the father is impatient with Gomez's attitude.
   c. the father is impatient with Omar's fear.
   d. Gomez mocks Omar for his fear of drowning.

3. When Omar makes his first dive, he
   a. forces himself to overcome his panic.
   b. darts to the surface when his breath begins to give out.
   c. feels no fear at all.
   d. fears the pink coral.

4. Of the various forms of sea-life mentioned, the one that is apparently of a variety of unusually large size is
   a. the coral.
   b. the clams.
   c. the sponges.
   d. the purple worms.

5. "With a quick glance he scanned the water below him and saw that most of the fish had disappeared into the countless alcoves of the reef." (lines 107–109) The reason for the disappearance of the fish is
   a. the nearness of a shark.
   b. the hot gusts of air from the desert.
   c. the coldness of the water.
   d. the activities of the spearfishermen.

6. The grip of the clam might not have trapped Gomez as it did if he
   a. had not let go his spear.
   b. were not panicked by the nearness of the shark.
   c. had not dived deeper than he should.
   d. had not stayed underwater too long.

7. Omar pries the clam loose from the coral rather than free Gomez from the clam's grip because he wants to
   a. avoid the flow of blood which would attract the shark.
   b. save time.
   c. keep the clam.
   d. kill the clam.

8. The shark finally shoots in to attack Omar because
   a. Omar showed signs of fear.
   b. the shark smelled blood.
   c. Gomez showed signs of fear.
   d. of reasons unknown.

9. Omar repels the shark by
   a. slapping the shark's nose.
   b. letting go of Gomez to confuse the shark.

    c. grabbing the shark's fins.

    d. staring the shark directly in the eye.

10. Once he is safe, Gomez's reaction towards Omar for rescuing him is best described as

    a. a return to his usual self.

    b. one of gratitude and love.

    c. one of increased rivalry and resentment.

    d. an anxiety to forget the whole thing.

11. It would seem that, as far as the father is concerned, Gomez

    a. told the whole story truthfully.

    b. gave no information.

    c. twisted the whole story around so that he was the rescuer.

    d. revealed as little as he had to and only under questioning.

12. The lesson in character development that *both brothers* probably learned can be said to revolve around

    a. cowardice vs. courage.

    b. respect for the father.

    c. taking no chances.

    d. reasonable self-confidence.

Literary and Language Skills

FORESHADOWING AND SUSPENSE

Will I pass the test? Will we win the game? Will Dad get a promotion? Will the date be a success? How will I do at the interview? Will the dentist hurt me? The story of real life is full of suspense as to how important events in the future will turn out. Suspense is also one important element that holds the reader's interest in a fictional story. The reader is held in suspense about how the characters will be affected by the shape that problems will take as the story unfolds and about how those problems will be worked out.

One way of creating suspense in fiction is through *foreshadowing*. Hints or suggestions are thrown out about problems and crises that will develop. ("Coming events cast their shadows before them.") As the reader sees these hints and watches them develop in the story, his interest and concern mount. He becomes engrossed in the action and experiences strong feelings at the final outcomes.

Exercise A

In *A Spear for Omar*, foreshadowing is used to help create suspense. Below are ten brief excerpts from the story. Seven of these are good examples of foreshadowing; the remaining three are not. Select the seven excerpts that are good examples of foreshadowing. Be ready to explain the reasons for your choices.

1. Omar knelt at the bottom of the small dugout canoe and let his hand drift in the balmy water of the Red Sea. (lines 1–2)

2. Today, however, there was no peace in Omar for he had failed again. (lines 8–9)

3. Deep inside he was thoroughly ashamed of his fear of drowning. (lines 26–27)

4. It is not well to show fear, but also it is not wise to disregard danger altogether as you so often do. (lines 32–33)

5. His father had promised him a spear of his own as soon as he had conquered his fear. (lines 37–38)

6. The minute the two brothers jumped into the crystal-clear water Omar forgot his disappointment that his brother had won the race over the burning sand. (lines 54–56)

7. Scattered over the coral like precious diamonds were thousands and thousands of sparkling sea gems. (lines 82–84)

8. With their wide-open jaws they seemed to be just waiting for Omar. (lines 86–87)

9. Then as he hung onto the canoe he suddenly went limp all over. (lines 103–104)

10. There was no sign of Gomez. (line 118)

Exercise B

Recall a real situation that involved a great deal of suspense for you or someone you know about. What was the suspenseful situation? How did it come out? Was there any foreshadowing of how things would go?

Vocabulary in Context

A. Carefully examine each word in its context; then decide which definition is most appropriate.

1. **balmy** (line 2)
   a. cold
   b. rough
   c. salty
   d. soothing

2. **smirked** (line 52)
   a. protested loudly
   b. attacked unfairly
   c. smiled mockingly
   d. agreed silently

3. **gaping** (line 89)
   a. imitating
   b. gnawing
   c. wide open
   d. poisonous

4. **protruding** (line 120)
   a. sticking out
   b. welcome

> c. rocky
>
> d. imaginary

5. **hovering** (line 150)
   a. waiting about
   b. growing
   c. disappearing silently
   d. getting darker

B. Match meaning and sentence context by writing the word which most suitably fills the blank in each sentence. (Note that two words, 6 and 7, from the previous lesson are included for review.)

1. **balmy**	6. **vicious**
2. **smirked**	7. **mute**
3. **gaping**	
4. **protruding**	
5. **hovering**	

a. We watched the helicopter that was ___?___ above us as though it were going to land on the roof of our house.

b. The lollipops were handed out to all the little guests at the birthday party, and in two seconds every child had a stick ___?___ from his mouth.

c. It was one of those ___?___ days in May when one wants to sit on a park bench and enjoy the feeling of spring.

d. The batter said nothing but ___?___ at the plate umpire when a third strike was called.

e. The wolf is actually a harmless and peaceful animal, not the ___?___ beast he has so long been pictured to be.

f. The opening of the great cave stood ___?___ before us like the mouth of a giant about to swallow us.

g. We gazed at the voiceless, ___?___ stones of the ancient ruins and wondered what tales they could tell if they could speak.

129

READING 10

We passed through the scullery to the kitchen—arranged as
a living-room with uncomfortable carved mahogany furniture,
and diced varnished wallpaper which reflected the furious
echoes of a "waggity" clock. Having told me to sit down and
5   rest, Mama removed the long pins from her hat and held
them in her mouth while she folded her veil. She then pinned
hat and veil together, hung them with her coat in the cur-
tained recess and, putting on a blue wrapper that hung behind the door, began with greater confidence to move to and
10 fro over the worn brown linoleum, giving me soft encouraging
looks while I sat, stiff and scarcely breathing in this alien
house, on the edge of a horsehair-covered chair beside the
range.
    "We're having our dinner in the evening, dear, seeing I
15 was away. When Papa comes in, try and not let him see you
crying. It's been a great grief for him as well. And he has a
lot to worry him—such a responsible position in the town.
Kate, my other daughter, will be in any minute, too. She's a
pupil teacher. . . . Maybe your mother told you." As my lip
20 drooped she went on hurriedly: "Oh, I know it's confusing,
even for a big man like yourself, to be meeting all his mother's
folks for the first time. And there's more to come." She
was trying, amidst her preoccupations, to coax a smile from
me. "There's Adam, my oldest son, who is doing wonder-
25 fully in the insurance business in Winton—he doesn't stay
with us, but runs down when he can manage. Then there's
Papa's mother. . . . She's away visiting some friends just now

Excerpt from THE GREEN YEARS, by A. J. Cronin, by permission of
Little, Brown and Co. Copyright 1944 by A. J. Cronin.

. . . but she spends about half of her time with us. And lastly, there's my father who lives here always—he's your great-grandpa Gow." While my head reeled with this jumble of unknown relatives her faint smile ventured forth again. "It isn't every boy who has a great-grandpa, I can tell you. It's quite an honor. You can just call him 'Grandpa,' though, for short. When I have his tray ready you can take it upstairs to him. Say how do you do, and help me at the same time."

Besides laying the table for five, she had, with a practised hand, prepared a battered black japanned tray, oval-shaped and with a rose painted in the centre, setting upon it a moustache cup of ribbed white china filled with tea, a plate of jam, cheese, and three slices of bread.

Watching her, I wondered, aloud, rather huskily: "Does Grandpa not eat his food downstairs?"

Mama seemed slightly embarrassed. "No, dear, he has it in his room." She lifted the tray and held it out to me. "Can you manage? Right up to the top floor. Be careful and not fall."

Bearing the tray, I climbed the unfamiliar stairs shakily, confused by the steep treads and the shiny, waxcloth "runner." Only a fragment of the dwindling afternoon was admitted by the high skylight. On the second landing opposite a boxed-in cistern, I tried the first of the two doors. It was locked. The other, however, yielded to my uncertain touch.

I entered a strange, interesting, dreadfully untidy room. The high brass bed in the corner, with its patchwork quilt and lopsided knobs, was still unmade; the bearskin hearthrug was rumpled; the towel on the splashed mahogany washstand hung awry. My eye was caught by a black marble timepiece of the "presentation" variety lying upon its side on the littered mantelpiece with its inside in pieces beside it. I felt a queer smell of tobacco smoke and past meals, a blending of complex and intricate smells, forming, as it were, the bouquet of a room much lived-in.

Wearing burst green carpet slippers and dilapidated home-

spun, my great-grandpa was sunk deeply in the massive ruin
of a horsehair armchair by the rusty fireplace, steadily driving
a pen over a long thick sheet of paper which lay, with the
original document he was copying, on the yellow-green cover
of the low table before him. On one hand stood a formidable
collection of walking sticks, on the other a box of newssheet
spills and a long rack of clay pipes, with metal caps, filled
and ready.

He was a large-framed man, of more than average height,
perhaps about seventy, with a pink complexion and a mane
of still faintly ruddy hair flying gallantly behind his collar.
It was, in fact, red hair which had lost a little of its ardour
without yet turning white, and the result was a remarkable
shade, golden in some lights. His beard and moustache,
which curled belligerently, were of the same tinge. Though
the whites of his eyes were peculiarly specked with yellow
the pupils remained clear, penetrating and blue, not the faded
blue of Mama's eyes, but a virile and electric blue, a forget-
me-not blue, conspicuous and altogether charming. But his
most remarkable feature was his nose. It was a large nose,
large, red and bulbous; as I gazed, awestruck, I could think
of no more apt simile than to liken it to a ripe, enormous
strawberry, for it was of the identical colour, and was even
peppered with tiny holes like the seed pits of that luscious
fruit. The organ dominated his entire visage; I had never seen
such a curious nose, never.

By this time he had ceased to write and, bestowing his pen
behind his ear, he turned slowly to regard me. The broken
springs of the seat, despite the brown paper stuffed around
them, twanged musically at the shifting of his weight, as
though ushering in the drama of our acquaintance. We stared
at each other in silence and, forgetting the momentary fas-
cination of his nose, I flushed to think of the wretched
picture I must make for him standing there in my ready-
made black suit, one stocking falling down, shoelaces loose,
my face pale and tear-stained, my hair inescapably red.

Still silent, he pushed aside his papers, made a gesture, 100
nervous but forceful, towards the cleared space on the table.
I put the tray down on it. Barely taking his eyes off me, he
began to eat, rapidly, and with a sort of grand indifference,
partaking of cheese and jam indiscriminately, folding over
his bread, soaking his crusts in his tea, washing everything 105
down with a final draught. Then, wiping his whiskers with a
downward sweep, he reached out instinctively—as though the
business of eating was a mere preamble to tobacco, or even
better things—and lit a pipe.

"So you are Robert Shannon?" His voice was reserved, 110
yet companionable.

"Yes, Grandpa." Though my answer came strained and
apologetic, I had remembered the instruction to omit his
"great."

"Did you have a good journey?" 115

"I think so, Grandpa."

"Ay, ay, they're nice boats, the *Adder* and the *Viper*. I
used to see them berth when I was in the excise. The *Adder*
has a white line on her understrake, that's how you tell the
difference between them. Can you play draughts?" 120

"No, Grandpa."

He nodded encouragingly, yet with a trace of condescen-
sion.

"You will in due course, boy, if you stay here. I understand you *are* going to stay." 125

"Yes, Grandpa. Mrs. Chapman said there was no place else
for me to go." A forlorn wave, warm with self-pity, gushed
over me.

Suddenly I had a wild craving for his sympathy, an unbearable longing to unbosom myself of my terrible predicament. 130
Did he know that my father had died of consumption, the
spectral family malady which had carried off his two sisters
before him—which had infected and, with terrible rapidity,
destroyed my mother—which, it was whispered, had even laid
a little finger, beguilingly, on me . . . ? 135

But Grandpa, taking a few musing puffs, looking me through and through with an ironic twist to his lips, had already turned the subject.

"You're eight, aren't you?"

140 "Almost, Grandpa."

I wished to make myself as young as possible but Grandpa was implacable. "It's an age when a boy should stand up for himself. . . . Though I will say there might be more of ye. Do you like to walk?"

Reading Comprehension

The exercises that follow are based on the passage you have just read. Each exercise consists of an incomplete statement followed by four choices. Select the choice that best completes the statement. Go back to the passage for rereading to whatever extent is necessary to help you choose your answer.

1. The boy who is the central character and narrator in this story is
   a. Mama's youngest child.
   b. unrelated to the other people in the house.
   c. an orphan.
   d. in his own home.

2. The description in the opening paragraph suggests that this is the household of
   a. a wealthy family.
   b. a family of modest economic circumstances.
   c. a stingy family.
   d. a foreign family.

3. The opening sentence of the second paragraph suggests that
   a. the main meal is customarily eaten in the middle of the day.

134

b. the main meal is customarily eaten quite late in the evening.

c. there is little or no food in the house.

d. the speaker resents the presence of another mouth to feed.

4. It is very likely that the relationship of Kate (line 18) to the boy is
   a. mother.
   b. aunt.
   c. cousin.
   d. none of the above.

5. "Besides laying the table for five . . ." (line 36) The one of the following that is included among the five is
   a. Papa's mother.
   b. Adam.
   c. Great-Grandpa Gow.
   d. Kate.

6. The chief impression given by the description of Grandpa's physical appearance, an impression supported by the mention of objects in the room, is one of
   a. vitality and energy.
   b. distasteful ugliness.
   c. orderliness and purpose.
   d. dismaying coldness.

7. A physical trait mentioned that establishes a clear link between Grandpa and the boy can be found in
   a. eye color.
   b. hair color.
   c. nose shape.
   d. skin complexion.

8. Grandpa's remarks and questions to the boy suggest that
   a. Grandpa is looking forward to a close companionship.
   b. Grandpa wants to establish the fact that the boy is not warmly welcomed.
   c. Grandpa wants the boy to be aware of the debt he owes to the family.

d. Grandpa wants the boy to understand that he will not be coddled as a child, that he is to assume his share of responsibilities as though he were a man.

9. "Though I will say there might be more of ye." (line 143) Grandpa means
    a. the boy is undersized for his age.
    b. other relatives may be coming to live in the house.
    c. the boy strikes him as one who will stand up for himself.
    d. he would like to see the boy improve his manners.

Literary and Language Skills

SENTENCE COMPOSITION

Look at the following three sentences.

1. **At dawn, we arose and saddled our horses.**
2. **We arose at dawn and saddled our horses.**
3. **We arose and saddled our horses at dawn.**

What do you notice about these sentences? You can see that all three use exactly the same words and say the same thing. Yet each sentence is different because the words do not come in the same order. To put it in another way, although the same words are used in the sentence, each sentence is put together, or *composed*, in a different way.

Sentence composition is one important element of writing style. By proper use of sentence composition, a writer can achieve greater variety and interest in his writing and, through the rhythms of his words, can add to the strength of the mood or emotion he wishes to create. If you know something about sentence composition, you will be helped towards becoming a better writer yourself as well as becoming a better reader.

Now look at the three sentences again. You can see that the specific difference among them is that in each case the prepositional phrase *at dawn* is placed in a different position. Where is the prepositional phrase *at dawn* placed in the first sentence? the second? the third? The placement of prepositional phrases in a sentence is one important way to achieve variety in sentence composition.

Exercise A

Each of the five sentences below contains a prepositional phrase. Re-compose each sentence *twice*, placing the prepositional phrase in a different position each time. Do not change any words.

1. In the pasture, the cows nibbled at the grass.

2. The boys shoved the boulder aside with a mighty effort.

3. We saw in the sky the long white jet stream.

4. Out of the wild, desolate surf, there suddenly emerged the black-clad scuba diver, a strange apparition.

5. We saw through the microscope the strange, wondrous, normally invisible creatures.

Now look at the following three sentences.

1. **Wearing his new clothes, the child proudly entered the room.**

2. **The child, wearing his new clothes, proudly entered the room.**

3. **The child proudly entered the room wearing his new clothes.**

Here, again, are three sentences all using the same words and saying the same thing. Again, each sentence is composed differently. In these examples, the specific difference is that the participial phrase, *wearing his new clothes*, is placed in a different position. The placement of participial phrases in a sentence is another important way to achieve variety in sentence composition.

Exercise B

Each of the five sentences below contains a participial phrase. Re-compose each sentence *twice*, placing the participial phrase in a different position each time. Do not change any words.

1. Blowing the trees fiercely, the wind swept through the orchard.
2. The mother, calling her son anxiously, hurried inside.
3. Casey struck out, swinging his bat mightily.
4. The cat watched the rolling ball intently, twitching his tail ever so slightly.
5. Munching the delicious frankfurters, we strolled contentedly along the boardwalk.

Exercise C

The writing of A. J. Cronin in *The Green Years* is characterized by skillful sentence composition. Among the ways Cronin achieves the stylistic effects he is after is *to begin sentences with prepositional phrases and participial phrases*. Below are ten sentences from the passage. Some are sentences that begin with a prepositional phrase. Some are sentences that begin with a participial phrase. Some belong in neither class.

   a. Identify the sentences that begin with a prepositional phrase.
   b. Identify the sentences that begin with a participial phrase.
   c. Select any five sentences that begin with either a prepositional or a participial phrase and re-compose each sentence by placing the phrase in a different position in the sentence.

1. Having told me to sit down and rest, Mama removed the long pins from her hat and held them in her mouth while she folded her veil.

2. We're having our dinner in the evening, dear, seeing I was away.

3. Besides laying the table for five, she had, with a practised hand, prepared a battered black japanned tray, oval-shaped and with a rose painted in the centre . . .

4. Bearing the tray, I climbed the unfamiliar stairs shakily, confused by the steep treads and the shiny, waxcloth "runner."

5. On the second landing opposite a boxed-in cistern, I tried the first of the two doors.

6. Wearing burst green carpet slippers and dilapidated homespun, my great-grandpa was sunk deeply in the massive ruin of a horsehair armchair by the rusty fireplace . . .

7. It was, in fact, red hair which had lost a little of its ardour without yet turning white, and the result was a remarkable shade, golden in some lights.

8. By this time he had ceased to write and, bestowing his pen behind his ear, he turned slowly to regard me.

9. Barely taking his eyes off me, he began to eat, rapidly, and with a sort of grand indifference, partaking of cheese and jam indiscriminately, folding over his bread, soaking his crusts in his tea, washing everything down with a final draught.

10. Suddenly I had a wild craving for his sympathy, an unbearable longing to unbosom myself of my terrible predicament.

Vocabulary in Context

A. Carefully examine each word in its context; then decide which definition is most appropriate.

1. **dwindling** (line 49)
   a. bright
   b. interesting

c. happy
d. fading

2. **formidable** (line 68)
   a. expensive
   b. awe-inspiring
   c. well-shaped
   d. deformed

3. **belligerently** (line 78)
   a. thinly
   b. fashionably
   c. untidily
   d. aggressively

4. **virile** (line 81)
   a. manly
   b. unpleasant
   c. washed-out
   d. greenish

5. **visage** (line 88)
   a. room
   b. view
   c. face
   d. nose

B. Match meaning and sentence context by writing the word which most suitably fills the blank in each sentence. (Note that two words, 6 and 7, from the previous lesson are included for review.)

1. **dwindling**
2. **formidable**
3. **belligerently**
4. **virile**
5. **visage**

6. **balmy**
7. **hovering**

a. Despite his age, the coach remained youthful, energetic, and ——?—— in appearance.

b. It was a ——?—— football team to face, the players averaging well over 225 pounds in weight and six feet in height.

c. The peace talks broke down because both sides acted as ——?—— around the discussion table as they had in the fields of battle.

d. ——?—— above the flowers, the hummingbird appeared to be suspended motionless in midair.

e. We let our boat drift, and the easy rhythm of the gentle, ——?—— lake waters made us drowsy.

f. The ——?—— supplies of oil and other sources of energy make it appear that rationing may be necessary.

g. The detective's ——?——, with its piercing eyes and hawklike nose, seemed to go well with his profession.

GROWING
(Unit Two)

Vocabulary in Context

WORD LIST

1. amazed	14. mute
2. avid	15. persuade
3. balmy	16. protruding
4. belligerently	17. reconciled
5. dwindling	18. retaliate
6. eliminated	19. smirked
7. fictitious	20. submission
8. formidable	21. token
9. gaping	22. vicious
10. heave	23. vigor
11. hovering	24. virile
12. insatiable	25. visage
13. level	

Exercise A—USE

Complete each phrase below by adding a list word that is the same part of speech named and that makes the best sense when added. After you have written each complete phrase, compose an original sentence in which the phrase is included. The first question is answered for you as an example.

WORD LIST

amazed	reconciled
balmy	retaliate
dwindling	smirked
formidable	submission
insatiable	token

1. *verb* their differences

   ANSWER: reconciled their differences

   The two former political opponents reconciled their differences.

143

2. *adjective* day in spring

3. *noun* of friendship

4. *adjective (verb form)* expression

5. *adjective* opponent

6. *adjective* curiosity of a child

7. *verb* nastily

8. *verb* vengefully

9. *adjective (verb form)* value of the dollar

10. meek *noun*

Exercise B—ETYMOLOGY

Etymology, the history of words, is a fascinating and important study. Every good dictionary tells you something about the etymology of words. Look at each of the dictionary entries below and answer the questions that follow them.

cur-few (kûr′fū) n. [ME *courfew* <OFr *covrefeu*, cover fire <*covrir* cover + feu, fire] a time set, generally in the evening, after which people may not appear in the streets

vil-lain (vil′ən) n. [ME *vilein* <OFr *vilain* <L. *villanus*, a farm servant] wicked person; scoundrel

re-ject (ri-jekt′) v.t. [<L. *rejectus* pp. of *rejicere*, to throw back or fling back <*re*, back + *jacere*, to throw] to refuse; to discard

1. What punctuation marks come before and after the etymology of the word in each entry?

2. What does the symbol < stand for?

3. Give the names of three ancient languages that are abbreviated in the etymologies.

4. What was the meaning of the old word from which our word "curfew" comes? What connection do you see?

144

5. What was the meaning of the old word from which our word "villain" comes? How does the present meaning reflect the class prejudice of the Middle Ages?

6. What is the past participle of the Latin word *rejicere?*

7. The stem of the word *reject* comes from the Latin root *ject* meaning *to throw.* Give at least three other English words that come from the same root.

Exercise C—MORE ETYMOLOGY

Try a little etymological detective work with some of the list words given in the column to the left. In the column to the right, in scrambled order, are the "ancestors," with meanings, of the stems (main parts) of these list words. Match them correctly. (Remember that sometimes the "ancestors" are similar to the stems of the modern words in both spelling and meaning. Sometimes changes in one or both have taken place.)

1. amazed	L. *vir*	—a man
2. belligerently	L. *limen*	—threshold, door
3. eliminated	AS. *hebban*	—seize, grasp
4. heave	L. *visus*	—a look, a seeing
5. insatiable	L. *trudere*	—thrust
6. protruding	L. *bellum*	—war
7. reconciled	AS. *amasod*	—puzzled, confused
8. vigor	L. *satis*	—enough, sufficient
9. virile	L. *vigere*	—to be strong
10. visage	L. *concilium*	—a meeting

Exercise D—MORE ETYMOLOGY

Try a little more etymological detective work. The ten words that follow are "cousins" of the list words given in Exercise C. That is, their stems are derived from the same "ancestors." Pair the "cousins." (Look for the best combination of similarities of meaning and spelling. Some are tricky!)

145

1. maze	6. council
2. satisfied	7. preliminary
3. visible	8. intrusion
4. invigorating	9. rebellion
5. virtue	10. hawk

Exercise E—CONTEXTS

Which list word to the right is most closely associated with each reference to the left?

1. Goliath, as he appeared to David	**protruding**
2. the crater of Vesuvius	**mute**
3. Pinocchio's nose	**formidable**
4. the name, Mark Twain	**gaping**
5. the Indian vow of silence	**fictitious**

Exercise F—MORE CONTEXTS

In the two lists below are words or forms of the words from Unit One and Unit Two. Pair the words from the two lists which are most nearly *opposite* in meaning

UNIT ONE	UNIT TWO
1. indifferent	*a.* persuasion
2. integrity	*b.* vigor
3. subdued	*c.* avid
4. injunction	*d.* viciousness
5. evanescence	*e.* belligerent

Exercise G—ANALOGIES

Decide what the relationship is between the pair of words given first. From the four choices, select the pair of words that comes closest to expressing the same relationship as the given pair.

1. amazed : open-mouthed
    a. running : breathless
    b. caught : act
    c. disappointed : frowning
    d. melt : ice

2. heave : boulder
    a. blow : feather
    b. jack : tire
    c. rolling : stone
    d. coin : flip

3. reconciled : stubborn
    a. friend : foe
    b. argue : talk
    c. bent : inflexible
    d. curved : straight

4. insatiable : appetite
    a. food : eat
    b. meal : devour
    c. unquenchable : thirst
    d. satisfying : need

5. visage : forehead
    a. thumb : toe
    b. exit : skyscraper
    c. body : chest
    d. appearance : character

Literary and Language Skills

Exercise H—SIMILES

Here are ten similes taken from the works of seven great writers. The key part of each simile (the imaginative picture) has been omitted. The omitted parts are listed in scrambled order at the bottom of the exercise. Complete each simile by selecting the missing part that best goes with it.

1. The *Hispaniola* was under her main-sail and two jibs, and the beautiful white canvas shone in the sun like ___ ? ___.
   —*Treasure Island*, Robert Louis Stevenson

2. I stood straight up against the wall, my heart still going like ___ ? ___.
   —*Treasure Island*, Robert Louis Stevenson

3. Every animal was motionless as though ___ ? ___.
   —*The Call of the Wild*, Jack London

4. From below came the fatal roaring where the wild current went wilder and was rent in shreds and spray by the rocks which thrust through like ___ ? ___.
   —*The Call of the Wild*, Jack London

5. Presently, he began to feel the effects of the atmosphere—a blistering sweat, a sensation that his eyeballs were about to crack like ___ ? ___.
   —*The Red Badge of Courage*, Stephen Crane

6. They [the retreating army] charged down upon him like ___ ? ___.
   —*The Red Badge of Courage*, Stephen Crane

7. It [the winter] came on in stealthy and measured glides like ___ ? ___.
   —*Tess of the D'Urbervilles*, Thomas Hardy

8. Here and there through the city, machine guns and rifles broke the silence of the night, spasmodically, like ___ ? ___.
   —*The Sniper*, Liam O'Flaherty

9. The fence, too, had lost many of its pickets and stood propped against the tangle like ____ ? ____.

—*Nancy*, Elizabeth Enright

10. They drove through heat waves rippling like ____ ? ____.

—*A Time of Learning*, Jessamyn West

    a. terrified buffaloes
    b. lake water
    c. a sledge hammer
    d. the moves of a chess-player
    e. dogs barking on a lone farm
    f. snow or silver
    g. a large comb with teeth missing
    h. hot stones
    i. turned to stone
    j. the teeth of an enormous comb

Exercise I—*AND* AND OTHER CONJUNCTIONS

You have learned that the conjunction *and* can have various meanings (page 111). That is, it can show various kinds of connections. Other conjunctions are used to show a more specific connection between parts of a sentence. Each sentence below is a compound sentence, one in which *and* is used to connect two independent clauses. Following each sentence in parentheses is another, more specific conjunction. Rewrite the sentence substituting the specific conjunction for *and*. Do not change any other words. You may, however, change the order of the two clauses, the capitalization, and the punctuation if necessary. Also, the specific conjunction may occur at a point other than the point where *and* appears in the original sentence.

1. It began to rain and the lady opened her umbrella. (*because*)
2. It was very late and I was tired. (*moreover*)
3. I bathed and I got dressed. (*after*)
4. We expected them at nine and they didn't arrive until ten. (*but*)
5. Ann cooked supper and Bill walked the dog. (*while*)
6. His friend left and George has been studying. (*since*)
7. The sun set and we turned on the lights. (*after*)
8. The room was getting uncomfortably hot and the host decided to turn on the air conditioning. (*because*)
9. The climbers set out for the peak with confidence and they got no more than half-way up. (*but*)
10. The future seemed pretty hopeless and things began to take a turn for the better. (*when*)

Exercise J—SENTENCE COMPOSITION

Rewrite each of the following sentences, adding an interesting *prepositional phrase*. Try to vary the position in which your phrases occur in each sentence.

1. The train suddenly and sharply stopped.
2. The crowd roared its approval.
3. I stared.
4. The grapes looked beautiful.
5. Andy laughed.

Rewrite each of the following sentences by adding an interesting *participial phrase*. Try to vary the position in which your phrases occur in each sentence.

6. The people hurried home.
7. Monkeys chattered and jungle birds screamed.
8. We ate as much food as our stomachs could hold.
9. Amy slammed the door.
10. The seagull floated and soared.

Themes for Growing

FOR THINKING

Where do I belong? How do I fit in? Am I any good? These are important and troubling questions for young people during the growing years. In practically everyone's life, during those years, there are conditions and experiences which tend to produce negative answers to those questions—feelings of uncertainty, self-doubt, insecurity. Bottles Barton was a poor athlete and he had to work after school. Leonardo da Vinci was "different," and therefore misunderstood and mistreated. Moss Hart was poor and felt deprived. Omar, as a young boy, felt fear about his ability to be successful in the dangerous career he had to learn. The boy-narrator of *The Green Years* was orphaned and had to go to live in a strange home. What are some other common conditions or experiences of the growing years you know about that may tend to produce feelings of self-doubt or feelings of not fitting in?

FOR DISCUSSION

Leonardo da Vinci seemed little bothered by the fact that he was misunderstood and mistreated by his father and the other boys. Moss Hart actually grew up to be one of America's most successful playwrights. (He specialized in bright, happy comedies!) In a supreme trial, Omar successfully overcame his self-doubts. On the other hand, Bottles Barton couldn't face up to his difficulties at all and withdrew into dreams and fantasies of success, probably to remain an unhappy failure all his life. What makes the difference? Why do some young people rise above the conditions that tend to produce self-doubt and insecurity while others are forever damaged by them?

FOR WRITING

Economic problems—poverty—were a factor in the life of most

of the main characters in this unit during their growing years. How important a role does poverty play in shaping the future adult life? Is it all-important? Partly important? Unimportant? Write a composition in which you state and explain your opinion. Try to illustrate your thoughts with specific examples you know about.

UNIT THREE

(Reading 11-15)

READING 11

There was a time when my brother David was a small boy and I was twelve or so that my mother seemed to favor him more than she did me. It seemed that she was always being nicer to him. He was a good-looking boy with large brown eyes and deep dimples and pudgy soft hands, and I did not have brown eyes or deep dimples or pudgy soft hands; not that I wanted them. I was tall and skinny and my face was starting to come out with pimples.

One time when I was out in the back yard I thought about my brother. I hid behind a bush and watched my mother spread a piece of jelly bread for him and noticed how tender she was and the way she not only handed him the jelly bread but kissed him on the forehead. It wasn't that I wanted to be kissed on the forehead; it was just the fact that she didn't have to do it to David. While I sat under the bush in the back yard I began to think how sad it would be if I ran off. I don't mean how sad I would feel but how sad my mother would feel, losing her twelve-year-old son and all. I guess when you came right down to it I wasn't much to have or not have; it was just that I was the older child and had been around a long time. I knew my mother would fret and be sorry. I don't think she ever realized that she wasn't spreading jelly bread for me any more. Maybe she thought I was old enough to do it myself. Just the same she never did it

---

WHEN YOU RUN AWAY by George H. Freitag, reprinted by permission of Mrs. Tencie B. Freitag.

any more, but all David had to do when he wanted a slice of jelly bread was look hungry and undernourished and he got it.

In a way it made me a little sad myself at the thought of my mother's feeling sad that I might leave. I spent some time drawing maps of ways to run away. I showed the icehouse and the train tracks and the large maple tree; things that would serve as specific places. The weather was nice; it was summer and the lilacs were in bloom and the nights were filled with lovely sounds and scents. There wouldn't be any problem about it. I thought for a while that I might go around and say farewell to my friends. But I liked them too well to have them feel sad at my going away. I was at an age when one is apt to make a very important decision quite by accident. And I did not want to let anyone know I was going. When you are old you make planned decisions, everything carefully worked out, but when you are a boy of twelve there is still time to make a few accidental decisions that change the course of your life.

I used to pity my father, who was tied so to my mother's apron strings. He went about his life in such a calculated way, doing all the proper things like going to work and coming home and wiping his mouth with a napkin during meals, coming and going with punctual regularity. I guess the town clock was even set by his routine. He did not have a thought of his own. He went to work and worked. He came home and was home. On the lines that were woven across my father's forehead was written the word "obligation." Poor, poor man.

A fellow knows pretty much what he is about at twelve. So just to try out my brother, I asked him to fetch me things. I wanted him to refuse so that I could have more reason to run away. "Go fetch me my lousy shoes, David," I yelled at him. He was four years old. He went to where I had hidden my shoes and brought them back.

"Here's your shoes," he said.

"Go fetch me a pencil and paper and an eraser and a box of crayons and don't come back until you have everything."

My little brother went out of the room and in about an hour he came back with everything; he even found the lost crayons. Then he made more trips and brought back things I never knew we had.

"See what a nice brother you have?" my mother said, giving him a smack-kiss on the cheek, but I only glowered at my mother. Then I spent more time drawing maps and getting my clothes together, a shirt, a pair of sandals to keep from getting stone bruises, my spyglass that I got with breakfast cereal, the one where the magnifying glass came in one box and another part in a different box until after forty-three boxes of breakfast cereal I had the spyglass. You don't know how many parts a spyglass has until you commence to eat breakfast cereal. I put my slingshot in the pack, too, and a calendar to know what day it was and how long I was gone, and a picture of my mother and father taken coming out of the Ritz-Balou picture show carrying a potted fern that my mother had won. I had other things in the pack, too, things like rope and a candle and a piece of moving-picture film of Rin Tin Tin moving his head from one side of the picture to the other, and a harmonica. Everybody who runs away carries a harmonica and sometimes it is just on the strength of one that a fellow gets a free meal somewhere.

The night I went away was very quiet and peaceful. My mother and my brother had gone to bed early. My father had been marched off to work, carrying his dinner bucket, and was already doing his job because the whole sky was ablaze. My father worked in a steel mill and you could see the reflection of fire in the sky. That was my father opening the furnace doors of the mill. I looked into the sky and my father seemed to be all over it, skipping around in the fleecy clouds like a spirit. He was working hard just so he could come back home in the morning and walk down the street and nod good morning to all the neighbors who were getting up and having their breakfast and start the dogs to barking and the cats to scurrying over the back-yard fences.

Men coming home in the evening can be just as tired as men coming home in the morning, but in the evening the sun is going down and one does not see the tiredness on a worker's face. In the morning the sun is fresh and new and it seeks out all kinds of things about a man's face and you can see fatigue on it then.

My father came home under the gaze of the new clean sun. Then he fitted himself back in the mold of being a husband and a father, of sprinkling the lawn and mowing it, of picking things up if my mother dropped them.

I was going to let myself down from the second-story window of my bedroom, but even though my mother had forgotten to bring in the mattress that she had put out to air, the drop was too much for a fellow my age, and I tiptoed down the stairs with my sack of things thrown over my shoulder. When I got outside I turned around and looked the neighborhood over. I had never seen it that late except once when my father and I had to find a doctor for my mother. All of my father's garden lay under a film of dew and was so still that you could hear the things grow. When a leaf died you could hear it drop from the stalk and fall to the ground. I remembered watching my grandfather die a year or so before. He had been a shoemaker. He lay in the long white bed and his long tapered fingers spread out across his chest and he said to me in German: "It is like being a petal on a flower. First you are a part of the flower, then you are growing into a grandfather, and after you are a grandfather you commence to shrivel up and I am shriveling up now." In the way the silence of the night spread itself across the expanse of yard, I remembered my grandfather's voice as it died. I remembered the cold room and the fragrance of sickness in the room. I remembered the light that flickered by my grandfather's bed. I never smell a pair of good shoes that I do not think of my grandfather's hands.

157

I said good-bye to the yard where my father's garden lay.
I said good-bye to the alley and even the rotten clothesline
135 post at the corner of the lot. I turned and grew sadder still at
the darkness of the whole house and at the windows that
looked empty and evil, like a toothless woman. As I walked
in the direction of the railroad tracks, the light my father
made in the sky, now pink, now a deep vermilion, followed
140 me. It pranced about and cavorted with the clouds and rolled
and billowed like a wave of fire. I wanted to wake everyone
up and say to them: "That is my father doing the fire," like
you would say of someone on the stage: "The sound you
hear is my brother making the wind blow."

145   Finally I heard the train. I swung the pack over my
shoulder and went through the back yards of houses until I
saw the whirling, searching headlights of the train. Then the
whistle blew, two long utterances of sound the way I always
heard them while I lay in my bed in my own room and made
150 up stories in my head about where the train would take me.
And now I was there close to it, so close, in fact, that I could
feel the suction of air and the pressure of steam and the
vibration of its energy upon the ground. Then I got on and
lifted myself into an open boxcar that didn't really seem to
155 want to belong to the rest, for it swayed and pulled always in
opposite ways from the others, and I said to myself, that it,
too, was a part of a plan of things just like my father.

The buildings of my own town went by, the back yards of
houses went by, and the fences and street lights and churches.
160 Then we went into a strange kind of place and I looked out
again to find that the train was coming to a stop and all the
boxcars were being sidetracked. We were in the freightyards
and a man said, his face against the flickering lantern: "I
guess that winds it up for tonight." Then the engine itself
165 went somewhere and the engineer climbed down and soon
the whole place, like my own back yard, was still. I crawled
down out of the car and I knew the night was growing old.
I looked into the sky; there was just a flicker of my father

glowing there, just a flash now and then of him opening the furnace doors. I walked over to the engine. "How do I get back to the place you found me?" I cried, but the engine was still. It gasped once or twice, as if from indigestion, but it was cooling down and resting. The thirty-one cars that had comprised the full train stood scattered at every conceivable angle, yellow cars, white and red cars, blue and black. 170 175

I began to follow the tracks; there were so many. Some did nothing more than circle; others went out and stopped. It was difficult to find the one I wanted. In the distance I heard a dog. The dog seemed to be calling for its master. Where could the master be? I walked in every direction for a short while, then doubled back. Then I sat down and rested. I opened the pack to get out my red sweater, the one I used to wear selling garden seeds house to house. My harmonica fell out, so I played a few tunes on it just to hear how a harmonica sounded in the freightyard. It sounded weak. When I put the harmonica back was when a sandwich that my mother must have fixed for me fell out, and an orange. I ripped off the wax paper and commenced to eat. It was my mother's way, I guess, of fitting me to the mold; you never know what a woman has in her head. I ate the whole sandwich and the orange, too, and played my harmonica again. Then I stood up and commenced to run, wiping my mouth with the back of my hand. I don't know why I was in such a hurry, unless I was afraid the sun would soon come out and show the homesickness written across my face. 180 185 190 195

Reading Comprehension

The exercises that follow are based on the passage you have just read. Each exercise consists of an incomplete statement followed by four choices. Select the choice that best completes the statement. Go back to the passage for rereading to whatever extent is necessary to help you choose your answer.

1. "While I sat under the bush in the back yard I began to think how sad it would be if I ran off." (lines 15–16) The best description of the feelings of the narrator towards the scene he is imagining is

   a. he is ashamed and guilty about his own imaginings.

   b. the imagined scene makes him realize that his mother loves him as much as she loves David.

   c. he is enjoying the scene only because he knows that it will never become a reality.

   d. the scene gives him the satisfaction of expressing his feelings of self-pity and resentment towards his mother.

2. From the first three paragraphs, it would appear that the best way to sum up the narrator's feelings about the position of older brother versus that of younger brother is

   a. he would like to have the best of both worlds.

   b. he would prefer the role of the younger brother.

   c. he prefers the position of older brother.

   d. he is envious only of David's good looks.

3. The best judgment of the narrator's remarks concerning his father (lines 44–53) is that

   a. they show the immaturity of a twelve-year-old boy's thinking.

   b. they show that the boy's father was a weak individual.

   c. they explain the boy's feelings towards his mother.

   d. they explain the boy's feelings towards his brother.

4. "A fellow knows pretty much what he is about at twelve." (line 54) A good reader will see that these words should be read to mean

   a. a fellow mistakenly thinks he knows pretty much what he is about at twelve.

   b. a fellow knows pretty much what he is about at twelve because young people have a wisdom that adults do not.

160

    c. a fellow knows pretty much what he is about at twelve because his goals are clear and simple.

    d. just what they say.

5. The narrator's scheme of sending David to fetch things
    a. works out just as he intended.
    b. works out in such a way as to show the narrator how wrong he was.
    c. doesn't accomplish anything.
    d. achieves the narrator's goal in a way opposite from what he intended.

6. The narrator's preparation of belongings to take with him when he runs away shows that
    a. he is thorough and practical.
    b. he is going to miss his breakfast cereal.
    c. he is governed by fantasies as well as realities.
    d. he has no serious intention of running away.

7. The narrator's remarks about his father (lines 87–108) show that
    a. the father is cold and insensitive.
    b. the narrator can be observant and sensitive.
    c. the family is wealthy.
    d. the narrator dislikes his father.

8. As the twelve-year-old boy leaves the house, he is filled with feelings of
    a. excitement and adventure.
    b. determination to overcome fears and regrets.
    c. close ties to family and home.
    d. self-reliance.

9. While he is on the train and in the freightyards, the twelve-year-old boy's mind seems to be haunted most with thoughts of his
    a. father.   *c.* mother.
    b. brother.   *d.* grandfather.

10. The expression "fitting me to the mold" (line 189) can probably best be translated as meaning
    a. showing me her love.   *c.* fitting me for manhood.
    b. teaching me a lesson.   *d.* whipping me into shape.

11. At the end of the story, the boy is in such a hurry because
    a. he is homesick.
    b. he is afraid of the freightyards.
    c. he is more than ever convinced that he must run away.
    d. the day is almost over.

12. The most accurate description of the five members of the family in the story is
    a. typically, each is pretty much wrapped up with his own needs and concerns.
    b. they are average people, good in some ways, bad in others.
    c. the mother seems to be an exceptionally fine person, but the others are rather selfish.
    d. though quite realistically human, all five are exceptionally decent, attractive people.

Literary and Language Skills

POINT OF VIEW

Have you ever witnessed a "discussion" between the two drivers after an automobile accident? If so, you will know that usually there will be an astonishing difference in their two versions of just what happened. What's more, as time goes by and the two have had a chance to calm down and review the events of the accident in their minds, the differences in their reports of just what happened will tend to grow wider and deeper.

Such natural human differences in *point of view* were made the basis for a very interesting Japanese motion picture called *Rashomon*. There were three characters—a businessman, his wife, and a robber—involved in an incident. The movie simply retold the incident three times, each time as it was seen through the eyes of one of the characters. The result was an unusual and very good movie. The audience was left impressed with the remarkable effects of differences in point of view and was led to think about what the real truth was of what actually had happened.

Exercise A

The striking effects of point of view are neatly summed up in the often quoted wish: "If we could only see ourselves as others see us!"

1. What do you think are some of the reasons for the frequent expression of this wish?

2. Do you think the wish is more often made by the speaker about himself or by the speaker about someone else? Why do you think so?

Point of view is very important to the technique of telling a story. The story itself will be different depending on whose point of view it is told from. The questions that the reader will be led to think about will vary according to the point of view from which the story is told. In fiction, three important points of view from which a story may be told are—

1. *The first-person narrator (central character)*

> The central character is one who is personally involved in the events of the story. As the first-person narrator, he tells the events of the story as he sees them through his own eyes. His view of events is shaped by the limits of his own knowledge, understanding, and feeling. The story is told mainly in the first person (I).

2. *The first-person narrator (secondary character)*

> A minor character in the story, who observes the events of the story but is not as personally involved in them as the main characters, tells the story. Some of the story will be

told in the first person (I) but much will be told in the third person (he, she, they, or the names of characters).

3. *The "omniscient" author*

This is the most common point of view from which a story is told. The teller of the story is the author, who is not in the story at all. He is able to know everything (omniscient). He is able to know what every character is doing at every moment of time. He is able to know what the characters are thinking and feeling as well as saying and doing. He knows what has happened, what is happening, and what will happen. Of course, the author makes his own choice as to which knowledge he will share with the reader and when he will do it.

Exercise B

Below are listed the titles of the stories from which passages you have read so far have been taken. By using the numbers 1, 2, and 3, indicate the *point of view* from which each story has been told. Be ready to explain your choices.

    a. The City Boy
    b. So Big
    c. Cress Delahanty
    d. Ride Out the Storm
    e. That's What Happened to Me
    f. The Green Years

Exercise C

Here is the first sentence of *When You Run Away*.

There was a time when my brother David was a small boy and I was twelve or so that my mother seemed to favor him more than she did me.

When You Run Away is told in the first person by the central character, as this sentence shows. The story might also have been told from the point of view of

1. the omniscient author.
2. the mother as first-person narrator.
3. the father as first-person narrator.
4. David as first-person narrator.

Below are four different versions of the original first sentence. For each version, decide from which one of the above four points of view the story is now being told. (Assume the name of the central character—the twelve-year-old boy—is Jim.) Be ready to give the reasons for your choices.

a. As is the case with many a twelve year old faced with the presence of an attention-getting baby brother, Jim was torn between the attractions of babyhood and the satisfactions of growing up.

b. Himself troubled by the attentions that little David needed and got, Jim was going through a stage troublesome for all of us; but his mother, I knew, could be counted on to understand and bring him through.

c. Even now, I can dimly remember how I loved Jim at that distant period, even respecting as somehow important and manly what I now realize to be his rather unreasonable behavior.

d. When Jim was twelve, I began to see that he was torn between the attractions of being a baby and those of being a man and that I had to be very careful in helping him make the right choice.

PSYCHOLOGICAL FICTION

Some stories are based on the inner workings of human behavior. Such stories are sometimes called *psychological fiction*. What are the feelings that lie beneath a person's acts? Why does a person sometimes act in a way that is clearly harmful to himself? Why will a person sometimes be blind to the feelings of another? These are some of the questions dealt with in psychological fiction. The writer of such a story will often find it suitable to tell his story from the point of view of the central character as first-person narrator. *When You Run Away* is a good example of psychological fiction.

Most experts would agree that the mature and well-adjusted person usually has strong inner feelings towards himself of respect. He is glad to be himself; he has *self-esteem*. This same type of person can have strong inner feelings towards others of appreciation, affection, and love. He is able to feel *love for others*. The immature and poorly adjusted person has an opposite pair of inner feelings. He is not happy to be himself. He has feelings of *self-dislike*. Towards others, he has inner feelings of resentment, envy, hate. Towards others, he has feelings of *hostility*.

Finally, the experts would say, practically everybody represents a mixture of all four of these feelings: *self-esteem*, *love for others*, *self-dislike*, *hostility*. It is even possible for opposite feelings to be active at the same time. However, there will be differences among people in the strength and influence of each of the four feelings. *When You Run Away* is a story that shows how these inner feelings work in the central character as well as in the others.

Exercise D

Here are the four important inner feelings that we have briefly discussed.

1. Self-esteem   3. Self-dislike
2. Love for others 4. Hostility

These inner feelings are all mixed up in the central character of *When You Run Away*. Below are five statements of the central character. As these statements occur in the context of the story, which inner feelings are revealed by each? (Note that there may be more than one inner feeling in each case even though these

166

feelings may contradict each other.) Be ready to explain your answers.

a. He was a good-looking boy with large brown eyes and deep dimples and pudgy soft hands, and I did not have brown eyes or deep dimples or pudgy soft hands; not that I wanted them. I was tall and skinny and my face was starting to come out in pimples.

b. I don't mean how sad I would feel but how sad my mother would feel, losing her twelve-year-old son and all.

c. My little brother went out of the room and in about an hour he came back with everything; he even found the lost crayons.

d. I looked into the sky and my father seemed to be all over it, skipping around the fleecy clouds like a spirit.

e. I ate the whole sandwich and the orange, too, and played my harmonica again.

Exercise E

Which inner feelings seem to be strongest in each of the following characters? Prove your answer.

    1. the mother   3. David
    2. the father   4. the grandfather

Vocabulary in Context

A. Carefully examine each word in its context; then decide which definition is most appropriate.

1. **fret** (line 21)
   a. think
   b. shriek

    c. punish

    d. worry

2. **obligation** (line 52)
    a. responsibility
    b. expense
    c. trouble
    d. politeness

3. **cavorted** (line 140)
    a. burned
    b. changed quickly
    c. leaped about
    d. fought

4. **utterances** (line 148)
    a. groans
    b. symphonies
    c. squeals
    d. statements

5. **conceivable** (line 174)
    a. sharp
    b. imaginable
    c. manageable
    d. outrageous

B. Match meaning and sentence context by writing the word which most suitably fills the blank in each sentence. (Note that two words, 6 and 7, from the previous lesson are included for review.)

1. **fret**	6. **dwindling**
2. **obligation**	7. **belligerently**
3. **cavorted**	
4. **utterances**	
5. **conceivable**	

a. When the lion began to roar and snarl ___?___, the keeper decided to get out of the cage fast.

b. In the ___?___ light of dusk, we found it harder and harder to pick our way along the trail.

c. In a democracy, voting is not only the right of the citizen but also his ___?___.

d. We tried to make sense of the excited ___?___ of the natives, but their language was too strange for us.

e. The housewives first began to ___?___ over the rising cost of food and then turned to expressing their worry in petitions and protest marches.

f. The horse ___?___ so energetically that the rider had all he could do to stay in the saddle.

g. Though we were seeing it with our own eyes, it did not seem ___?___ that men were walking on the moon.

READING 12

Hunger stole upon me so slowly that at first I was not aware of what hunger really meant. Hunger had always been more or less at my elbow when I played, but now I began to wake up at night to find hunger standing at my bedside,
5 staring at me gauntly. The hunger I had known before this had been no grim, hostile stranger; it had been a normal hunger that had made me beg constantly for bread, and when I ate a crust or two I was satisfied. But this new hunger baffled me, scared me, made me angry and insistent. When-
10 ever I begged for food now my mother would pour me a cup of tea which would still the clamor in my stomach for a moment or two; but a little later I would feel hunger nudging my ribs, twisting my empty guts until they ached. I would grow dizzy and my vision would dim. I became less active in
15 my play, and for the first time in my life I had to pause and think of what was happening to me.

"Mama, I'm hungry," I complained one afternoon.

"Jump up and catch a kungry," she said, trying to make me laugh and forget.

20 "What's a *kungry?*"

"It's what little boys eat when they get hungry," she said.

"What does it taste like?"

"I don't know."

"Then why do you tell me to catch one?"

25 "Because you said that you were hungry," she said, smiling.

I sensed that she was teasing me and it made me angry.

"But I'm hungry. I want to eat."

Excerpt from pages 13–16 in BLACK BOY by Richard Wright. Copyright 1937, 1942, 1944, 1945 by Richard Wright. Reprinted by permission of Harper & Row, Publishers, Inc.

"You'll have to wait."

"But I want to eat now."

"But there's nothing to eat," she told me.

"Why?"

"Just because there's none," she explained.

"But I want to eat," I said, beginning to cry.

"You'll just have to wait," she said again.

"But why?"

"For God to send some food."

"When is He going to send it?"

"I don't know."

"But I'm hungry!"

She was ironing and she paused and looked at me with tears in her eyes.

"Where's your father?" she asked me.

I stared in bewilderment. Yes, it was true that my father had not come home to sleep for many days now and I could make as much noise as I wanted. Though I had not known why he was absent, I had been glad that he was not there to shout his restrictions at me. But it had never occurred to me that his absence would mean that there would be no food.

"I don't know," I said.

"Who brings food into the house?" my mother asked me.

"Papa," I said. "He always brought food."

"Well, your father isn't here now," she said.

"Where is he?"

"I don't know," she said.

"But I'm hungry," I whimpered, stomping my feet.

"You'll have to wait until I get a job and buy food," she said.

As the days slid past the image of my father became associated with my pangs of hunger, and whenever I felt hunger I thought of him with a deep biological bitterness.

My mother finally went to work as a cook and left me and my brother alone in the flat each day with a loaf of bread and a pot of tea. When she returned at evening she would be tired and dispirited and would cry a lot. Sometimes, when she was in despair, she would call us to her and talk to us for hours, telling us that we now had no father, that our lives would be different from those of other children, that we must learn as soon as possible to take care of ourselves, to dress ourselves, to prepare our own food; that we must take upon ourselves the responsibility of the flat while she worked. Half frightened, we would promise solemnly. We did not understand what had happened between our father and our mother and the most that these long talks did to us was to make us feel a vague dread. Whenever we asked why father had left, she would tell us that we were too young to know.

One evening my mother told me that thereafter I would have to do the shopping for food. She took me to the corner store to show me the way. I was proud; I felt like a grownup. The next afternoon I looped the basket over my arm and went down the pavement toward the store. When I reached the corner, a gang of boys grabbed me, knocked me down, snatched the basket, took the money, and sent me running home in panic. That evening I told my mother what had happened, but she made no comment; she sat down at once, wrote another note, gave me more money, and sent me out to the grocery again. I crept down the steps and saw the same gang of boys playing down the street. I ran back into the house.

"What's the matter?" my mother asked.

"It's those same boys," I said. "They'll beat me."

"You've got to get over that," she said. "Now, go on."

"I'm scared," I said.

"Go on and don't pay any attention to them," she said.

I went out of the door and walked briskly down the sidewalk, praying that the gang would not molest me. But when I came abreast of them someone shouted.

"There he is!"

They came toward me and I broke into a wild run toward home. They overtook me and flung me to the pavement. I

yelled, pleaded, kicked, but they wrenched the money out 100
of my hand. They yanked me to my feet, gave me a few
slaps, and sent me home sobbing. My mother met me at the
door.

"They b-beat m-me," I gasped. "They t-t-took the
m-money." 105

I started up the steps, seeking the shelter of the house.

"Don't you come in here," my mother warned me.

I froze in my tracks and stared at her.

"But they're coming after me," I said.

"You just stay right where you are," she said in a deadly 110
tone. "I'm going to teach you this night to stand up and
fight for yourself."

She went into the house and I waited, terrified, wondering
what she was about. Presently she returned with more money
and another note; she also had a long heavy stick. 115

"Take this money, this note, and this stick," she said. "Go
to the store and buy those groceries. If those boys bother
you, then fight."

I was baffled. My mother was telling me to fight, a thing
that she had never done before. 120

"But I'm scared," I said.

"Don't you come into this house until you've gotten those
groceries," she said.

"They'll beat me; they'll beat me," I said.

"Then stay in the streets; don't come back here!" 125

I ran up the steps and tried to force my way past her into
the house. A stinging slap came on my jaw. I stood on the
sidewalk, crying.

"Please, let me wait until tomorrow," I begged.

"No," she said. "Go now! If you come back into this 130
house without those groceries, I'll whip you!"

She slammed the door and I heard the key turn in the lock.
I shook with fright. I was alone upon the dark, hostile streets
and gangs were after me. I had the choice of being beaten at
home or away from home. I clutched the stick, crying, trying 135

to reason. If I were beaten at home, there was absolutely nothing that I could do about it; but if I were beaten in the streets, I had a chance to fight and defend myself. I walked slowly down the sidewalk, coming closer to the gang of boys,
140 holding the stick tightly. I was so full of fear that I could scarcely breathe. I was almost upon them now.

"There he is again!" the cry went up.

They surrounded me quickly and began to grab for my hand.

145 "I'll kill you!" I threatened.

They closed in. In blind fear I let the stick fly, feeling it crack against a boy's skull. I swung again, lamming another skull, then another. Realizing that they would retaliate if I let up for but a second, I fought to lay them low, to knock
150 them cold, to kill them so that they could not strike back at me. I flayed with tears in my eyes, teeth clenched, stark fear making me throw every ounce of my strength behind each blow. I hit again and again, dropping the money and the grocery list. The boys scattered, yelling, nursing their
155 heads, staring at me in utter disbelief. They had never seen such frenzy. I stood panting, egging them on, taunting them to come on and fight. When they refused, I ran after them and they tore out for their homes, screaming. The parents of the boys rushed into the streets and threatened me, and for
160 the first time in my life I shouted at grownups, telling them that I would give them the same if they bothered me. I finally found my grocery list and the money and went to the store. On my way back I kept my stick poised for instant use, but there was not a single boy in sight. That night I won
165 the right to the streets of Memphis.

Reading Comprehension

The exercises that follow are based on the passage you have just read. Each exercise consists of an incomplete statement followed by four choices. Select the choice that best completes the statement. Go back to the passage for rereading to whatever extent is necessary to help you choose your answer.

1. A chief intent of the discussion of hunger in the first paragraph is to
   a. give a picture of the enormous appetites of a growing boy.
   b. show the boy's growing awareness of the difference between appetite and starvation.
   c. show that hunger is sometimes a mental need rather than a physical one.
   d. suggest that the boy's symptoms are being caused by some illness or disease.

2. "Jump up and catch a kungry." (line 18) This remark really shows Mama's
   a. gaiety.
   b. anger.
   c. hopefulness.
   d. desperation.

3. "Where's your father?" she asked me. (line 42) Mama asks this question because
   a. she thinks the boy may know something she doesn't.
   b. she wants to help the boy to understand the realities of their situation.
   c. the boy has been partly responsible for the family problem.
   d. the boy didn't know that the father had been missing for many days.

4. The chief impression that the boy has apparently had of his father is that of
   a. breadwinner.
   b. tyrant.
   c. friend.
   d. stranger.

5. After she obtains a job as a cook, the mother has long talks with the boy and his brother. The chief effect of these talks is to
   a. make the boys fearful.
   b. give the boys a sense of grown-up responsibility.
   c. help the boys understand the problem between their parents.
   d. make the boys realize they must find jobs.

6. When the boy is first told that he will have to do the shopping for food, he feels
   a. proud.
   b. angry.
   c. frightened.
   d. puzzled.

7. The main motive of the attacks by the gang appears to be
   a. hatred of "outsiders."
   b. prejudice.
   c. robbery.
   d. unclear.

8. After two beatings by the gang, the mother insists that the boy go once more and fight back. She acts so harshly because she
   a. is disgusted with her son.
   b. doesn't know what she's doing.
   c. is full of hate for a world that has treated her cruelly.
   d. knows it is necessary.

9. "That night I won the right to the streets of Memphis." (lines 164–165) This sentence means that
   a. the boy feels that he "owns" the town.
   b. the family is going to move to Memphis.
   c. the boy can walk in the streets without fear.
   d. the boy will become a member of the street gang.

10. The moral or lesson that the boy appears to have learned from his experiences as told in this account is best summed up in the phrase
   a. in a jungle world, the law is survival of the fittest.
   b. love conquers all.
   c. necessity is the mother of invention.
   d. most men lead lives of quiet desperation.

Literary and Language Skills

THE EXACT WORD

An important part of the passage from *Black Boy* consists of dialogue. Here is an example.

"It's what little boys eat when they get hungry," she said.

As in this example, the general word *said* is used most often in the writing of dialogue. But, if the dialogue is lengthy, the repetition of *said* can become monotonous. In addition, *said* is vague and general in its meaning. Now, look at this second example from the passage.

"But I'm hungry," I whimpered, stomping my feet.

Here the writer has used a much more specific, exact synonym for *said*. The word *whimpered* (meaning "spoke in low, whining sounds") tells us not only that the boy spoke the words but also suggests how he sounded and felt as he spoke them. The use of the exact synonym *whimpered* adds force, interest, and variety to the writing.

Exercise A

Find in the passage five examples of the use of more exact synonyms for *said*.

Exercise B

Give yourself three minutes. How many synonyms for *said* can you jot down?

Exercise C

Here are five examples of dialogue from the passage in which the general word *said* has been used. Can you substitute a suitable more exact synonym for *said* in each case?

1. "Take this money, this note, and this stick," she *said*. "Go to the store and buy those groceries. If those boys bother you, then fight."

2. "But I'm scared," I *said*.

3. "Don't you come into this house until you've gotten those groceries," she *said*.

4. "They'll beat me; they'll beat me," I *said*.

5. "No," she *said*. "Go now! If you come back into this house without those groceries, I'll whip you!"

Exercise D

How many synonyms for *said* were you able to jot down in Exercise B? In this exercise you will be given one hundred synonyms for *said* (and there are more)!

Each group of ten synonyms for *said* given below is followed by three examples of dialogue. In each example, the general word *said* is used. From the ten synonyms, select the one that can be best substituted for *said* in each example. A sample is done for you in group I.

I

1. accused	6. argued
2. advised	7. asked
3. affirmed	8. asserted
4. answered	9. bargained
5. apologized	10. barked

SAMPLE:

"I'm truly sorry, Jim," *said* Mary, "but I won't be able to keep our date for Saturday night."

"I'm truly sorry, Jim." *apologized* Mary, "but I won't be able to keep our date for Saturday night."

a. "With your aptitudes, you should think of a career in law," the counselor *said*.

b. "Straighten up that line!" *said* the top sergeant.

c. "Throw in radial tires and it's a deal," the customer *said*.

II

11. begged	16. chattered
12. beseeched	17. claimed
13. blurted	18. coaxed
14. boasted	19. commanded
15. breathed	20. complained

a. "Don't answer the bell and don't make a sound," she *said*. "It's that neighbor wanting to borrow something and I don't want her to know we're home."

b. The child *said*, "Jimmy told me not to tell you he tore his new sweater."

c. "Eat up all your egg," *said* the mother, "and Mommy will buy you a new toy."

179

21. conceded	26. contradicted
22. concluded	27. cried
23. confessed	28. declaimed
24. confided	29. declared
25. consented	30. denied

a. "You are quite mistaken, officer," the driver *said*. "The light was green, not red, when I passed it."

b. "I'll tell you this completely off the record and for your ears only," the senator *said*, "but I have no intention of running for another term."

c. "What a rotten break!" *said* the coach. "Another inch and he'd have had a touchdown."

IV

31. dictated	36. exaggerated
32. disclosed	37. exclaimed
33. divulged	38. flattered
34. echoed	39. gossiped
35. emphasized	40. groaned

a. "I was so hungry I ate three steaks for dinner," the boy *said*.

b. "I don't care whether you believe it or not," Mary *said*, "but I heard that last week Harvey had dates with three different girls."

c. "From tomorrow on," the office manager *said*, "every employee is to be at his desk at 8:45 A.M."

V

41. growled	46. hissed
42. grunted	47. insisted
43. guessed	48. interjected
44. harangued	49. interrupted
45. hinted	50. intoned

a. "And, my fellow citizens," *said* the street corner speaker, "each and every one of us must fight to bring down this weak government and replace it with a strong one under which we can all unite once more to bring back the ancient power and glory of the motherland."

b. "Your honor," the defense attorney *said*, "I object to the prosecutor's harassment of the witness."

c. The jury foreman *said*, "We find the defendant guilty on the first count, guilty on the second count, guilty on the third count."

VI

51. jeered	56. moaned
52. jested	57. mocked
53. laughed	58. murmured
54. lied	59. narrated
55. mentioned	60. objected

a. "The pain in my leg is unbearable, Dr. Welby," *said* the patient.

b. Andy *said*, "I suppose you're going to tell us you dropped the ball because the sun was in your eyes."

c. "There's a special on canned soups today, Mrs. Smith," *said* the grocer.

VII

61. persisted	66. predicted
62. pleaded	67. proclaimed
63. prattled	68. promised
64. prayed	69. questioned
65. preached	70. raged

a. "There will be heavy snow tomorrow," *said* the weather man.

b. The little leaguer *said*, "Give me one more chance at bat. I know I can get a hit."

c. "Did you remember to mail the letters?" Mother *said*.

VIII

71. ranted	76. reprimanded
72. raved	77. requested
73. recited	78. responded
74. remarked	79. roared
75. repeated	80. scolded

a. The crowd *said*, "We want a touchdown!"

b. "The sum of the angles of a triangle," *said* the student, "is 180 degrees."

c. "Johnny, your room is a mess again. Aren't you ever going to learn to keep it neat?" Mrs. Harris *said*.

IX

81. screamed	86. sneered
82. sermonized	87. specified
83. sighed	88. stammered
84. snapped	89. suggested
85. snarled	90. squawked

a. "Jim is so handsome," *said* Mary. "If only he would pay a little attention to me."

b. "Don't you think it would be a good idea to open the window and let in a little fresh air?" Dick *said*.

c. "I'm t-t-terribly sorry, Miss," *said* the young man. "I th-thought you were someone else."

X

91. stuttered	96. warned
92. summarized	97. whimpered
93. threatened	98. whispered
94. thundered	99. wondered
95. urged	100. yelled

a. "Should I go to the movies or study for the test?" Tom *said.*

b. "If we don't cut down on our consumption of energy," *said* the scientist, "there will be a serious shortage."

c. "Please don't make me go to bed," *said* the child. "I never get a chance to watch my T.V. programs anymore."

Vocabulary in Context

A. Carefully examine each word in its context; then decide which definition is most appropriate.

1. **grim** (line 6)
   a. imaginary
   b. nutritious
   c. fierce
   d. laughing

2. **baffled** (line 9)
   a. excited
   b. confused
   c. taught
   d. calmed

3. **restrictions** (line 47)
   a. limitations
   b. advice
   c. conversations
   d. explanations

4. **dread** (line 74)
   a. hope
   b. feeling
   c. respect
   d. fear

5. **taunting** (line 156)
   a. ridiculing
   b. resisting
   c. forcing
   d. fearing

B. Match meaning and sentence context by writing the word which most suitably fills the blank in each sentence. (Note that two words, 6 and 7, from the previous lesson are included for review.)

1. grim
2. baffled
3. restrictions
4. dread
5. taunting
6. fret
7. obligation

a. After the first round, the champion knew that his young opponent was to be no easy victim, that instead he would put up a —— ? ——, tough challenge.

b. There is something so evil and dangerous about the appearance of sharks that even experienced divers are filled with a sense of —— ? —— by the sight of the beasts.

c. —— ? —— by all the attention given to his new baby brother, the boy became sullen and withdrawn.

d. The audience showed its hostility towards the speaker by its jeering, —— ? ——, and booing.

e. Nowadays, more and more people are placing themselves on dietary —— ? —— of various kinds, almost as though food regulation were a cure-all.

f. According to the law, a bank has an —— ? —— to explain fully the interest rate it charges on loans.

g. A self-confident person does not worry, hesitate, and —— ? —— every time he has to make a decision.

READING 13

The children were to be driven, as a special treat, to the sands at Jagborough. Nicholas was not to be of the party; he was in disgrace. Only that morning he had refused to eat his wholesome bread-and-milk on the seemingly frivolous ground that there was a frog in it. Older and wiser and better people 5
had told him that there could not possibly be a frog in his bread-and-milk and that he was not to talk nonsense; he continued, nevertheless, to talk what seemed the veriest nonsense, and described with much detail the coloration and markings of the alleged frog. The dramatic part of the inci- 10
dent was that there really was a frog in Nicholas' basin of bread-and-milk; he had put it there himself, so he felt entitled to know something about it. The sin of taking a frog from the garden and putting it into a bowl of wholesome bread-and-milk was enlarged on at great length, but the fact that 15
stood out clearest in the whole affair, as it presented itself to the mind of Nicholas, was that the older, wiser, and better people had been proved to be profoundly in error in matters about which they had expressed the utmost assurance.

"You said there couldn't possibly be a frog in my bread- 20
and-milk; there *was* a frog in my bread-and-milk," he repeated, with the insistence of a skilled tactician who does not intend to shift from favourable ground.

So his boy-cousin and girl-cousin and his quite uninteresting younger brother were to be taken to Jagborough sands 25
that afternoon and he was to stay at home. His cousins'

aunt, who insisted, by an unwarranted stretch of imagination, in styling herself his aunt also, had hastily invented the Jagborough expedition in order to impress on Nicholas the delights that he had justly forfeited by his disgraceful conduct at the breakfast table. It was her habit, whenever one of the children fell from grace, to improvise something of a festival nature from which the offender would be rigorously debarred; if all the children sinned collectively they were suddenly informed of a circus in a neighbouring town, a circus of unrivalled merit and uncounted elephants, to which, but for their depravity, they would have been taken that very day.

A few decent tears were looked for on the part of Nicholas when the moment for the departure of the expedition arrived. As a matter-of-fact, however, all the crying was done by his girl-cousin, who scraped her knee rather painfully against the step of the carriage as she was scrambling in.

"How she did howl," said Nicholas cheerfully, as the party drove off without any of the elation of high spirits that should have characterized it.

"She'll soon get over that," said the *soi-disant* aunt; "it will be a glorious afternoon for racing about over those beautiful sands. How they will enjoy themselves!"

"Bobby won't enjoy himself much, and he won't race much either," said Nicholas with a grim chuckle; "his boots are hurting him. They're too tight."

"Why didn't he tell me they were hurting?" asked the aunt with some asperity.

"He told you twice, but you weren't listening. You often don't listen when we tell you important things."

"You are not to go into the gooseberry garden," said the aunt, changing the subject.

"Why not?" demanded Nicholas.

"Because you are in disgrace," said the aunt loftily.

Nicholas did not admit the flawlessness of the reasoning; he felt perfectly capable of being in disgrace and in a gooseberry garden at the same moment. His face took on an expression of considerable obstinacy. It was clear to his aunt that he was determined to get into the gooseberry garden, "only," as she remarked to herself, "because I have told him he is not to." 65

Now the gooseberry garden had two doors by which it might be entered, and once a small person like Nicholas could slip in there he could effectually disappear from view amid the masking growth of artichokes, raspberry canes, and fruit 70 bushes. The aunt had many other things to do that afternoon, but she spent an hour or two in trivial gardening operations among flower beds and shrubberies, whence she could keep a watchful eye on the two doors that led to the forbidden paradise. She was a woman of few ideas, with immense 75 powers of concentration.

Nicholas made one or two sorties into the front garden, wriggling his way with obvious stealth of purpose towards one or other of the doors, but never able for a moment to evade the aunt's watchful eye. As a matter-of-fact, he had no 80 intention of trying to get into the gooseberry garden, but it was extremely convenient for him that his aunt should believe that he had; it was a belief that would keep her on self-imposed sentry duty for the greater part of the afternoon. Having thoroughly confirmed and fortified her suspicions, 85 Nicholas slipped back into the house and rapidly put into execution a plan of action that had long germinated in his brain. By standing on a chair in the library one could reach a shelf on which reposed a fat, important-looking key. The key was as important as it looked; it was the instrument 90 which kept the mysteries of the lumber room secure from unauthorized intrusion, which opened a way only for aunts and suchlike privileged persons. Nicholas had not had much experience of the art of fitting keys into keyholes and turning locks, but for some days past he had practised with the 95 key of the schoolroom door; he did not believe in trusting too much to luck and accident. The key turned stiffly in the lock, but it turned. The door opened, and Nicholas was in an

unknown land, compared with which the gooseberry garden
100 was a stale delight, a mere material pleasure.

Often and often Nicholas had pictured to himself what the
lumber room might be like, that region that was so carefully
sealed from youthful eyes and concerning which no questions
were ever answered. It came up to his expectations. In the
105 first place it was large and dimly lit, one high window opening on to the forbidden garden being its only source of illu-
mination. In the second place it was a storehouse of un-
imagined treasures. The aunt-by-assertion was one of those
people who think that things spoil by use and consign them
110 to dust and damp by way of preserving them. Such parts of
the house as Nicholas knew best were rather bare and cheer-
less, but here there were wonderful things for the eye to
feast on. First and foremost there was a piece of framed
tapestry that was evidently meant to be a fire screen. To
115 Nicholas it was a living, breathing story; he sat down on a roll
of Indian hangings, glowing in wonderful colours beneath a
layer of dust, and took in all the details of the tapestry
picture. A man, dressed in the hunting costume of some
remote period, had just transfixed a stag with an arrow; it
120 could not have been a difficult shot because the stag was
only one or two paces away from him; in the thickly growing
vegetation that the picture suggested it would not have been
difficult to creep up to a feeding stag, and the two spotted
dogs that were springing forward to join in the chase had
125 evidently been trained to keep to heel till the arrow was
discharged. That part of the picture was simple, if interesting, but did the huntsman see, what Nicholas saw, that four
galloping wolves were coming in his direction through the
wood? There might be more than four of them hidden be-
130 hind the trees, and in any case would the man and his dogs be
able to cope with the four wolves if they made an attack?
The man had only two arrows left in his quiver, and he might
miss with one or both of them; all one knew about his skill
in shooting was that he could hit a large stag at a ridiculously

188

short range. Nicholas sat for many golden minutes revolving 135
the possibilities of the scene; he was inclined to think that
there were more than four wolves and that the man and his
dogs were in a tight corner.

But there were other objects of delight and interest claim-
ing his instant attention: there were quaint twisted candle- 140
sticks in the shape of snakes, and a teapot fashioned like a
china duck, out of whose open beak the tea was supposed to
come. How dull and shapeless the nursery teapot seemed in
comparison! And there was a carved sandalwood box packed
tight with aromatic cotton wool, and between the layers of 145
cotton wool were little brass figures, hump-necked bulls, and
peacocks and goblins, delightful to see and to handle. Less
promising in appearance was a large square book with plain
black covers; Nicholas peeped into it, and, behold, it was full
of coloured pictures of birds. And such birds! In the garden, 150
and in the lanes when he went for a walk, Nicholas came
across a few birds, of which the largest were an occasional
magpie or wood pigeon; here were herons and bustards, kites,
toucans, tiger bitterns, brush turkeys, ibises, golden pheas-
ants, a whole portrait gallery of undreamed-of creatures. And 155
as he was admiring the colouring of the mandarin duck and
assigning a life history to it, the voice of his aunt in shrill
vociferation of his name came from the gooseberry garden
without. She had grown suspicious at his long disappearance,
and had leapt to the conclusion that he had climbed over the 160
wall behind the sheltering screen of the lilac bushes; she was
now engaged in energetic and rather hopeless search for him
among the artichokes and raspberry canes.

"Nicholas, Nicholas!" she screamed, "you are to come out
of this at once. It's no use trying to hide there; I can see you 165
all the time."

It was probably the first time for twenty years that any
one had smiled in that lumber room.

Presently the angry repetitions of Nicholas' name gave way
to a shriek, and a cry for somebody to come quickly. Nicho- 170

las shut the book, restored it carefully to its place in a corner, and shook some dust from a neighbouring pile of newspapers over it. Then he crept from the room, locked the door, and replaced the key exactly where he had found it. His aunt was still calling his name when he sauntered into the front garden.

"Who's calling?" he asked.

"Me," came the answer from the other side of the wall; "didn't you hear me? I've been looking for you in the gooseberry garden, and I've slipped into the rain-water tank. Luckily there's no water in it, but the sides are slippery and I can't get out. Fetch the little ladder from under the cherry tree——"

"I was told I wasn't to go into the gooseberry garden," said Nicholas promptly.

"I told you not to, and now I tell you that you may," came the voice from the rain-water tank, rather impatiently.

"Your voice doesn't sound like aunt's," objected Nicholas; "you may be the Evil One tempting me to be disobedient. Aunt often tells me that the Evil One tempts me and that I always yield. This time I'm not going to yield."

"Don't talk nonsense," said the prisoner in the tank; "go and fetch the ladder."

"Will there be strawberry jam for tea?" asked Nicholas innocently.

"Certainly there will be," said the aunt, privately resolving that Nicholas should have none of it.

"Now I know that you are the Evil One and not aunt," shouted Nicholas gleefully; "when we asked for strawberry jam yesterday she said there wasn't any. I know there are four jars of it in the store cupboard, because I looked, and of course you know it's there, but *she* doesn't, because she said there wasn't any. Oh, Devil, you *have* sold yourself!"

There was an unusual sense of luxury in being able to talk to an aunt as though one was talking to the Evil One, but Nicholas knew, with childish discernment, that such luxuries were not to be overindulged in. He walked noisily away, and

190

it was a kitchenmaid, in search of parsley, who eventually rescued the aunt from the rain-water tank.

Tea that evening was partaken of in a fearsome silence. The tide had been at its highest when the children had arrived 210 at Jagborough Cove, so there had been no sands to play on—a circumstance that the aunt had overlooked in the haste of organizing her punitive expedition. The tightness of Bobby's boots had had disastrous effect on his temper the whole of the afternoon, and altogether the children could not have 215 been said to have enjoyed themselves. The aunt maintained the frozen muteness of one who has suffered undignified and unmerited detention in a rain-water tank for thirty-five minutes. As for Nicholas, he, too, was silent, in the absorption of one who has much to think about; it was just possible, he 220 considered, that the huntsman would escape with his hounds while the wolves feasted on the stricken stag.

Reading Comprehension

The exercises that follow are based on the passage you have just read. Each exercise consists of an incomplete statement followed by four choices. Select the choice that best completes the statement. Go back to the passage for rereading to whatever extent is necessary to help you choose your answer.

1. Nicholas is punished by being barred from the outing to Jagborough mainly because he has
    a. refused to eat his bread-and-milk.
    b. claimed that there was a frog in his bread-and-milk.
    c. actually put a frog in his bread-and-milk.
    d. gone into the garden.

2. The main point of the whole frog incident, as far as Nicholas is concerned, is that
   a. the older, wiser, better people had said there was no frog in the bread-and-milk, and there was.
   b. his "aunt" was not really his aunt.
   c. he had been unjustly accused of wrongdoing.
   d. he hadn't wanted to go to Jagborough anyway.

3. "It was her habit, whenever one of the children fell from grace, to improvise something of a festival nature from which the offender would be rigorously debarred . . ." (lines 31–33) This habit suggests that the aunt
   a. believes in a system of rewards rather than punishments.
   b. is a firm but fair disciplinarian.
   c. is too easygoing to be a disciplinarian.
   d. has a cruel streak in her, besides being foolish.

4. Concerning the trip to Jagborough, it can be inferred that
   a. the aunt did not go.
   b. Nicholas finally got to go.
   c. nobody got to go.
   d. the girl-cousin did not go.

5. From the context, you can infer that the French term *soi-disant* (line 46) probably means
   a. so-called.
   b. sympathetic.
   c. distant.
   d. glorious.

6. The aunt probably did not hear Bobby's complaints about his shoes because
   a. she didn't want to spoil Bobby's afternoon.
   b. she was paying attention to the crying girl-cousin.
   c. she is slightly hard of hearing.
   d. she was more intent on Nicholas's punishment than on the other children's pleasures.

7. Nicholas wriggled his way with obvious stealth towards the doors of the gooseberry garden to
   a. sneak past the aunt.
   b. mislead the aunt as to his true intentions.
   c. prove to himself that he can get into the garden if he wants to.
   d. discourage the aunt from her watch over the doors.

8. The lumber room (a term used more in England than America) seems to be
   a. a room for drying lumber.
   b. a kind of storage room for house furnishings.
   c. a living room with a fireplace.
   d. the aunt's room.

9. In the lumber room, Nicholas proves himself to be
   a. mischievous and happy-go-lucky.
   b. malicious and destructive.
   c. sensitive and imaginative.
   d. healthy and active.

10. "Will there be strawberry jam for tea?" (line 193) Nicholas asks this question to
    a. trap the aunt into revealing herself as having lied about there being no strawberry jam.
    b. force the aunt into giving him strawberry jam for tea.
    c. prove to himself that it is not really the aunt in the tank.
    d. show how innocent he is.

11. At tea, Nicholas was occupied with
    a. enjoying the unhappiness of the aunt.
    b. sympathizing with the unhappiness of the children.
    c. enjoying the luxury of his strawberry jam.
    d. thoughts having nothing to do with the people or activities of the moment.

Literary and Language Skills

THE ENGLISH LANGUAGE

We usually think of the English language as one language. It is a language, however, that has many different forms and shapes. It would not be far from the truth to say that there are many English languages.

- The English that a person uses when he is speaking is different in many ways from the English he uses when he is writing.

- The English spoken by persons from Boston, Massachusetts; Brooklyn, New York; Biloxi, Mississippi; and Butte, Montana, will all sound quite different from each other.

- There will be many differences in the English of an American, an Englishman, and an Australian.

- The English you use in writing a letter to a close friend will be different from the English you use in writing an application for a job.

- The English used by football players in a huddle will be different from the English used in a meeting of nuclear physicists or in a conference of sales managers of a corporation.

Exercise A

The same word can have very different meanings according to the person who uses it or the circumstances under which it is used. What different meaning may each of the following words have to the three users named after the word? If you need help, refer to a good dictionary.

1. **run**
   a. a baseball player
   b. a banker
   c. a girl concerned about her appearance

2. **strain**
   a. a cattlebreeder
   b. a weight lifter
   c. a cook

3. **earth**
   a. a farmer
   b. an astronaut
   c. a religious leader

4. **watch**
   a. a sailor
   b. a spectator
   c. a jeweler

5. **stock**
   a. an investor
   b. a storekeeper
   c. a ranchowner

Exercise B

We tend to use a different vocabulary in *formal* and *informal* situations. For example, in informal conversation, one might use the word "kids," whereas in formal writing one might prefer "children." Give an informal equivalent of each of the formal words below.

1. frankfurter
2. obese
3. physical education
4. physician
5. domicile

Exercise C

Americans are likely to read the works of some of the great British authors of past and present, see British plays or movies, hear Britons on television. They will notice the many differences between British English and American English in pronunciation, vocabulary, phrasing, and spelling. You may have noticed some of these differences in the story *The Lumber Room*. H. H. Munro, whose pen-name is "Saki," is British. If necessary, refer to an unabridged dictionary to help you answer the following questions based on Munro's story.

1. How might you tell from the title of the story itself that the author is British?

2. What is the difference in meaning of the word "tea" to an Englishman and an American?

3. The following words occur in the story: favourable, neighbouring, colours, coloured. What conclusion can you draw about one difference in British and American spelling? Give two other words of your own that are covered by the same rule.

4. Here are three words that occur in the story. What word would an American be more likely to use instead?
   a. sands (line 48)
   b. boots (line 50)
   c. cupboard (line 200)

5. Here are ten common British words. What are the American equivalents?

a. underground		*f.* petrol	
b. lift		*g.* cooker	
c. pram		*h.* nappie	
d. greengrocer		*i.* lorry	
e. pub		*j.* pudding	

Exercise D

A good unabridged dictionary is rich in information about word meanings as they relate to the many varieties of the English language, as well as many other kinds of information. On the next page are the entries for the word *pan* from the unabridged Webster's New International Dictionary, Second Edition. Answer the following questions based on the entry.

1. Name at least five different professions, trades, or occupations in which *pan* has specialized meaning.

2. In what cases of special usage does each of the following meanings of *pan* apply?
   a. the cranium
   b. of the thigh bone
   c. fit; agree
   d. to ridicule mercilessly
   e. a wall plate
   f. to harden or cake
   g. to yield a result

3. As what parts of speech may *pan* be used?

4. Give five words in which *pan* is used as a combining form.

5. In what foreign language is *pan* used as a title of nobility? How is it pronounced in this use? What sign is used to show when a foreign word has been taken directly into English?

6. From what ancient language is the word *pan*, when it means "a dish," thought to be derived?

7. Sometimes the use of a word is illustrated by quoting from a famous author. What author is quoted in this entry? What are the quoted words?

8. What special meaning might *pan* have for each of the following: (*a*) a ship's captain in winter; (*b*) a South African; (*c*) a pistol collector; (*d*) a Newfoundland sealer?

9. Name eight specific kinds of information that an unabridged dictionary gives about a word. Illustrate each from the entry for *pan*.

pan, *n.* [ME. *panne,* fr. AS. *panne;* cf. D. *pan,* G. *pfanne,* OHG. *pfanna,* ON., Sw., & ML. *panna;* perh. fr. L. *patina.* See PATEN; cf. PENNY.] **1.** A metal or earthenware dish or vessel for domestic uses, commonly broad and shallow, and often open. "A bowl or a *pan.*" *Chaucer.*
2. Any of various other more or less similar vessels or articles; as: **a** Either of the receptacles for the weights or the bodies weighed in a pair of scales or a balance. **b** A vessel for evaporating, as salt brine. **c** A vessel for grinding and amalgamating ores; also, a vessel for separating gold, stream tin, etc., from gravel, crushed rock, etc.
3. A depressed or hollowed part of, or place in, something, suggesting the hollow of a pan; as: **a** In old guns or pistols, the hollow part of the lock to receive the priming. **b** *Obs.* Of the thigh bone, the acetabulum. **c** A natural basin or depression, esp. one containing standing water or mud and, as in South Africa, in the dry season often dried up, leaving a salt deposit; also, an artificial basin, as for evaporating brine.
4. The brainpan; the cranium. *Obs. exc. Scot. & Dial.*
5. A hard subsoil; hardpan. See HARDPAN.
6. A fragment of the flat, relatively thin ice which forms in bays or fiords or along the shore and then becomes free and drifts about the sea. Some pans have upturned edges formed when a number bump together in wind or storm.
7. A pile of sealskins left temporarily on ice, as by Newfoundland sealers.
8. *Carp.* A recess, or bed, for the leaf of a hinge.
9. *Elec.* = SHOE, *n.,* 7.
10. *Organ Building.* The channel board.
11. *Railroads.* The head of a tamping bar.
12. *Trapping.* The round flat disk of metal on a steel trap on which the animal steps to spring the trap.
13. *Whaling.* The broad posterior part of the lower jawbone of a whale.

-pan (-păn). A combining form of the noun *pan,* often written separately, as in:

ashpan	dishpan	piepan
bakepan	dustpan	saucepan
bedpan	flashpan	scalepan
brainpan	frying pan	stewpan
bread pan	kneepan	warming pan
cake pan	pattypan	

pan (păn), *v.;* PANNED (pănd); PAN′NING. *Transitive:* **To** treat in a pan; specif.: **a** *Mining.* To wash in a kind of pan for the purpose of separating heavy particles; to separate by such a process; as, to *pan* dirt or gravel for gold. **b** To extract (salt) by evaporation in a pan. **c** To cook in a pan in a small quantity of fat or water. **d** To pour with a pan; — often with *out.* **e** *Slang.* To attack with harsh criticism; to ridicule mercilessly.
——, *Intransitive:* **1.** *Mining.* **a** To wash earth, gravel, etc., in a pan in searching for gold. **b** To yield gold in or as in the process of panning; to yield precious metal; — usually with *out;* as, the gravel *panned* out richly; the dirt *panned* out 40 ounces of gold to the ton.
2. To yield a result; to turn out (profitably or unprofitably); to result; — used with *out;* as, the investigation, or the speculation, *panned* out poorly. *Colloq.*
3. To harden or cake superficially, as ground. *Dial. Eng.*
pan (păn), *n.* [F. *panne.*] *Arch.* A wall plate. *Eng.*
pan, *v. t. & i.* To join or fit together; to unite; fit; agree. *Scot. & Dial. Eng.*
pan (pän), *n.* [Hind. *pān,* fr. Skr. *parṇa* leaf.] The betel leaf; also, the masticatory made of it.
‖**pan** (pän), *n.; pl.* PANOWIE (pä·nô′vyĕ). [Pol.] A title of nobility, used honorifically; sir.

Vocabulary in Context

A. Carefully examine each word in its context; then decide which definition is most appropriate.

1. **frivolous** (line 4)
   - *a.* complete
   - *b.* stated
   - *c.* silly
   - *d.* perfect

2. **improvise** (line 32)
   - *a.* prove completely
   - *b.* insist firmly on
   - *c.* imitate accurately
   - *d.* invent quickly

3. **depravity** (line 37)
   - *a.* wickedness
   - *b.* appetite
   - *c.* age
   - *d.* demands

4. **asperity** (line 53)
   - *a.* grace
   - *b.* harshness
   - *c.* temptation
   - *d.* remedy

5. **punitive** (line 213)
   - *a.* inflicting punishment
   - *b.* exploring territory
   - *c.* happy
   - *d.* granting mercy

B. Match meaning and sentence context by writing the word which most suitably fills the blank in each sentence. (Note that two words, 6 and 7, from the previous lesson are included for review.)

1. frivolous
2. improvise
3. depravity
4. asperity
5. punitive

6. baffled
7. restrictions

a. The dictator took such severe ___?___ action against those who had opposed him before he rose to power that the world was shocked.

b. As a student, he occupied himself with ___?___ ideas and activities, but once in the world of work he was devoted to serious and important matters.

c. The cruelty and ___?___ of the tyrant could no longer be tolerated and the people rose against him.

d. Most Americans who try to understand the English game of cricket are completely ___?___ even though, like baseball, it is played with bat and ball.

e. A soldier's life is much freer today since many of the old ___?___ are no longer enforced.

f. Even when he was a child, his musical genius showed itself in the way he could sit down at the piano and effortlessly ___?___ original, lively melodies.

g. He was a judge known for the ___?___ of his decisions, and some thought his harshness to be excessive.

READING 14

Portrait of a Boy

After the whipping, he crawled into bed;
Accepting the harsh fact with no great weeping.
How funny uncle's hat had looked striped red!
He chuckled silently. The moon came, sweeping
A black frayed rag of tattered cloud before   5
In scorning; very pure and pale she seemed,
Flooding his bed with radiance. On the floor
Fat motes danced. He sobbed; closed his eyes and dreamed.

Warm sand flowed round him. Blurts of crimson light
Splashed the white grains like blood. Past the cave's mouth   10
Shone with a large fierce splendor, wildly bright,
The crooked constellations of the South;
Here the Cross swung; and there, affronting Mars,
The Centaur stormed aside a froth of stars.
Within, great casks like wattled aldermen   15
Sighed of enormous feasts, and cloth of gold
Glowed on the walls like hot desire. Again,
Beside webbed purples from some galleon's hold,
A black chest bore the skull and bones in white
Above a scrawled "Gunpowder!" By the flames,   20
Decked out in crimson, gemmed with syenite,
Hailing their fellows by outrageous names
The pirates sat and diced. Their eyes were moons.
"Doubloons!" they said. The words crashed gold.
    "Doubloons!"

Reading Comprehension

The exercises that follow are based on the passage you have just read. Each exercise consists of an incomplete statement followed by four choices. Select the choice that best completes the statement. Go back to the passage for rereading to whatever extent is necessary to help you choose your answer.

1. At the opening of the poem, the boy is
    a. in bed at night awake.
    b. on a ship.
    c. dreaming.
    d. eating dinner.

2. The boy has received a whipping because he
    a. wore his uncle's hat.
    b. tore his uncle's hat.
    c. put red stripes on his uncle's hat.
    d. laughed at his uncle's hat.

3. The boy's reaction to the earlier events of the day is
    a. resentment at the harsh treatment he had received.
    b. amusement in recalling his own mischief.
    c. great weeping over his pain.
    d. a determination to run away.

4. The boy sees the moon
    a. as he crosses the fields.
    b. in his imagination.
    c. shining into his room through a window.
    d. after he falls asleep.

5. In his dream, the boy is first
    a. in a cave.
    b. dancing on the floor.
    c. swimming for his life in tropical waters.
    d. on a beach, probably in the Southern Hemisphere.

6. The Cross and the Centaur are the names of
    a. constellations.
    b. pirates.
    c. animals.
    d. stars.

7. The word "Within" (line 15) refers to
    a. the beach.
    b. the stars.
    c. the Centaur.
    d. the cave.

8. The black chest contained
    a. gold.
    b. webbed purples.
    c. gunpowder.
    d. skulls and bones.

9. The cave is occupied by
    a. no one.
    b. ghosts doing a dance.
    c. moons chanting.
    d. pirates playing dice.

10. As the poem ends, the boy
    a. is waking.
    b. is dreaming.
    c. has been unable to fall asleep.
    d. is reading.

Literary and Language Skills

THE LANGUAGE OF POETRY—SOUND

> Twinkle, twinkle little star
> How I wonder what you are,
> Up above the world so high,
> Like a diamond in the sky.

Millions of children have known and enjoyed nursery rhymes like this one. Why? Say it aloud yourself and you will know that one important reason is that children enjoy the *sound* of these words.

- They enjoy the regular *rhythms* created by the arrangement of the words in lines. In this verse, the words are arranged so that there are seven syllables in each line. The syllables have a rhythmic beat.

- They enjoy the sound of the *rhymes*. Each pair of two lines rhymes, ending with the same sound. The first two lines end in the sound *ahr* and the second two in the sound *ah-ee*. We can describe the rhyme scheme by using the letters of the alphabet. For this verse, the rhyme scheme is

  a
  a
  b
  b

- We repeat the letter when the sound is repeated. We change the letter when the sound changes.

In poems, certain words or phrases may have a special sound effect of their own. In this verse, the word "twinkle" is an example. Its sound is pleasant and seems to go with the meaning. The sound of the words "pure and pale" (line 6) in *Portrait of a Boy* have a similar appeal.

Exercise A

How many syllables are there in *most* of the lines of *Portrait of a Boy?*

Exercise B

Use the letters of the alphabet to show the rhyme scheme of *Portrait of a Boy*. (Hint: you will need to use the letters *a* through *l*.) You will find that at two points in the poem the rhyme scheme changes. Why do you think the poet made these changes?

Exercise C

Read the poem aloud yourself and listen for words and phrases whose sound have a special quality for you. Give three examples of words or phrases whose sound adds appeal or force to the poem.

THE LANGUAGE OF POETRY—IMAGES

You have learned that a poet is a writer who is also something of a musician in the way he uses words. The poet is also something of a painter, who, in part, expresses himself through verbal images.

Exercise D

1. What are three vivid pictures that the boy sees either in his mind or in the room about him before he falls asleep?
2. What are three vivid pictures that the boy sees in his dream after he falls asleep?

Exercise E

Color and light are important tools of the painter of pictures. List at least seven colors and references to kinds of light that are used in the poem.

Exercise F

The star in the sky is like a diamond.

This statement is a rewording of the nursery rhyme. It contains an imaginative comparison. The star is compared to a diamond. The word *like* is used to express the imaginative comparison. The statement is therefore a *simile*, about which you have already learned (page 88).

The star in the sky is a diamond.

In this statement the same imaginative comparison is being made. It doesn't really mean that the star is a diamond. It means that the star is similar to a diamond in the way it shines. It is an imaginative comparison from which the comparing words *like* or *as* are omitted. It is called a *metaphor*. A metaphor is often defined as an implied (suggested) imaginative comparison.

The images or pictures of poetry are often in the form of similes and metaphors. Each of the following is a simile. Change it to a metaphor. What two things are compared imaginatively in both simile and metaphor forms?

1. The sea was like glass.

2. His mind was like a machine, with gears and pistons pounding away.

3. Time is like an accordion in the way it sometimes stretches out and sometimes folds up.

4. His face was as wrinkled as a prune.

5. My love is like a red, red rose.

Exercise G

Here are six excerpts from *Portrait of a Boy*. Which two of these are simply literal statements? Which two are similes? Which

206

two are metaphors? What two things are compared in the similes and metaphors?

1. "After the whipping, he crawled into bed" (line 1)

2. "A black frayed rag of tattered cloud" (line 5)

3. "Blurts of crimson light
   Splashed the white grains like blood." (lines 9–10)

4. "great casks like wattled aldermen" (line 15)

5. "A black chest bore the skull and bones in white" (line 19)

6. "Their eyes were moons." (line 23)

Vocabulary in Context

A. Carefully examine each word in its context; then decide which definition is most appropriate.

1. **frayed** (line 5)
   - *a.* white
   - *b.* ragged
   - *c.* enormous
   - *d.* fearful

2. **radiance** (line 7)
   - *a.* wealth
   - *b.* power
   - *c.* sound
   - *d.* brightness

3. **affronting** (line 13)
   - *a.* running rapidly at
   - *b.* talking to
   - *c.* rising from the earth
   - *d.* facing defiantly

4. **gemmed** (line 21)
   - *a.* adorned with jewels

b. poor and ugly
c. cautiously hopeful
d. sitting

5. **outrageous** (line 22)
    a. brave
    b. friendly
    c. shocking
    d. unfamiliar

B. Match meaning and sentence context by writing the word which most suitably fills the blank in each sentence. (Note that two words, 6 and 7, from the previous lesson are included for review.)

1. **frayed**   6. **improvise**
2. **radiance**   7. **punitive**
3. **affronting**
4. **gemmed**
5. **outrageous**

a. Many people feel that oil spills in the oceans are an ——?—— threat to the environment.

b. The dancing flames in the fireplace lit the room with their ——?——.

c. The old man's clothes were so worn and ——?—— they hardly protected him from the cold.

d. With no fear whatsoever, David stood ——?—— the giant Goliath and ready to do him battle.

e. Should severe ——?—— actions be taken against criminals, or should the emphasis be on helping them to reform?

f. The crown was ——?—— with diamonds, rubies, and sapphires.

g. The singer suddenly forgot the words of the song, but he was able to ——?—— new ones so cleverly that no one knew the difference.

READING 15

Reflections on a Gift of Watermelon Pickle
Received from a Friend Called Felicity

During that summer
When unicorns were still possible;
When the purpose of knees
Was to be skinned;
When shiny horse chestnuts   5
   (Hollowed out
   Fitted with straws
   Crammed with tobacco
   Stolen from butts
   In family ashtrays)   10
Were puffed in green lizard silence
While straddling thick branches
Far above and away
From the softening effects
Of civilization;   15

During that summer—
Which may never have been at all;
But which has become more real
Than the one that was—
Watermelons ruled.   20

Reprinted from NEW MEXICO QUARTERLY, Spring 1961 Issue, Volume XXXI:1, page 45, copyrighted by the University of New Mexico Press 1961, with permission of the author, John Tobias.

Thick pink imperial slices
Melting frigidly on sun-parched tongues
Dribbling from chins;
Leaving the best part,
25   The black bullet seeds,
To be spit out in rapid fire
Against the wall
Against the wind
Against each other;

30   And when the ammunition was spent,
There was always another bite:
It was a summer of limitless bites,
Of hungers quickly felt
And quickly forgotten
35   With the next careless gorging.

The bites are fewer now.
Each one is savored lingeringly,
Swallowed reluctantly.

But in a jar put up by Felicity,
40   The summer which maybe never was
Has been captured and preserved.
And when we unscrew the lid
And slice off a piece
And let it linger on our tongue:
45   Unicorns become possible again.

Reading Comprehension

The exercises that follow are based on the passage you have just
read. Each exercise consists of an incomplete statement followed

by four choices. Select the choice that best completes the statement. Go back to the passage for rereading to whatever extent is necessary to help you choose your answer.

1. "... unicorns were still possible" (line 2) because it was the time of
   a. young childhood.
   b. summer.
   c. the middle ages.
   d. sleep and dreams.

2. The horse chestnuts were
   a. eaten as a summer delicacy.
   b. gotten by climbing trees.
   c. made into the bowl of a smoking pipe.
   d. thrown around in play.

3. The silence is described as "green lizard silence" (line 11) because
   a. the children were sitting still in tree branches.
   b. the green lizards sat silently all about the children.
   c. summer is green and peaceful.
   d. the children were puffing silently.

4. "During that summer—
   Which may never have been at all;
   But which has become more real
   Than the one that was—"

   The common expression that comes closest to paralleling the meaning suggested by the above lines is
   a. hope springs eternal.
   b. tried and true.
   c. the good old days.
   d. live for today.

5. The greatest pleasure of the summer was
   a. smoking.

b. swimming.

   c. pickles.

   d. watermelon.

6. The best part of the watermelons was

   a. spitting the seeds.

   b. the appearance of the pink slices.

   c. the coldness on "sun-parched" tongues.

   d. the juice "dribbling from chins."

7. "The bites are fewer now." (line 36) The "now" is

   a. fall.

   b. winter.

   c. adulthood.

   d. reality.

8. The last stanza probably really refers to

   a. remembrance.

   b. a girl.

   c. a jar of preserved watermelon.

   d. sadness.

Literary and Language Skills

THE LANGUAGE OF POETRY—THE POET'S VISION

If you were to take a drop of water from a pond and look at it with your eye, you would see nothing but an uninteresting bit of wetness. If you looked at the drop under a microscope, you would see that in the tiny drop of water is a complex world of living things. You would have an entirely new vision of that drop of water and of the ordinarily unseen world about you in general.

The instruments of science can give you a new and special vision and understanding of the world about you. The poet, in a different way, offers new visions of reality. His instrument is words which he puts together in an original and creative way, so that the reader can see beneath the surface of things and beyond the ordinary reach of understanding.

Here is an example. In Shakespeare's famous play, *Romeo and Juliet*, there are two noble families, the Montagues and the Capulets, between whom there is a blood feud. Juliet, the young heroine, meets and falls deeply in love with Romeo. Shortly after, Juliet, who is a Capulet, is shocked to learn that Romeo is a Montague. In thinking about the fact that the young man she loves so dearly bears the name of a hated enemy of her family, Juliet says

> "What's in a name? That which we call a rose
> By any other name would smell as sweet."

In these few words, Shakespeare opens up a whole new vision. Juliet is saying, of course, that it is Romeo, the individual, that counts, not Romeo as a member of a family group. But, a much broader vision is also expressed by her words. She is saying that while there is a great difference between the reality of a thing and the word we use for it, sometimes the word becomes more important for us than the reality, and so we can confuse and mislead ourselves. This great vision of Shakespeare has been simply expressed by the artistry in which he puts a few simple words together. They are words that make us stop and think, ask questions, and come up with answers that, like the microscope, give us a new vision.

Exercise A

Reflections on a Gift of Watermelon Pickle Received from a Friend Called Felicity begins with the lines

> "During that summer
> When unicorns were still possible"

Unicorns are legendary horse-like animals, generally of very gentle nature, with one horn protruding from the forehead.

1. Do these lines mean that unicorns, now extinct, once really existed, or do they refer to medieval times, when people believed in unicorns? Explain your answer.

2. If neither is true, what *is* meant by "unicorns were still possible."

3. Why does the poet say "unicorns were still possible" instead of "unicorns were still thought to be possible"? What is the poet's vision concerning the outlook of childhood versus the outlook of adulthood?

Exercise B

> "When the purpose of knees
> Was to be skinned"

1. In what way do these words turn a usual attitude inside out?
2. What understanding does the poet express by his way of putting things in these lines?

Exercise C

> "During that summer—
> Which may never have been at all;
> But which has become more real
> Than the one that was—"

1. What contradiction appears in these lines?
2. What underlying meaning explains the contradiction?

THE LANGUAGE OF POETRY—METAPHOR

This poem contains several interesting metaphors. Looking at them closely will help you to greater understanding and appreciation of metaphorical language.

Exercise D

"Watermelons ruled." (line 20)

1. Explain the metaphor in this line.
2. Which one word in line 21 continues the metaphor? Explain.

Exercise E

"But in a jar put up by Felicity,
The summer which maybe never was
Has been captured and preserved.
And when we unscrew the lid
And slice off a piece
And let it linger on our tongue:
Unicorns become possible again."

This is a complicated metaphor. In the metaphor what does each of the following stand for?

1. Felicity
2. the jar
3. captured and preserved
4. unscrewing the lid and slicing off a piece
5. letting it linger on our tongue
6. unicorns become possible again

Vocabulary in Context

A. Carefully examine each word in its context; then decide which definition is most appropriate.

1. **imperial** (line 21)
   a. intoxicating
   b. tall
   c. kingly
   d. warm

2. **frigidly** (line 22)
   a. freezingly
   b. freely
   c. frighteningly
   d. slowly

3. **gorging** (line 35)
   a. expecting the worst
   b. acting carelessly
   c. growing tired
   d. eating to the full

4. **savored** (line 37)
   a. saved
   b. enjoyed
   c. wasted
   d. swallowed

5. **reluctantly** (line 38)
   a. greedily
   b. unwillingly
   c. hastily
   d. truly

B. Match meaning and sentence context by writing the word which most suitably fills the blank in each sentence. (Note that two words, 6 and 7, from the previous lesson are included for review.)

1. **imperial**	6. **frayed**
2. **frigidly**	7. **radiance**
3. **gorging**	
4. **savored**	
5. **reluctantly**	

a. He had the habit of ___?___ himself at every meal as though he would never have the opportunity to eat again.

216

b. The terrible storm had left the sails badly ___ ? ___ and torn so that the vessel was almost crippled.

c. The actor had the ___ ? ___ bearing of one accustomed to having his every wish instantly obeyed.

d. The dog followed his master into the house ___ ? ___, for romping outdoors was a pleasure he always hated to end.

e. The winter storm swept ___ ? ___ into the village driving everyone to the warm shelter.

f. The divers were equipped with torches of a powerful ___ ? ___ so that they could now explore even the darkest undersea caverns.

g. Hungry as we were, we ___ ? ___ the simple meal as though it were the finest of feasts.

GROWING
(Unit Three)

Vocabulary in Context

Exercise A—VERB FORMS

All verbs have forms called *participles*. Regular verbs form the present participle by adding *ing* and the past participle by adding *ed*. Some examples are

> want, wanting, wanted
> fear, fearing, feared
> laugh, laughing, laughed

If the regular verb ends in *e*, the present participle is formed by dropping the *e* and then adding *ing*, and the past participle is formed by adding *d*. Some examples are

> face, facing, faced
> blame, blaming, blamed
> cure, curing, cured

Participles may be used either by themselves as adjectives or with various helping verbs to form a number of different tenses. Some examples are

>The *crying* baby kept us awake.
>The baby *was crying* all night.

>The *rested* hikers resumed their climb.
>The hikers *had rested* and resumed their climb.

Select the participle from the word list that best completes the meaning of each of the following sentences.

1. The boys are __?__ themselves as though they would never have an opportunity to eat another meal.

2. He had __?__ his mother's excellent cooking through all his growing years, so his future wife was to face a hard challenge.

3. The sweater was in excellent condition generally but the elbows had __?__ because of excessive contact with table tops.

4. It was a crime whose solution would have __?__ even Sherlock Holmes.

5. The fans were __?__ their own team because it appeared that the players weren't even trying.

Exercise B—VERB FORMS

Use a participial form of the verb on the list that best completes the meaning of each sentence below. To make the correct choice, you may have to use a list word that is already a participle or you may have to change a list verb to the proper participial form. After you have made your choice, state whether the participle in each case is used as an adjective or as part of a verb.

1. The richly __?__ crown shone with dazzling diamonds, rubies, and sapphires.

2. The exhausted troops had been ___?___ the superior enemy forces for weeks without relief.

3. They were known as ___?___ musicians who created remarkably original variations on melodies.

4. For years Mr. Smith had ___?___ about his ever receding hairline, and finally he decided to stop worrying and do something.

5. Ever since his master came home, the dog has ___?___ and romped to express his delight.

Exercise C—CONTEXTS

In the columns to the left are references to the passages you have read. What list word in the columns to the right is most closely associated with each reference? Do Group 1 and Group 2 separately.

Group 1

1. Remarks made by his schoolmates to Bottles Barton.
2. Lisbeth's reaction to going away.
3. What Richard Wright's father imposed on him.
4. The kind of Christmas Moss Hart expected when his aunt left.
5. How Nicholas's "aunt" felt when she looked for him in the gooseberry garden.

grim
taunting
fret
baffled
restrictions

Group 2

1. A quality Herbie saw in his "angels."
2. The action taken for the striping of the hat.
3. The temperature of the water just before Omar saw the shark.
4. What Cress did with the story of King Midas.

improvise
punitive
radiance
depravity
frigid

5. What Leonardo's way with horses meant to some.

Exercise D—ANALOGIES

Decide what the relationship is between the pair of words given first. From the four choices, select the pair of words that comes closest to expressing the same relationship as the given pair.

1. depravity : mischief
   a. smashed : scratched
   b. bad : good
   c. youth : adult
   d. crime : criminal

2. gemmed : thriftiness
   a. money : investment
   b. needle : thread
   c. clothes : man
   d. armed : pacifism

3. imperial : crown
   a. ruler : ruled
   b. shack : hut
   c. military : helmet
   d. prince : dagger

4. punitive : rewarding
   a. jail : hospital
   b. policeman : judge
   c. justice : psychology
   d. fine : prize

5. utterances : mouth
   a. ear : hear
   b. orchestra : music
   c. smoke : chimney
   d. speak : words

Literary and Language Skills

Exercise E—THE EXACT WORD

You have learned that some words, like *said*, are more general (or *abstract*), while others are more exact (or *concrete*). This exercise will help you to understand better the relationship between abstract and concrete words. Rearrange each of the four groups of words below in order, beginning with the most abstract and ending with the most concrete. Here is a sample exercise.

WORDS: color   scarlet   appearance   red
ANSWER: appearance   color   red   scarlet

1. evergreen   tree   plant   spruce
2. profession   occupation   cardiology   medicine
3. biology   science   study   botany
4. cantaloupe   melon   food   fruit
5. robbery   crime   felony   act
6. beef   meat   porterhouse   steak
7. aria   music   song   sound
8. granite   matter   rock   solid
9. business   economics   retail   sales
10. awareness   sensation   pain   toothache

Exercise F—MORE OF THE EXACT WORD

From the columns to the right choose the more concrete word that goes with the more abstract word to the left.

ABSTRACT WORDS   CONCRETE WORDS

1. singer   6. bird   thumb   conjunction
2. tool   7. emotion   knife   carpenter
3. word   8. vehicle   sparrow   anger
4. furniture   9. gait   wagon   tenor
5. craftsman   10. finger   chair   gallop

Exercise G—AND MORE OF THE EXACT WORD

There are quite a few frequently used words like *said* (studied on page 177) for which more exact synonyms can be substituted. Among such words are *walk*, *eat*, and *look*. In the groups below substitute the best-fitting exact word from the column to the right which replaces the general word in each sentence.

Group 1—walk

1. The weary fighter just managed to *walk* back to his corner.
2. The hikers *walked* through the forest enjoying the scenery.
3. The tired troops *walked* silently along, mile after mile.
4. We saw the angry colonel *walk* out of the room.
5. Before we had a chance to move, the mouse *walked* under the stove.

stride
stagger
rambled
scampered
trudged

Use in sentences of your own: *scurry, toddle, plod.*

Group 2—eat

1. It was such a lovely spring day that the family decided to *eat* out of doors with a blanket spread on the grass.
2. We could tell the child wasn't feeling well by the listless way she *ate* her food.
3. The pelican *ate* the fish down in one great swallow.
4. The dog *ate* at the bone methodically.
5. The stout man decided to *eat* carefully, counting every calorie.

diet
nibbled
gobbled
gnawed
picnic

Use in sentences of your own: *banquet, breakfast, dine.*

Group 3—look

1. The timid squirrel *looked* at us from behind a tree.
2. The sentry *looked* intently into the dark trying to make out the shadows.
3. The defendant *looked* angrily at his accuser.
4. George merely *looked* quickly through a few pages and told himself he had studied.
5. He *looked* and *looked* at us as though he couldn't believe his eyes.

glared
stared
peered
glanced
peeked

Use in sentences of your own: *gaze, squint, inspect.*

Exercise H—THE LANGUAGE OF POETRY

Poets put words together in an original and creative way. The person who knows how to read the language of poetry is given a new vision—a new way of looking at things, new thoughts, new ways of feeling. The language of poetry makes the reader stop and ask, "Now just what do these words mean?" In answering his own question the reader is led to new visions, just as one can be led to new visions by looking into a microscope.

This exercise will help you to learn to read the language of poetry more rewardingly. You are given ten short quotations from poems. After each quotation, step one is done for you. The right questions are asked (though you may want to add a few of your own). First, read each quotation aloud several times. Then, tackle the questions. As you think about your answers and try to express them as fully as you can, you will find that your "vision" is improving remarkably.

1. Home is the place where, when you have to go there,
   They have to take you in.

   —Robert Frost

   Why might one *have* to go home? Who are *they* and why do they *have* to take you in?

2. Much Madness is divinest Sense

—Emily Dickinson

How can this statement itself make sense? What special meaning can "Madness" have so that it does make sense? What are some examples? Why are Madness and Sense capitalized?

3. Glory be to God for dappled things—
For skies as coupled-colored as a brindled cow

—Gerard Manley Hopkins

What meaning do "dappled," "couple-colored," and "brindled" all have? Why does the poet praise God for dappled things? Do you feel the same way? Why?

4. All the world's a stage,
And all the men and women merely players
They have their exits and their entrances;
And one man in his time plays many parts

—William Shakespeare

In what way are all people players (actors) on a stage? What "exits" and "entrances" do they have? What are some of the many parts (roles) that one person plays?

5. Progress is
The law of life: man is not Man as yet.

—Robert Browning

What meanings does the poet have in mind for the words "man" and "Man"? What does he think is the case now and what does he look forward to? Do you agree?

6. The force that through the green fuse drives the flower
Drives my green age.

—Dylan Thomas

What time of a person's life is described as the "green age"? What is the "green fuse" through which a flower is driven? What is the "force" that drives both the flower and the green age?

7. The world is too much with us; late and soon
   Getting and spending, we lay waste our powers
                                —William Wordsworth

   What meaning does "getting" have as it is paired with "spending" in these lines? If "world" is explained by the phrase "getting and spending," what does "world" mean here? What powers are being wasted? How can they be better used?

8. But words are things, and a small drop of ink
   Falling like dew upon a thought, produces
   That which makes thousands, perhaps millions, think.
                                        —Lord Byron

   When Byron says that words are "things," does he mean they are weak and vague or does he mean they are strong and solid? How do you know? What common act is Byron referring to when he says ". . . ink falling . . . upon a thought"?

9. in the street of the sky night walks scattering poems
                                        —e. e. cummings

   What are some "poems" that night scatters (name as many as you can)? Why is night described as walking rather than standing still?

10. If you ask your mother for one fried egg for breakfast and she gives you two fried eggs and you eat both of them, who is better in arithmetic, you or your mother?
                                        —Carl Sandburg

   Well, who *is* better in arithmetic? What humorous comment is Sandburg making about arithmetic?

Themes for Growing

FOR THINKING

Most young people restlessly await adulthood. They look forward to being free and independent, to being "their own boss," to having the whole world of experience open to them. But John Tobias, in "Reflections on a Gift of Watermelon Pickle Received from a Friend Called Felicity," takes an opposite point of view. He feels that childhood is the time of freedom and of having open access to the widest world of experience. What do you think? What is the correct point of view?

FOR DISCUSSION

In most of the passages in this unit, the influence of their elders on young people is stressed. Think about these elders: the mother and father of the boy in *When You Run Away;* the mother of Richard Wright; the "aunt" of Nicholas; the boy and his parents (though they are not directly mentioned) in "Portrait of a Boy." What is your judgment of these elders? In which ways is each wise and good? In which ways is each foolish and bad? Which did you like best? Which least? Why?

FOR WRITING

A famous psychologist has said that being a good parent is by far the most difficult and important job there is. Write a composition explaining why being a good parent is a difficult and important job. Try to include your own thoughts on two or three *musts* for being a good parent.

UNIT FOUR

(Reading 16-20)

READING 16

The country school-house was three miles from my uncle's
farm. It stood in a clearing in the woods and would hold
about twenty-five boys and girls. We attended the school
with more or less regularity once or twice a week in summer,
5 walking to it in the cool of the morning by the forest paths,
and back in the gloaming at the end of the day. All the
pupils brought their dinners in baskets—corn dodger, butter-
milk, and other good things—and sat in the shade of the trees
at noon and ate them. It is the part of my education which .
10 look back upon with the most satisfaction. My first visit to
the school was when I was seven. A strapping girl of fifteen
in the customary sunbonnet and calico dress, asked me if .
"used tobacco," meaning did I chew it. I said no. It rousec
her scorn. She reported me to all the crowd and said:
15   "Here is a boy seven years old who can't chew tobacco."
By the looks and comments which this produced I realizec
that I was a degraded object, and was cruelly ashamed o
myself. I determined to reform. But I only made mysel
sick; I was not able to learn to chew tobacco. I learned to
20 smoke fairly well but that did not conciliate anybody and
remained a poor thing, and characterless. I longed to be
respected but I never was able to rise. Children have bu
little charity for each other's defects.
As I have said, I spent some part of every year at the farm
25 until I was twelve or thirteen years old. The life which I led

Excerpt from pages 109–114 in MARK TWAIN'S AUTOBIOGRAPHY, Vol
ume I by Mark Twain. Copyright 1924 by Clara Gabrilowitsch; renewe
1952 by Clara Clemens Samossoud. Reprinted by permission of Harper &
Row, Publishers, Inc.

here with my cousins was full of charm and so is the memory of it yet. I can call back the solemn twilight and mystery of the deep woods, the earthy smells, the faint odors of the wild flowers, the sheen of rainwashed foliage, the rattling clatter of drops when the wind shook the trees, the far-off hammering of woodpeckers and the muffled drumming of wood-pheasants in the remoteness of the forest, the snapshot glimpses of disturbed wild creatures scurrying through the grass—I can call it all back and make it as real as it ever was, and as blessed. I can call back the prairie, and its loneliness and peace, and a vast hawk hanging motionless in the sky with his wings spread wide and the blue of the vault showing through the fringe of their end-feathers. I can see the woods in their autumn dress, the oaks purple, the hickories washed with gold, the maples and the sumachs luminous with crimson fires, and I can hear the rustle made by the fallen leaves as we plowed through them. I can see the blue clusters of wild grapes hanging amongst the foliage of the saplings, and I remember the taste of them and the smell. I know how the wild blackberries looked and how they tasted; and the same with the pawpaws, the hazelnuts, and the persimmons; and I can feel the thumping rain upon my head of hickory-nuts and walnuts when we were out in the frosty dawn to scramble for them with the pigs, and the gusts of wind loosed them and sent them down. I know the stain of blackberries and how pretty it is, and I know the stain of walnut hulls and how little it minds soap and water, also what grudged experience I had of either of them. I know the taste of maple sap and when to gather it, and how to arrange the troughs and the delivery tubes, and how to boil down the juice, and how to cook the sugar after it is made; also how much better hooked sugar tastes than any that is honestly come by, let bigots say what they will.

I know how a prize watermelon looks when it is sunning its fat rotundity among pumpkin vines and "simblins"; I know how to tell when it is ripe without "plugging" it. I

231

know how inviting it looks when it is cooling itself in a tub o
water under the bed, waiting; I know how it looks when i
lies on the table in the sheltered great floor-space betwee
65 house and kitchen, and the children gathered for the sacrific
and their mouths watering. I know the crackling sound i
makes when the carving knife enters its end and I can see th
split fly along in front of the blade as the knife cleaves it
way to the other end; I can see its halves fall apart and displa
70 the rich red meat and the black seeds, and the heart standin
up, a luxury fit for the elect. I know how a boy looks be
hind a yard-long slice of that melon and I know how he feels
for I have been there. I know the taste of the watermelo
which has been honestly come by and I know the taste of th
75 watermelon which has been acquired by art. Both taste goo
but the experienced know which tastes best.

I know the look of green apples and peaches and pears o
the trees, and I know how entertaining they are when the
are inside of a person. I know how ripe ones look when the
80 are piled in pyramids under the trees, and how pretty the
are and how vivid their colors. I know how a frozen appl
looks in a barrel down celler in the wintertime, and how har
it is to bite and how the frost makes the teeth ache, and ye
how good it is notwithstanding. I know the disposition o
85 elderly people to select the specked apples for the childre
and I once knew ways to beat the game. I know the look o
an apple that is roasting and sizzling on a hearth on a winter'
evening, and I know the comfort that comes of eating it ho
along with some sugar and a drench of cream. I know th
90 delicate art and mystery of so cracking hickory-nuts and wa
nuts on a flatiron with a hammer that the kernels will be d
livered whole, and I know how the nuts, taken in conjunctio
with winter apples, cider, and doughnuts, make old people
old tales and old jokes sound fresh and crisp and enchantin
95 and juggle an evening away before you know what went wit
the time. I know the look of Uncle Dan'l's kitchen as it wa
on privileged nights when I was a child, and I can see th

232

white and black children grouped on the hearth, with fire-
light playing on their faces and the shadows flickering upon
the walls clear back toward the cavernous gloom of the rear, 100
and I can hear Uncle Dan'l telling the immortal tales which
Uncle Remus Harris was to gather into his book and charm
the world with, by and by. And I can feel again the creepy
joy which quivered through me when the time for the ghost
story was reached—and the sense of regret too which came 105
over me, for it was always the last story of the evening and
there was nothing between it and the unwelcome bed.

I can remember the bare wooden stairway in my uncle's
house and the turn to the left above the landing, and the
rafters and the slanting roof over my bed, and the squares of 110
moonlight on the floor and the white cold world of snow outside, seen through the curtainless window. I can remember
the howling of the wind and the quaking of the house on
stormy nights, and how snug and cozy one felt under the
blankets, listening; and how the powdery snow used to sift in 115
around the sashes and lie in little ridges on the floor, and
make the place look chilly in the morning and curb the wild
desire to get up—in case there was any. I can remember how
very dark that room was in the dark of the moon, and how
packed it was with ghostly stillness when one woke up by 120
accident away in the night, and forgotten sins came flocking
out of the secret chambers of the memory and wanted a hearing; and how ill-chosen the time seemed for this kind of
business and how dismal was the hoo-hooing of the owl and
the wailing of the wolf, sent mourning by on the night wind. 125

I remember the raging of the rain on that roof, summer
nights, and how pleasant it was to lie and listen to it and enjoy the white splendor of the lightning and the majestic
booming and crashing of the thunder. It was a very satis-
factory room, and there was a lightning rod which was reach- 130
able from the window, an adorable and skittish thing to climb
up and down, summer nights when there were duties on hand
of a sort to make privacy desirable.

I remember the 'coon and 'possum hunts, nights, with the
135 Negroes, and the long marches through the black gloom of
the woods and the excitement which fired everybody when
the distant bay of an experienced dog announced that the
game was treed; then the wild scramblings and stumblings
through briers and bushes and over roots to get to the spot;
140 then the lighting of a fire and the felling of the tree, the joy-
ful frenzy of the dogs and the Negroes, and the weird picture
it all made in the red glare—I remember it all well, and the delight that everyone got out of it, except the 'coon.

Reading Comprehension

The exercises that follow are based on the passage you have just
read. Each exercise consists of an incomplete statement followed
by four choices. Select the choice that best completes the statement. Go back to the passage for rereading to whatever extent is
necessary to help you choose your answer.

1. The first paragraph suggests that
    a. the children attended school faithfully every day even dur-
    ing the summer.
    b. the children were discouraged by the long walk to and
    from school.
    c. the noontime meal was called dinner.
    d. the writer found great satisfaction in his classes.

2. "Here is a boy seven years old who can't chew tobacco."
(line 15) The writer's main purpose in quoting this remark is
probably to
    a. show that in those days children reached maturity at an
    earlier age.
    b. have the reader enjoy the humor in the local attitudes of
    the time.
    c. explain why he began to smoke.
    d. support his views against the evils of tobacco.

3. In recalling the natural beauties of his years at the farm, the writer mentions each of the following birds EXCEPT
   a. woodpecker.
   b. wood-pheasant.
   c. hawk.
   d. eagle.

4. The colors of the autumn dress of the woods are
   a. purple, gold, crimson.
   b. black, brown, blue.
   c. orange, yellow, red.
   d. purple, black, orange.

5. ". . . I know the stain of walnut hulls and how little it minds soap and water, also what grudged experience it had of either of them." (lines 51–53) The author uses the words "grudged experience" as a humorous way of referring to
   a. the stubbornness of the stain of walnut hulls.
   b. the scarcity of soap and water.
   c. the infrequency of voluntary washing among the children.
   d. the inexperience of the farm children with city ways.

6. The word "hook" (line 56) is probably used to mean
   a. crystallize.
   b. steal.
   c. pour.
   d. sell.

7. The paragraph beginning "I know how a prize watermelon looks . . ." (line 59) is mainly a tribute to
   a. watermelons.
   b. pumpkins.
   c. "simblins".
   d. all three of the above.

8. The word "art" (line 75) means
   a. cutting.
   b. stealing.

    c. plugging.

    d. tasting.

9. "I know the disposition of elderly people to select the specked apples for the children . . ." (lines 84–85) Here the writer is

    a. poking fun at the older people.

    b. praising the older people.

    c. objectively describing the older people.

    d. speaking of himself, now, as an older person.

10. The highlight of a night in the kitchen on the farm was

    a. baked apples.

    b. cider.

    c. a tale of Uncle Remus.

    d. a ghost story.

11. The bed was "unwelcome" because

    a. the wind howled and the house quaked on stormy nights.

    b. the good time of the evening was over.

    c. guilty feelings came at night.

    d. snow blew into the bedroom.

Literary and Language Skills

APPRECIATING HUMOR

As this passage from his autobiography well illustrates, Mark Twain is a great American humorist. The last sentence of the passage is a typical example of Twain's humor.

> "I remember it all well, and the delight that everyone got out of it, except the 'coon."

You will recall (from page 32) that *incongruity* (a clashing, a non-fitting) is an important element of humor. The humor in this sentence is based on an incongruity of points of view. Twain describes at great length the pleasure the children had in the hunt. In this sentence, he sums up the delight of the humans. Then he suddenly and humorously switches to a different and incongruous point of view—that of the hunted animal, the raccoon.

Much of the humor of Mark Twain is based on incongruity of points of view. Sometimes the clash is between points of view of two characters he is writing about. Sometimes the clash is between the point of view of a character in the story and a point of view that is commonly held or believed in.

Mark Twain's humor sometimes has its serious side in that it makes the reader think critically about what is really right or wrong, good or bad.

Exercise A

Here are five examples of humor from the story. Explain the incongruity or clash of two points of view on which the humor in each case is based.

1. "Here is a boy seven years old who can't chew tobacco." (line 15)

2. "I know . . . also how much better hooked sugar tastes than any that is honestly come by, let bigots say what they will." (lines 56–58) (Comment on the use of the word *bigots*.)

3. "I know the taste of the watermelon which has been honestly come by and I know the taste of the watermelon which has been acquired by art. Both taste good but the experienced know which tastes best." (lines 73–76) (Comment on the use of the word *art*.)

4. ". . . how the powdery snow used to . . . curb the wild desire to get up—in case there was any." (lines 115–118)

5. ". . . there was a lightning rod which was reachable from the window, an adorable and skittish thing to climb up and down, summer nights when there were duties on hand of a sort to make privacy desirable." (lines 130–133) (Comment on the use of the words *adorable* and *duties*.)

Exercise B

Look through some of the other works of Mark Twain (*The Adventures of Tom Sawyer; The Adventures of Huckleberry Finn*) for at least one example of humor based on incongruity of point of view. Be ready to explain to the class the humor of incongruity in your example.

Exercise C

The humor of cartoons is often based on incongruity of points of view. On that basis, explain each of the following cartoons.

"Brother, what I mean, we sure got the dirty end of the stick when natural habitats were handed out."

Drawing by John Corcoran; © 1973
The New Yorker Magazine, Inc.

"Oh, to dream once more the untroubled dreams of childhood!"

Drawing by Whitney Darrow, Jr.; © 1973
The New Yorker Magazine, Inc.

239

"O.K., I'll try anything once."

SENSE IMPRESSIONS

The life of a child is largely a life of sense impressions of the world around him. Mark Twain had a vivid memory of his childhood life on a farm in the country and his *Autobiography* is rich in sense impressions of that life.

Exercise D

From the passage choose a favorite example of your own of a sense impression mainly involving

1. sight
2. sound
3. smell
4. taste
5. touch (feeling)

Vocabulary in Context

A. Carefully examine each word in its context; then decide which definition is most appropriate.

1. **degraded** (line 17)
   a. unusual
   b. interesting
   c. respected
   d. dishonored

2. **conciliate** (line 20)
   a. reform
   b. gain the favor of
   c. gain the attention of
   d. gain the disapproval of

3. **luminous** (line 40)
   a. shining
   b. delicious
   c. destroyed
   d. burned out

4. **bigots** (line 57)
   a. prejudiced people
   b. honest people
   c. newspapers
   d. gossips

5. **disposition** (line 84)
   a. tendency
   b. kindness
   c. selfishness
   d. fault

B. Match meaning and sentence context by writing the word which most suitably fills the blank in each sentence. (Note that two words, 6 and 7, from the previous lesson are included for review.)

1. **degraded**	6. **savored**
2. **conciliate**	7. **reluctantly**
3. **luminous**	
4. **bigots**	
5. **disposition**	

a. The child attempted to ___?___ his angry mother by smiling as sweetly and charmingly as he could.

b. We knew our neighbor had a ___?___ to talk entirely too much, so we tried to avoid her, particularly on that busy day.

c. When the corruption of his administration came to light, the once respected official became an object of contempt, the more ___?___ because of his violation of public trust.

d. Having survived the fearful ordeal of climbing Everest, the party now stood and ___?___ the pleasure of the magnificent sight that was spread before them.

e. Every so often there is an epidemic of claims of ___?___ objects in the air, asserted to be visitors from outer space.

f. Once the actions of ___?___ were subject to no legal controls, but now there is legislation that acts to limit prejudice-influenced actions, as in employment.

g. The campers began to pack ___?___, hating the thought of leaving the beauties of nature for the dirt and noise of the city.

READING 17

Sighing, she began to move. She took the packages out of the car, went outside (the heat was not brilliant), put them down, and, with deft angry motions in case Timmy was secretly watching, pulled down the garage door and locked
5   it. "There!" But when she turned, her confidence was distracted. She stared at the house. Shrubbery hiding the concrete slab—basements were not necessary this far south—rosebushes bobbing roses, vulnerable, insanely gaudy, the great picture window that made her think, always, someone
10 was slyly watching her, even the faint professional sweep of grass out to the road—all these in their elaborate planned splendor shouted mockery at her, mockery at themselves, as if they were safe from destruction! Annette fought off the inertia again, it passed close by her, a whiff of something
15 like death; the same darkness that had bothered her in the hospital, delivered of her child. She left the packages against the garage (though the ice cream in its special package might be melting) and, awkward in her high heels, hurried out the drive. She shielded her eyes: nothing in sight down the road.
20 It was a red clay road, a country road that would never be paved, and she and her husband had at first taken perverse pride in it. But it turned so, she had never noticed that before, and great bankings of foliage hid it, disguised its twistings, so that she could see not more than a quarter mile

away. Never before had the land seemed so flat.   25

She hurried. At the gate the sun caught up with her, without ceremony. She struggled to swing the gate around (a few
rusty, loosened prongs had caught in the grass), she felt
perspiration breaking out on her body, itching and prickling
her, under her arms, on her back. The white dress must have   30
hung damp and wrinkled about her legs. Panting with the
exertion, she managed to get the gate loose and drag it
around; it tilted down at a jocose angle, scraping the gravel;
then she saw that there was no lock, she would need a padlock, there was one in the garage somewhere, and in the same 35
instant, marveling at her stamina, she turned back.

Hurrying up the drive, she thought again of the little
Mexican boy. She saw his luxurious face, that strange
unhealthy grin inside his embracing arms—it sped toward her.
Cheeks drawn in as if by age, eyes protruding with—it must   40
have been hunger, dirty hands like claws reaching out, grab-
bing, demanding what? What would they demand of her?
If they were to come and shout for her out in the road, if
she were to offer them—something—milk, maybe, the choco-
late cookies Timmy loved so, maybe even money? Would   45
they go away then, would they thank her and run back to
their people? Would they continue their trip north, headed
for Oregon and Washington? What would happen? Violence
worried the look of the house, dizzied Annette! there were
the yellow roses she tended so fondly, rich and sprawling   50
against the orange brick. In the sunlight their petals, locked
intricately inside one another, were vivid, glaringly detailed,
as if their secret life were swelling up in rage at her for having
so endangered their beauty.

There the packages lay against the garage, and seeing them,   55
Annette forgot about the padlock. She stooped and picked
them up. When she turned again she saw Timmy standing
just inside the screen door. "Timmy, open the—" she said,
vexed, but he had already disappeared. Inside the kitchen
she slammed the bags down, fought back the impulse to cry,   60

stamped one heel on the linoleum so hard that her foot buzzed with pain. "Timmy," she said, her eyes shut tight, "come out in this kitchen."

He appeared, carrying a comic book. That was for the look of it, of course; he had not been reading. His face was wary. Fair, like his mother, blond-toned, smart for his age, he had still about his quiet plump face something that belonged to field animals, wood animals, shrewd, secret creatures that had little to say for themselves. He read the newspaper as his father did, cultivated the same thoughtful expression; encouraged, he talked critically about his schoolteacher with a precocity that delighted his father, frightened Annette (to her, even now, teachers were somehow *different* from other people); he had known the days of the week, months of the year, continents of the world, planets of the solar system, major star groupings of the universe, at an astonishing age—as a child he approached professional perfection; but Annette, staring at him, was not sure now that she could trust him. What if, when the shouting began outside, when "Missus! Missus!" demanded her, Timmy ran out to them, joined them, stared back at her in the midst of their white eyes and dirty arms? They stared at each other as if this question had been voiced.

"You almost killed him," Timmy said.

His voice was soft. Its innocence showed that he knew how daring he was; his eyes as well, neatly fringed by pale lashes, trembled slightly in their gaze. "What?" said Annette. "What?"

The electric clock, built into the big white range, whirred in the silence. Timmy swallowed, rustled his comic book, pretended to wipe his nose—a throwback to a habit long outgrown—hoping to mislead her, and looked importantly at the clock. "*He* hit the car. Two times," he said.

This was spoken differently. The ugly spell was over. "Yes, he certainly did," Annette said. She was suddenly busy. "He certainly did." After a moment Timmy put down the comic book to help her. They worked easily, in silence. Eyes avoided each other. But Annette felt feverishly excited; something had been decided, strengthened. Timmy, stooping to put vegetables in the bottom of the refrigerator, felt her staring at him and peered up, his little eyebrows raised in a classic look of wonder. "You going to call Daddy?" he said.

Annette had been thinking of this, but when Timmy suggested it, it was exposed for what it was—a child's idea. "That won't be necessary," she said. She folded bags noisily and righteously.

When they finished, mother and son wandered without enthusiasm into the dining room, into the living room, as if they did not really want to leave the kitchen. Annette's eyes flinched at what she saw: crystal, polished wood, white walls, aqua lampshades, white curtains, sand-toned rug, detailed, newly cleaned, spreading regally across the room— surely no one ever walked on that rug! That was what *they* would say if they saw it. And the glassware off in the corner, spearlike, transparent green, a great window behind it linking it with the green grass outside, denying a barrier, inviting in sunlight, wind, anyone's eyes approaching—Annette went to the window and pulled the draw drapes shut; that was better; she breathed gently, coaxed by the beauty of those drapes into a smile: they were white, perfectly hung, sculpted superbly in swirling curves. And fireproof, if it came to that. . . . Annette turned. Timmy stood before the big red swivel chair as if he were going to sit in it—he did not—and looked at her with such a queer, pinched expression, in spite of his round face, that Annette felt a sudden rush of shame. She was too easily satisfied, too easily deluded. In all directions her possessions stretched out about her, defining her, identifying her, and they were vulnerable and waiting, the dirt road led right to them; and she could be lured into smiling! That must be why Timmy looked at her so strangely. "I have something to do," she murmured, and

went back to the dining room. The window there was open; she pulled it down and locked it. She went to the wall
135 control and turned on the air conditioning. "Run, honey, and close the windows," she said. "In your room."

She went into the bedroom, closed the windows there and locked them. Outside there was nothing—smooth lawn, lawn furniture (fire-engine red) grouped casually together, as if
140 the chairs made of tubing and spirals were having a conversation. Annette went into the bathroom, locked that window, avoided her gaze in the mirror, went, at last, into the "sewing room" that faced the road, and stood for a while staring out the window. She had never liked the color of that clay,
145 really—it stretched up from Louisiana to Kentucky, sometimes an astonishing blood red, pulsating with heat. Now it ran watery in the sunlight at the bend. Nothing there. Annette waited craftily. But still nothing. She felt that, as soon as she turned away, the first black spots would appear—
150 coarse black hair—and the first splashes of color; but she could not wait. There was too much yet to do.

She found Timmy in the living room again, still not sitting in the chair. "I'll be right back, darling," she said. "Stay here. It's too hot outside for you. Put on the television—
155 Mommy will be right back."

She got the clipping shears out of the closet and went outside, still teetering in her high heels. There was no time to waste, no time. The yellow rosebush was farthest away, but most important. She clipped roses off, a generous
160 amount of stem. Though hurried—every few seconds she had to stare down the road—she took time to clip off some leaves as well. Then she went to the red bushes, which now exclaimed at her ignorance: she could see they were more beautiful, really, than the yellow roses. Red more beautiful
165 than yellow; yellow looked common, not stunning enough against the house. It took her perhaps ten minutes, and even then she had to tear her eyes away from the lesser flowers, over there in the circular bed, she did not have time for

248

them—unaccountably she was angry at them, as if they had betrayed her already, grateful to the migrant workers who 170 were coming to tear them to pieces! Their small stupid faces nodded in the hot wind.

Timmy awaited her in the kitchen. He looked surprised at all the roses. "The big vase," she commanded. In a flurry of activity, so pleased by what she was doing that she did not 175 notice the dozens of bleeding scratches on her hands, she lay the roses on the cupboard, clipped at leaves, arranged them, took down a slender copper vase and filled it with water, forced some roses in, abandoned it when Timmy came in with the milk-glass vase (wedding present from a remote aunt 180 of hers). The smell of roses filled the kitchen, sweetly drugged Annette's anxiety. Beauty, beauty—it was necessary to have beauty, to possess it, to keep it around oneself!—how well she understood that now.

Finished abruptly, she left the refuse on the cupboard and 185 brought the vases into the living room. She stood back from them, peered critically ... saw a stain on the wood of the table already, she must have spilled some water. And the roses were not arranged well, too heavy, too many flowers, an insane jumble of flowered faces, some facing one another 190 nose to nose, some staring down toward the water in the vase in an indecent way, some at the ceiling, some at Annette herself. But there was no time to worry over them, already new chores called to her, demanded her services. What should she do next?—The answer hit her like a blow; how 195 could she be so stupid? The doors were not even locked! Staggered by this, she ran to the front door, with trembling fingers locked it. How could she have overlooked this? Was something in her, some secret corner, conspiring with the Mexicans down the road? She ran stumbling to the back 200 door—even that had been left open, it could have been seen from the road! A few flies buzzed idly, she had no time for them. When she appeared, panting, in the doorway, she saw

Timmy by the big white vase trying to straighten the flowers.
205 ... "Timmy," she said sharply, "you'll cut yourself. Go
away, go into the other room, watch television."

He turned at once but did not look at her. She watched
him and felt, then, that it was a mistake to speak that way to
him—in fact, a deliberate error, like forgetting about the
210 doors; might not her child be separated from her if they
came, trapped in the other room? "No, no, Timmy," she
said, reaching out for him—he looked around, frightened—
"no, come here. Come here." He came slowly. His eyes
showed trust; his mouth, pursed and tightened, showed
215 wariness, fear of that trust. Annette saw all this—had she not
felt the same way about him, wishing him dead as soon as he
was born?—and flicked it aside, bent to embrace him. "Darling, I'll take care of you. Here. Sit here. I'll bring you
something to eat."

220 He allowed her to help him sit at the dining room table.
He was strangely quiet, his head bowed. There was a surface
mystery about that quietness! Annette thought, in the
kitchen, I'll get through that, I'll prove myself to him. At
first cunningly, then anxiously, she looked through the
225 refrigerator, touching things, rearranging things, even upsetting things—a jar of pickles—and then came back carrying
some strawberry tarts, made just the day before, and the
basket of new strawberries, and some apples. "Here, darling,"
she said. But Timmy hesitated; while Annette's own mouth
230 watered painfully, he could only blink in surprise. Impatiently she said, "Here, eat it, eat them. You love them.
Here." "No napkins," Timmy said fearfully. "Never mind
napkins, or a tablecloth, or plates," Annette said angrily—
how slow her child seemed to her, like one of those empty-
235 faced children she often saw along the road, country children,
staring at her red car. "Here. Eat it. Eat it." When she
turned to go back to the kitchen, she saw him lifting one of
the tarts slowly to his mouth.

She came back almost immediately—bringing the package

of ice cream, two spoons, a basket of raspberries, a plate of   240
sliced chicken wrapped loosely in wax paper—She was overcome by hunger. She pulled a chair beside Timmy, who had
not yet eaten—he stared gravely at her—and began to eat one
of the tarts. It convulsed her mouth, so delicious was it, so
sweet yet at the same time sour, tantalizing; she felt some-   245
thing like love for it, jealousy for it, and was already reaching
for another when she caught sight of Timmy's stare. "Won't
Daddy be home? Won't we have dinner?" he pleaded.

But he paused. His lips parted moistly and he stared at his
mother, who smiled back at him, reassuring him, comforting   250
him, pushing one of the tarts toward him with her polished
nails. Then something clicked in his eyes. His lips damp with
new saliva, he smiled at her, relieved, pleased. As if a secret
ripened to bursting between them, swollen with passion, they
smiled at each other. Timmy said, before biting into the tart,   255
"*He* can't hit the car again, it's all locked up." Annette said,
gesturing at him with sticky fingers, "Here, darling. Eat this.
Eat. *Eat*."

Reading Comprehension

The exercises that follow are based on the passage you have
just read. Each exercise consists of an incomplete statement followed by four choices. Select the choice that best completes the
statement. Go back to the passage for rereading to whatever
extent is necessary to help you choose your answer.

1. In the first paragraph, the emotions of the woman whose
   actions are being described seem to be dominated by
   a. pride in her possessions.
   b. nervous anxiety.
   c. confidence.
   d. anger.

2. Timmy carries a comic book when he is called because he
   a. has just been reading it.
   b. wants to show his defiance of the order not to read comic books.
   c. uses it as an excuse for ignoring Annette's call.
   d. wants to pretend that he is not aware that anything is wrong.

3. The situation narrated in this story has apparently been triggered by
   a. Annette's near running over of a Mexican boy while driving back from shopping.
   b. a family argument over whether to take a trip north to Oregon.
   c. the fact that Annette never wanted to have a child.
   d. Annette's resentment of the closeness between Timmy and his father.

4. "You almost killed him." (line 84) This statement is described as "daring" because it
   a. is a hostile and untrue accusation.
   b. brings into the open Annette's inner fear and guilt.
   c. shows that Timmy has a sick mind.
   d. is true.

5. The probable reason that Annette tells Timmy that she will not call her husband is that
   a. it is a childish idea.
   b. Timmy suggested it.
   c. she would have to give voice to the unreasoned fears she wishes to hide.
   d. she wants to call without Timmy's having to worry about it.

6. The italicized *they* (line 114) probably refers to
   a. the Mexicans.
   b. Annette's parents.
   c. Annette's husband.
   d. the world in general.

7. The best explanation of Annette's going out to clip the roses is that it is
   a. a semi-hysterical reaction to inner fear.
   b. a demonstration of love of beauty.
   c. merely the following of a daily routine.
   d. an unpleasant necessity because of the unusual heat.

8. The protection against fear that Annette finally provides for herself and appears to convey to Timmy is rooted in
   a. love.
   b. courage.
   c. possessions.
   d. humor.

9. Basically this is a story of
   a. rich versus poor.
   b. ethnic conflict.
   c. an emotionally unstable mother.
   d. family strength.

Literary and Language Skills

EXPLORING CHARACTER

Have you ever been alone in the house in the evening reading a mystery or a horror story? Have you then had fear quietly steal up on you so that you noticed noises and sounds and thought you saw movements that caused your fear to grow? How far did your fear go in taking over? Did you feel it was foolish? Or did you panic, quake with terror, phone for help? How did you feel about your experience in the light of the next day? Did you laugh at yourself or did the fear stay with you? Was there, to begin with, any real reason for your fear or was it purely manufactured by your own inner emotions?

Fear and the many other emotions—anger, loneliness, sadness, confidence—normally play a role in everyone's life. But, for each person the meaning of the emotion is different and can be understood only by exploring the individual's character. Some fiction writers explore character to shed light on the meaning of a person's emotions. In *First Views of the Enemy*, Joyce Carol Oates skillfully explores the character of Annette to shed light on the character's fear.

Exercise A

Annette is stricken with fear after she has almost run over a Mexican boy, one of a group of migrant workers, near her home. Why is she fearful? Is it because there is a real danger of attack as a result of the incident? Is it because Annette appears always to have been an inwardly anxious person, one who tends to look for and find reason to be afraid? Look at the following ten excerpts from the story. Which five seem best to suggest that Annette has *always* been an anxious and fearful person?

1. "... the great picture window that made her think, always, someone was slyly watching her ..." (lines 8–10)

2. "Annette fought off the inertia again, it passed close by her, a whiff of something like death; the same darkness that had bothered her in the hospital, delivered of her child." (lines 13–16)

3. "In the sunlight their petals, locked intricately inside one another, were vivid, glaringly detailed, as if their secret life were swelling up in rage at her for having so endangered their beauty." (lines 51–54)

4. "... encouraged, he talked critically about his schoolteacher with a precocity that delighted his father, frightened Annette (to her, even now, teachers were somehow *different* from other people) ..." (lines 71–74)

5. "What if, when the shouting began outside, when 'Missus! Missus!' demanded her, Timmy ran out to them, joined them, stared back at her . . . ?" (lines 79–81)

6. "And the glassware off in the corner, spearlike, transparent green, a great window behind it linking it with the green grass outside, denying a barrier, inviting in sunlight, wind, anyone's eyes approaching . . ." (lines 115–118)

7. "She had never liked the color of that clay, really—it stretched up from Louisiana to Kentucky, sometimes an astonishing blood red, pulsating with heat." (lines 144–146)

8. "She felt that, as soon as she turned away, the first black spots would appear—coarse black hair—and the first splashes of color . . ." (lines 148–150)

9. "She clipped roses off, a generous amount of stem." (lines 159–160)

10. "His eyes showed trust; his mouth, pursed and tightened, showed wariness, fear of that trust. Annette saw all this—had she not felt the same way about him, wishing him dead as soon as he was born? . . ." (lines 213–217)

Exercise B

Now look at the five excerpts which you did NOT choose in answer to Exercise A. These excerpts also help you to explore Annette's character, telling you something important about her fear. Which of the three statements below best summarizes what these five excerpts tell you about Annette's fear?

1. Annette encourages her imagination to feed her fear.

2. Annette's fear is based on racial and class prejudice.

3. Annette realizes that her lovely home is dangerously lonely and vulnerable.

Vocabulary in Context

A. Carefully examine each word in its context; then decide which definition is most appropriate.

1. **deft** (line 3)
   - *a.* delicate
   - *b.* hesitant
   - *c.* polite
   - *d.* skillful

2. **vulnerable** (line 8)
   - *a.* open to attack
   - *b.* straight
   - *c.* showy
   - *d.* full of thorns

3. **deluded** (line 127)
   - *a.* happy
   - *b.* hurt
   - *c.* determined
   - *d.* deceived

4. **wariness** (line 215)
   - *a.* caution
   - *b.* playfulness
   - *c.* anger
   - *d.* spitefulness

5. **tantalizing** (line 245)
   - *a.* aching
   - *b.* teasing
   - *c.* pleasing
   - *d.* sweet

B. Match meaning and sentence context by writing the word which most suitably fills the blank in each sentence. (Note that two words, 6 and 7, from the previous lesson are included for review.)

1. deft
2. vulnerable
3. deluded
4. wariness
5. tantalizing

6. conciliate
7. luminous

a. The young warrior's efforts to ___?___ the angry chief failed, and he was exiled from the tribe forever.

b. The country was protected by impassable mountains to the north, west, and south, but was ___?___ from the east.

c. The surface of the ocean gave off the ___?___ glow of millions of tiny phosphorescent animals.

d. The girl's determination to lose weight was mightily shaken when the ___?___ strawberry shortcake was put on the table.

e. Even as a child, the artist was remarkably ___?___ with a pencil and produced excellent sketches.

f. The mountain climber ascended the peak with great ___?___, for one slip of the foot meant a plunge to death.

g. The careful shopper does not allow himself to be ___?___ by misleading ads.

READING 18

The block: *my* block. It was on the Chester Street side of our house, between the grocery and the back wall of the old drugstore, that I was hammered into the shape of the streets. Everything beginning at Blake Avenue would always wear for
5   me some delightful strangeness and mildness, simply because it was not of my block, *the* block, where the clang of your head sounded against the pavement when you fell in a fist fight, and the rows of storelights on each side were pitiless, watching you. Anything away from the block was good: even
10   a school you never went to, two blocks away: there were vegetable gardens in the park across the street. Returning from "New York," I would take the longest routes home from the subway, get off a station ahead of our own, only for the unexpectedness of walking through Betsy Head Park
15   and hearing the gravel crunch under my feet as I went beyond the vegetable gardens, smelling the sweaty sweet dampness from the pool in summer and the dust on the leaves as I passed under the ailanthus trees. On the block itself everything rose up only to test me.
20   We worked every inch of it, from the cellars and the backyards to the sickening space between the roofs. Any wall, any stoop, any curving metal edge on a billboard sign made a place against which to knock a ball; any bottom rung of a fire escape ladder a goal in basketball; any sewer cover a base;
25   any crack in the pavement a "net" for the tense sharp tennis that we played by beating a soft ball back and forth with our hands between the squares. Betsy Head Park two blocks

---

away would always feel slightly foreign, for it belonged to the Amboys and the Bristols and the Hopkinsons as much as it did to us. *Our* life every day was fought out on the pavement and in the gutter, up against the walls of the houses and the glass fronts of the drugstore and the grocery, in and out of the fresh steaming piles of horse manure, the wheels of passing carts and automobiles, along the iron spikes of the stairway to the cellar, the jagged edge of the open garbage cans, the crumbly steps of the old farmhouses still left on one side of the street.

As I go back to the block now, and for a moment fold my body up again in its narrow arena—there, just there, between the black of the asphalt and the old women in their kerchiefs and flowered housedresses sitting on the tawny kitchen chairs —the back wall of the drugstore still rises up to test me. Every day we smashed a small black viciously hard regulation handball against it with fanatical cuts and drives and slams, beating and slashing at it almost in hatred for the blind strength of the wall itself. I was never good enough at handball, was always practicing some trick shot that might earn me esteem, and when I was weary of trying, would often bat a ball down Chester Street just to get myself to Blake Avenue. I have this memory of playing one-o'-cat by myself in the sleepy twilight, at a moment when everyone else had left the block. The sparrows floated down from the telephone wires to peck at every fresh pile of horse manure, and there was a smell of brine from the delicatessen store, of egg crates and of milk scum left in the great metal cans outside the grocery, of the thick white paste oozing out from behind the fresh Hecker's Flour ad on the metal signboard. I would throw the ball in the air, hit it with my bat, then with perfect satisfaction drop the bat to the ground and run to the next sewer cover. Over and over I did this, from sewer cover to sewer cover, until I had worked my way to Blake Avenue and could see the park.

With each clean triumphant ring of my bat against the

gutter leading me on, I did the whole length of our block up
and down, and never knew how happy I was just watching
the asphalt rise and fall, the curve of the steps up to an old
farmhouse. The farmhouses themselves were streaked red on
one side, brown on the other, but the steps themselves were
always gray. There was a tremor of pleasure at one place; I
held my breath in nausea at another. As I ran after my ball
with the bat heavy in my hand, the odd successiveness of
things in myself almost choked me, the world was so full as
I ran—past the cobblestoned yards into the old farmhouses,
where stray chickens still waddled along the stones; past the
little candy store where we went only if the big one on our
side of the block was out of Eskimo Pies; past the three
neighboring tenements where the last of the old women sat
on their kitchen chairs yawning before they went up to make
supper. Then came Mrs. Rosenwasser's house, the place on
the block I first identified with what was farthest from home,
and strangest, because it was a "private" house; then the
fences around the monument works, where black cranes rose
up above the yard and you could see the smooth gray slabs
that would be cut and carved into tombstones, some of them
already engraved with the names and dates and family virtues
of the dead.

Beyond Blake Avenue was the pool parlor outside which
we waited all through the tense September afternoons of the
World Series to hear the latest scores called off the ticker-
tape—and where as we waited, banging a ball against the
bottom of the wall and drinking water out of empty coke
bottles, I breathed the chalk off the cues and listened to the
clocks ringing in the fire station across the street. There was
an old warehouse next to the pool parlor; the oil on the
barrels and the iron staves had the same rusty smell. A block
away was the park, thick with the dusty gravel I liked to hear
my shoes crunch in as I ran round and round the track; then
a great open pavilion, the inside mysteriously dark, chill even
in summer; there I would wait in the sweaty coolness before

pushing on to the wading ring where they put up a shower on the hottest days.

Beyond the park the "fields" began, all those still unused lots where we could play hard ball in perfect peace—first shooing away the goats and then tearing up goldenrod before laying our bases. The smell and touch of those "fields," with their wild compost under the billboards of weeds, goldenrod, bricks, goat droppings, rusty cans, empty beer bottles, fresh new lumber, and damp cement, lives in my mind as Brownsville's great open door, the wastes that took us through to the west. I used to go round them in summer with my cousins selling near-beer to the carpenters, but always in a daze, would stare so long at the fibrous stalks of the goldenrod as I felt their harshness in my hand that I would forget to make a sale, and usually go off sick on the beer I drank up myself. Beyond! Beyond! Only to see something new, to get away from each day's narrow battleground between the grocery and the back wall of the drugstore! Even the other end of our block, when you got to Mrs. Rosenwasser's house and the monument works, was dear to me for the contrast. On summer nights, when we played Indian trail, running away from each other on prearranged signals, the greatest moment came when I could plunge into the darkness down the block for myself and hide behind the slabs in the monument works. I remember the air whistling around me as I ran, the panicky thud of my bones in my sneakers, and then the slabs rising in the light from the street lamps as I sped past the little candy store and crept under the fence.

In the darkness you could never see where the crane began. We liked to trap the enemy between the slabs and sometimes jumped them from great mounds of rock just in from the quarry. A boy once fell to his death that way, and they put a watchman there to keep us out. This made the slabs all the more impressive to me, and I always aimed first for that yard whenever we played follow-the-leader. Day after day the monument works became oppressively more mysterious and

remote, though it was only just down the block; I stood in
front of it every afternoon on my way back from school,
filling it with my fears. It was not death I felt there—the
slabs were usually faceless. It was the darkness itself, and the
140 wind howling around me whenever I stood poised on the edge
of a high slab waiting to jump. Then I would take in, along
with the fear, some amazement of joy that I had found my
way out that far.

Beyond! Beyond! *Beyond* was "the city," connected
145 only by interminable subway lines and some old Brooklyn-
Manhattan trolley car rattling across Manhattan Bridge. At
night, as the trolley ground its way home in the rain through
miles of unknown streets from some meeting in the Jewish
Daily *Forward* building on the East Side to which my father
150 had taken me, I saw the flickering light bulbs in the car, the
hard yellow benches on which we sat half asleep, the motor-
man's figure bulging the green curtain he had drawn against
the lights in the car, as a rickety cart stumbling through
infinite space—the driver taking us where? *Beyond* was the
155 wheeze of an accordion on the Staten Island ferry boat—the
music rocking in such unison with the vibration of the engines as the old man walked in and out of the cars on the
lower deck squeezing the tunes out of the pleats that never
after would I be able to take a ferry from South Ferry, from
160 Christopher Street, from 23rd, from Dyckman, from 125th,
without expecting that same man to come round with his
silver-backed accordian and his hat in his hand as he jangled a
few coins in a metal plate. *Beyond* was the long shivering
blast of the ferry starting out from the Battery in sight of the
165 big Colgate ad across the river in Jersey; the depth of peace as
the sun warmed the panels of the doors sliding out to the ob-
servation deck; the old Italian shoeshine men walking round
and round with their boxes between all those suddenly relaxed New Yorkers comfortably staring at each other in the
170 high wind on the top deck; a garbage scow burning in the upper bay just under Liberty's right arm; the minarets on Ellis

Island; the old prison walls under the trees of Governor's Island; then, floating back in the cold dusk toward the diamond-lighted wall of Manhattan skyscrapers, the way we huddled in the great wooden varnish-smelling cabin inside as if we were all getting under the same quilt on a cold night.

Beyond was the canvas awnings over an El station in summer. Inside, the florid red windows had curlicues running up and down their borders. I had never seen anything like them in all the gritty I.R.T. stations below. Those windows were richer than all my present. The long march of snails up and down and around the borders of those windows, the cursive scrolls in the middle patch forever turning back on themselves, promised to lead me straight into the old New York of gaslight and police stations I always looked for in the lower city. And of a winter afternoon—the time for which I most lovingly remember the El, for the color of the winter dusk as it fell through those painted windows, and the beauty of the snow on the black cars and iron rails and tar roofs we saw somewhere off Brooklyn Bridge—when the country stove next to the change booth blazed and blazed as some crusty old woman with a pince-nez gave out change, and the heavy turnstiles crashed with a roar inside the wooden shed—then, among the darkly huddled crowds waiting to go out to the train, looking out on Brooklyn Bridge all dark sweeping cable lines under drifts of snow, I pretended those were gaslights I saw in the streets below, that all old New Yorkers were my fathers, and that the train we waited for could finally take me back—back and back to that old New York of wood and brownstones and iron, where Theodore Roosevelt as Police Commissioner had walked every night.

Beyond was anything old and American—the name *Fraunces Tavern* repeated to us on a school excursion; the eighteenth-century muskets and glazed oil paintings on the wall; the very streets, the deeper you got into Brooklyn, named after generals of the Revolutionary War—Putnam, Gates, Kosciusko, DeKalb, Lafayette, Pulaski. *Beyond* was the sound of *Des-*

brosses Street that steaming July morning we crossed back on a Jersey ferry, and the smell of the salt air in the rotting
210 planks floating on the green scummy waters of the Hudson. *Beyond* was the watery floor of the Aquarium that smelled of the eternally wet skins of the seals in the great tank; the curve of lower Broadway around Bowling Green Park when you went up to Wall Street; the yellow wicker seats facing
215 each other in the middle of the El car; the dome of the Manhattan Savings Bank over Chinatown at the entrance to Manhattan Bridge, and then in Brooklyn again, after we had traveled from light into dark, dark into light, along the shuddering shadowy criss-cross of the bridge's pillars, the miles
220 and miles of Gentile cemeteries where crosses toppled up and down endless slopes. *Beyond* was that autumn morning in New Haven when I walked up and down two *red* broken paving stones, smelled the leaves burning in the yard, and played with black battered poker chips near the country
225 stove in an aunt's kitchen; it was the speckles on the bananas hanging in the window of the grocery store another aunt owned in the Negro streets just behind Union Station in Washington; the outrageously warm taste of milk fresh from a cow that summer my mother cooked with a dozen others
230 in the same Catskill boarding house; it was the open trolley cars going to Coney Island, the conductor swinging from bar to bar as he came around the ledge collecting fares; it was the *Robert Fulton* going up the Hudson to Indian Point, the ventilators on the upper deck smelling of soup.
235   *Beyond*, even in Brownsville, was the summer sound of *flax* when my mother talked of *der heym*. It was the Negroes singing as they passed under our windows late at night on their way back to Livonia Avenue. It was the Children's Library on Stone Avenue, because they had an awning over
240 the front door; in the long peaceful reading room there were storybook tiles over the fireplace and covered deep wooden benches on each side of it where I read my way year after year from every story of King Alfred the Great to *Twenty*

Thousand Leagues Under the Sea. Beyond was the burly
Jewish truckers from the wholesale fruit markets on Osborne   245
Street sitting in their dark smoky "Odessa" and "Roumanian"
tearooms, where each table had its own teapot, and where
the men sat over mounds of saucers smoking Turkish cigarettes
and beating time to the balalaíka. *Beyond* was the way to
the other end of Sutter Avenue, past a store I often went into   250
to buy buttons and thread for my mother, and where the
light simmered on the thin upturned curves of the pearl buttons in the window. *Beyond* was the roar in the Pennsylvania
freight yards on the way to East New York; even the snow
houses we built in the backyard of a cousin's house on Herzl   255
Street waiting to ambush those thieves from Bristol Street.
It was the knife grinder's horse and wagon when he stopped
on our block, and an "American" voice called up to every
window, *Sharpen knives! Sharpen knives!*—that man had
obviously come from a long way off.   260

Reading Comprehension

The exercises that follow are based on the passage you have just
read. Each exercise consists of an incomplete statement or a
question followed by four choices. Select the choice that best
completes the statement or best answers the question. Go back to
the passage for rereading to whatever extent is necessary to help
you choose your answer.

1. In this autobiographical account of the author's early life, the
   word *beyond* is used again and again to express
   a. the boy's fear of the world outside his own block.
   b. the boy's interest in the life of older times.
   c. the boy's general yearning to expand his experience of the
      world.
   d. the boy's wish to overcome his poverty.

2. The neighborhood in which the boy lived was apparently
   a. at the edge of the city.

    b. in the heart of an inner-city slum.

    c. in the country.

    d. an upper-middle-class residential area.

3. "We worked every inch of it, from the cellars and the backyards to the sickening space between the roofs." (lines 20–21) In this sentence, the word "worked" is used to mean

    a. tested.

    b. explored thoroughly.

    c. performed odd jobs to earn a few cents.

    d. put to use for games.

4. As suggested in the second and third paragraphs the emphasis in the "life style" being described is on

    a. physical activity.

    b. the emotions.

    c. thoughts and ideas.

    d. religion.

5. Mrs. Rosenwasser's place is "strange" mainly because it is

    a. a small candy store.

    b. a private house.

    c. a farmhouse.

    d. far.

6. At the time of this account, which of the following was apparently not a part of the boy's life?

    a. automobiles.

    b. subways.

    c. Coca-Cola.

    d. radios.

7. Some of the ingredients of the "wild compost" under the billboards in the fields suggest that

    a. construction work is going on.

    b. the goatherds drink a lot of beer.

    c. the area is isolated from "civilization."

    d. the boy's imagination is a little wild.

8. The boy's feelings towards the monument works were the result of
   a. fear of the death symbolized by the gravestones.
   b. fear resulting from the death of another boy.
   c. fear of the watchman.
   d. nameless fears within himself.

9. Among the trips remembered is each of the following EXCEPT
   a. a trip to the East Side of Manhattan on a Brooklyn-Manhattan trolley car.
   b. a trip on the Staten Island ferry.
   c. a school excursion to *Fraunces Tavern*.
   d. a family visit to Roumania.

10. The red windows inside the El station fascinated the boy particularly because
    a. they were reminders of the old New York.
    b. they were so beautiful in winter.
    c. they were a rich present.
    d. they were alive with crawling snails.

11. A hero whom the boy loved to read about was
    a. King Alfred.
    b. Theodore Roosevelt.
    c. General Desbrosses.
    d. Robert Fulton.

Literary and Language Skills

SENSE IMPRESSIONS

In an earlier lesson (page 44) you learned something about how verbal imagery can be used to create beauty. Sense impressions expressed in verbal images can be used also to give the impact of reality. A young person, such as Alfred Kazin in the account you have just read, is particularly alert to the sights, sounds, and smells of the world around him. The boyhood world that Kazin recaptures in words is made especially real for the reader because it is full of the sense impressions—the sights, the sounds, the smells—that were a basic part of his experience.

Exercise A

Here is one example from the passage of a vivid *sight* impression.

"... the rows of storelights on each side were pitiless, watching you."

Find and list at least three other examples of vivid *sight* impressions.

Exercise B

Here is one example from the passage of a vivid *sound* impression.

"With each clean triumphant ring of my bat against the gutter ..."

Find and list at least three other examples of vivid *sound* impressions.

Exercise C

Here is one example from the passage of a vivid *smell* impression.

"... the smell of the salt air in the rotting planks ..."

Find and list at least three other examples of vivid *smell* impressions.

Vocabulary in Context

A. Carefully examine each word in its context; then decide which definition is most appropriate.

1. **fanatical** (line 44)
    a. skillful
    b. unusually strong
    c. enthusiastic to an extreme
    d. spoiled

2. **esteem** (line 48)
    a. shyness
    b. stubbornness
    c. ambition
    d. respect

3. **florid** (line 178)
    a. ugly
    b. expensive
    c. new
    d. flowery

4. **excursion** (line 203)
    a. lesson
    b. short trip
    c. vehicle
    d. detour

5. **burly** (line 244)
    a. inactive
    b. cheerful
    c. husky
    d. thoughtful

B. Match meaning and sentence context by writing the word which most suitably fills the blank in each sentence. (Note that two words, 6 and 7, from the previous lesson are included for review.)

1. fanatical   6. deft
2. esteem   7. wariness
3. florid
4. excursion
5. burly

a. The audience showed its ——?—— for the famous cellist by rising to applaud as he appeared on the stage.

b. The class enjoyed its ——?—— to the zoo.

c. The ——?—— hands of the pianist moved so quickly and skillfully over the keys that we could hardly follow them.

d. Cats move instinctively with great ——?——, ready to run and hide at the slightest suggestion of danger.

e. He was a writer of ——?——, emotional, colorful style.

f. The ——?—— woodsman was built as thick and strong as the great trees he cut down.

g. He was so ——?—— a tennis player that no one ever saw him without a racquet in his hand.

READING 19

Sometimes we act, go in and out, do this and that, and everything is easy, casual, and unforced; seemingly it could all be done differently. And sometimes, other times, nothing could be done differently, nothing is unforced and easy, and every breath we take is controlled by some outside power and heavy with fate. 5

What we call the good deeds of our lives, the ones we find easy to tell about, are almost all of that first, "easy" kind, and we easily forget them. Other acts, which we find hard to talk about, we never forget; they seem to be more ours than 10 the others, and they cast long shadows over all the days of our lives.

Our father's house stood tall and bright on a sunlit street. You entered it through a high gate and at once found yourself embraced by coolness, dusk, and stony moist air. A high 15 dark hall silently received you; the red sandstone squares of the flooring led at a slight incline to the stairs, which lay far at the rear, in semidarkness. Many thousands of times I entered through that high gate, and never did I pay attention to gate and hallway, stone flooring and stairs. For these were 20 always merely a passage into another world, "our" world. The hall smelled of stone; it was dusky and high. At the rear of it, the stairs led up out of the dim coolness into light and bright coziness. But the hall and the somber duskiness always came first. There was something of Father about it, some- 25 thing of dignity and power, something of punishment and

Excerpt from "A Child's Heart." Reprinted with the permission of Farrar, Straus & Giroux, Inc. from KLINGSOR'S LAST SUMMER by Hermann Hesse, translated by Richard and Clara Winston, translation © 1970 by Farrar, Straus & Giroux, Inc.

guilty conscience. A thousand times I passed through, laughing. But sometimes I stepped inside and at once felt crushed and reduced, afraid, and I hurried to the liberating stairs.

30   One day when I was eleven years old I came home from school. It was one of those days when fate lurks in the corners, when something can easily happen. On such days every failing and disturbance in our own souls seems to be reflected in our surroundings, distorting them. Uneasiness
35   and anxiety grip our hearts, and we seek and find their presumed cause outside us. We see the world as ill-arranged and are met by obstacles everywhere.

That was how it was on that day. From early morning on, I was dogged by a sense of guilty conscience. Who knows
40   what its source was—perhaps dreams of the night. For I had done nothing particularly bad. That morning my father's face had worn a suffering and reproachful expression. The breakfast milk had been lukewarm and insipid. Although I had not run into any trouble at school, everything had once
45   more felt dreary, lifeless, and discouraging; everything had combined to form that already familiar feeling of helplessness and despair which tells us that time is endless, that eternally and forever we shall be small and powerless and remain under the rule of this stupid, stinking school, for years and years,
50   and that this whole life is senseless and loathsome.

I had also been vexed by my best friend on that day. Lately I had struck up a friendship with Oskar Weber, the son of a locomotive engineer, without really knowing what drew me to him. He had recently boasted that his father earned
55   seven marks a day, and I had answered at random that my father earned fourteen. He had let that impress him without argument, and that had been the beginning of the thing. Before the week was out I formed a league with Weber. We set up a joint savings account to be used later to buy a pistol.
60   The pistol was displayed in a hardware shop's window, a massive weapon with two blued steel barrels. And Weber had calculated that we only had to save hard for a while and we

272

would be able to buy it. Money was easy to come by; he was often given ten pfennig for errands, or picked up a tip here and there, and sometimes you found money on the street, or things worth money, like horseshoes, pieces of lead, and other things that could be easily sold. Moreover, he promptly contributed a ten-pfennig piece for our savings, and that convinced me and made our whole plan seem both feasible and hopeful.

As I entered the hall of our house that noon and in the cool, cellarlike air felt dark admonishments of a thousand bothersome and hateful things and systems wafting into my face, my thoughts were preoccupied with Oskar Weber. I felt that I did not love him, although I rather liked his good-natured face, which reminded me of a washerwoman's. What attracted me to him was not himself but something else—I might say, his class. It was something that he shared with almost all boys of his type and origins: a kind of cheeky facility with life, a thick skin that protected him from danger and humiliation, a familiarity with the small, practical affairs of life, with money, stores and workshops, with goods and prices, with kitchens and laundries and things of that sort. Boys like Weber, who seemed impervious to the blows dealt out in school, who were kindred to and friendly with hired hands, draymen, and factory girls, stood differently and more securely in the world than I did. They knew how much their fathers earned in a day and undoubtedly knew many other things about which I was wholly inexperienced. They laughed at expressions and jokes that I did not understand. Altogether, they could laugh in a way that was closed to me, in a filthy and coarse but undeniably grownup and "manly" way. It did not help that I was smarter than they and knew more in school. It did not help that I was better dressed, combed, and washed. On the contrary, these very differences were to their credit. It seemed to me that boys like Weber could enter without trouble into the "world," as it appeared to me in a nimbus of strangeness and glamour, while the

"world" was so utterly closed to me that I would have to
conquer each of its gates by a wearisome, endless process of
growing older, sitting in school, examinations, and upbring-
ing. It was only natural that such boys also found horseshoes, money, and pieces of lead in the street, that they were
paid for errands, received all sorts of gifts in shops, and
thrived in every possible way.

I felt obscurely that my friendship with Weber and his
savings was nothing but a wild longing for that "world."
There was nothing lovable about Weber but his great secret,
by virtue of which he stood closer to adults than I did and
lived in a more naked, less veiled, more robust world than I
did with my dreams and wishes. And I sensed beforehand
that he would disappoint me, that I would not be able to
wrest from him his secret and the magic key to life.

He had just left me and I knew he was now on his way
home, thickset and smug, whistling and cheerful, troubled
by no longings, no forebodings. When he met the housemaids
and factory girls and saw them leading their mysterious,
perhaps wonderful, perhaps criminal life, it was no mystery
to him, no vast secret, no danger; it was nothing wild and
exciting, but as natural, familiar, and homelike as water is to
a duck. That was how it was. And I, for my part, would
always stand outside, alone and uncertain, full of intimations
but without certainty.

Altogether, on that day life once again tasted hopelessly
pallid. The day had some of the quality of a Monday,
although it was a Saturday. It smelled of Monday, three
times as long and three times as dreary as the other days. Life
was damned and disgusting, horrid and full of falsehood. The
grownups acted as if the world were perfect and as if they
themselves were demigods, we children nothing but scum.
These teachers . . . ! I felt striving and ambition within myself; I made sincere and passionate efforts to be good, whether
in learning the Greek irregular verbs or in keeping my clothes
clean. I struggled to achieve obedience to my parents or si-

lent stoicism before all pain and humiliation. Again and again 135
I rose up, ardent and devout, prepared to dedicate myself to
God and to tread the ideal, pure, noble path toward the
heights, to practice virtue, to suffer evil silently, to help
others. And alas, again and again it remained only a beginning, an attempt, a brief fluttering flight! Again and again, 140
after a few days, even after a few hours, something happened
that should not have been allowed, something wretched, de-
pressing, and shaming. Again and again, in the midst of the
noblest and staunchest decisions and vows, I fell abruptly,
inescapably, into sin and wickedness, into ordinary bad 145
habits. Why was it this way? Why could I recognize so
clearly the beauty and rightness of good intentions, could
feel them so deeply within my heart, when all of life (including the adults) reeked everlastingly of ordinariness and everything was so arranged that shabbiness and vulgarity tri- 150
umphed? How could it be that in the morning, on my knees
at my bedside, or at night before lighted candles, I could
pledge myself to goodness and the light, could appeal to God
and renounce all sin forever and ever—only to commit,
perhaps but a few hours later, the most wretched betrayals 155
of this same solemn oath and the sincerest resolution, if only
by chiming in with tempting laughter, or by lending an ear to
a stupid schoolboy joke? Why was that so? Was it different
for others? Had heroes, the Romans and Greeks, the knights,
the first Christians—had all these others been different from 160
myself, better, more perfect, without bad impulses, equipped
with some organ that I lacked, which prevented them from
forever falling back from heaven into everyday life, from the
sublime into inadequacy and wretchedness? Was original sin
unknown to heroes and saints? Was holiness and nobility 165
possible only for a few rare, elect souls? But why, if I were
not one of the elect, why was this impulse toward beauty
and nobility innate in me? Why did I have this wild, painful
longing for purity, goodness, and virtue? Was I being made
mock of? Could it possibly be, in God's world, that a person, 170

275

a boy, would simultaneously have all the sublime and all the evil impulses within himself and be forced to suffer and despair, to cut an unhappy and ridiculous figure, for the amusement of God as he looked on? Could that be so?
175 Rather, wasn't—yes, wasn't the whole world a joke of the devil that ought to be spewed out? If that were so, then was not God a monster, insane, a stupid, horrible prankster? . . . And even as I had this thought, with a faint savor of voluptuous delight in rebellion, my fearful heart punished me for
180 the blasphemy by pounding furiously!

How clearly I see, after thirty years, that stairwell with the tall opaque windows giving on the wall of the house next door and casting so little light, with the white-scoured pine steps and risers and the smooth wooden banister polished
185 from my innumerable sliding descents. Distant as my childhood is, and incomprehensible and fabulous though it seems to me on the whole, I still sharply remember all the suffering and doubts I felt at the time, in the midst of happiness. All those reelings existed in the child's heart, where they have
190 been ever since: doubt of my own worth, vacillation between self-esteem and discouragement, between idealistic contempt for the world and ordinary sensuality. And just as I did then, I later continued to regard these aspects of my nature sometimes as a miserable morbidity, sometimes as a distinction.
195 At times I believed that God wished to lead me on this painful path to a special isolation and deepening of my nature, at other times I took it all as nothing but the signs of shabby weakness of character, of a neurosis such as thousands of people bear wearisomely through their lives.
200 If I were to reduce all my feelings and their painful conflicts to a single name, I can think of no other word but: dread. It was dread, dread and uncertainty, that I felt in all those hours of shattered childhood felicity: dread of punishment, dread of my own conscience, dread of stirrings in my
205 soul which I considered forbidden and criminal.

At that hour I have been speaking of, this sense of dread

once again struck me as I drew nearer to the glass door at the top of the stairs, where the light grew brighter and brighter. The feeling began with a tightness in my stomach that rose to my throat and there became a choking or gagging sensation. Along with this at such moments, and now also, I felt a painful sense of embarrassment, a distrust of all observers, an urge to be alone and to hide.

With this repulsive feeling, truly the feeling of a criminal, I entered the hall and then the living room. I sensed that the devil was afoot today, that something was going to happen. I sensed it as the barometer senses a change in the pressure of the air, with utterly helpless passivity. Ah, here it was again, the inexpressible horror. The demon was skulking through the house. Original sin gnawed at my heart. Vast and invisible, a ghost stood behind every wall, a father and judge.

As yet I knew nothing. It was all mere foreboding, a gnawing, anticipatory uneasiness. In such situations it was often best to fall ill, to throw up and go to bed. Then the dangerous time sometimes passed harmlessly; Mother or Sister came in, I would be given tea and felt surrounded by loving solicitude. I could cry or sleep, and afterwards waken sound and cheerful in a wholly transformed, relaxed, and bright world.

My mother was not in the living room, and only the maid was in the kitchen. I decided to go up to Father's study at the top of a narrow flight of stairs. Although I was also afraid of him, it was sometimes good to turn to him whom I had to ask forgiveness for so many things. With Mother it was easier and simpler to find comfort; but Father's comfort was more valuable. It meant peace with the judging conscience, reconciliation and a new covenant with the good powers. After nasty scenes, interrogations, confessions, and punishments I had often emerged good and pure from Father's room, punished and reproved, to be sure, but full of fresh resolutions, strengthened by the pact with power against the evil enemy. I decided to visit Father and tell him that I was feeling ill.

245 And so I climbed the short flight of stairs that led to the study. These stairs, with their own special wallpaper smell and the dry sound of the light, hollow wooden treads, were infinitely more fraught with significance and fatefulness than even the entrance hall. Many important causes had led me
250 up these steps; a hundred times I had dragged dread and a tormented conscience up them, or defiance and wild anger, and quite often I had returned down them with absolution and new security. In the dwelling below, mother and child were at home; the atmosphere was mild there. Up here
255 power and spirit dwelt; up here were the courthouse and temple and the "realm of the father."

Rather timidly, as always, I pressed down the old-fashioned latch and opened the door halfway. The smell of the paternal study flowed toward me, the familiar smell of books
260 and ink, attenuated by blue air from half-opened windows, by white, clean curtains, a faint dash of cologne water, and an apple on the desk. But the room was empty.

With a sensation half of disappointment and half of relief, I entered. I checked my thumping footsteps, walked on
265 tiptoe, as we often had to up here when Father was napping or had a headache. And as soon as I became aware of how quietly I was moving, my heart began to pound and I again felt, intensified, the anxious pressure in my stomach and my throat. I moved on, skulking and frightened, took a step and
270 another step, and already I had ceased to be a harmless visitor and petitioner and had become an intruder. More than once I had secretly crept into Father's two rooms during his absence, had explored his secret realm, and twice I had filched something from it.

275 The memory of these thefts came at once and filled me, and I knew at once that disaster was upon me. Now something was going to happen, now I was doing something forbidden and evil. I had no thought of flight! Rather, I did

think of it, thought fervently and longingly of running away, down the stairs and into my own room or into the garden— but I knew that I was not going to, that I could not. How I wished that my father might stir in the adjacent room and come in and break the terrible spell that held me in its grip. If only he would come! If only he would come, scolding for all I cared, but come before it was too late!

I coughed to announce my presence, and when there was no answer I called softly: "Papa!" All remained still; the many books on the walls gave no answer. A pane of the casement window moved in the wind, casting a glint of sunlight on the floor. No one redeemed me, and inside myself I had no freedom to do anything but the demon's bidding. A feeling of criminality contracted my stomach and made my fingertips cold; my heart fluttered with dread. As yet I had no idea what I would do. I knew only that it would be something naughty.

Now I was at the desk. I picked up a book and read a title in English which I did not understand. I hated English—my father always spoke it with Mother when we children were not supposed to understand, and also when they were quarreling. In a bowl lay all sorts of small objects, toothpicks, pen points, tacks. I took two of the pen points and pocketed them. God knows why; I did not need them, had no lack of pens. I did it only to obey the compulsion that was almost choking me, the compulsion to do something bad, to harm myself, to load myself with guilt. I leafed through my father's papers, saw a letter he had begun, read the words, "We and the children are very well, thank God," and the Latin letters of his handwriting looked at me like so many eyes.

Then I stole softly into the bedroom. There stood Father's iron army bed, his brown house slippers under it, a handkerchief on the night table. I inhaled the paternal air in the cool, bright room, and the image of my father rose plainly before my eyes, while reverence and rebellion con-

315 tested in my overladen heart. For moments I hated him, remembering with spite and malice how he sometimes, on headache days, lay still and flat on his low cot, stretched out at great length, a wet towel on his forehead, sometimes sighing. Certainly I had an inkling that he, too, for all his power,
320 had no easy life; that he, of whom I stood in such awe, also experienced timidity and doubts of himself. In a moment my strange hatred evaporated and was followed by pity and sentiment. But in the meanwhile I had opened one of the drawers of his chest. There his linens lay in neat layers,
325 and a bottle of cologne water, which he was fond of. I wanted to sniff it, but the bottle was still unopened and firmly capped; I put it back. Next to it I found a small round box of lozenges which had a licorice taste. I popped a few of them into my mouth. A sense of disappointment overcame
330 me, and at the same time I was glad not to have found and taken anything more.

Already renouncing and preparing to leave, I playfully pulled at one more drawer, my heart somewhat lightened, so that I could promise myself to replace the two stolen pen
335 points. Perhaps a return to grace was possible. Perhaps all could be made good again and I would be saved. God's hand above me might be stronger than all temptation. . . .

Reading Comprehension

The exercises that follow are based on the passage you have just read. Each exercise consists of an incomplete statement followed by four choices. Select the choice that best completes the statement. Go back to the passage for rereading to whatever extent is necessary to help you choose your answer.

1. "What we call the good deeds of our lives, the ones we find easy to tell about, are almost all of that first 'easy' kind, and we easily forget them. Other acts, which we find hard to

talk about, we never forget; they seem to be more ours than the others, and they cast long shadows over all the days of our lives." (lines 7–12) The narrator is here suggesting that the deeds which have a more lasting and personal effect on our lives are those about which we feel
   a. certain
   b. guilty
   c. proud
   d. happy

2. The phrase in the third paragraph that would be likely to strike the average reader of today as strange, but which, at the same time, seems to be in keeping with the dominant relationship of this story is
   a. "Our father's house."
   b. "never did I pay attention to gate and hallway."
   c. "something of dignity and power."
   d. "A thousand times I passed through, laughing."

3. "One day when I was eleven years old I came home from school." (lines 30–31) The boy's mood on that day is apparently best explained by the words
   a. "It was one of those days when fate lurks in the corners . . ." (lines 31–32)
   b. "Uneasiness and anxiety grip our hearts, and we seek and find their presumed cause outside us." (lines 34–36)
   c. "That morning my father's face had worn a suffering and reproachful expression." (lines 41–42)
   d. "I had also been vexed by my best friend on that day." (line 51)

4. "He had recently boasted that his father earned seven marks a day, and I had answered at random that my father earned fourteen." (lines 54–56) It is most likely that
   a. the narrator is telling the truth.
   b. the narrator is lying because he knows his father is in serious financial difficulties.

    c. the narrator has no idea how much his father earns but that the amount is probably less than he has given.

    d. the narrator has no idea how much his father earns but it is undoubtedly far more than he has stated.

5. Oskar has "a thick skin that protected him from danger and humiliation." This is apparently true because

    a. Oskar has grown up among the poorer classes and has learned to be tough and self-reliant.

    b. Oskar has been sheltered and protected from hardship.

    c. Oskar is fourteen, while the narrator is eleven.

    d. Oskar's father is a professional man.

6. The narrator admires Oskar for his "secret." This "secret" is the fact that

    a. Oskar is smarter than the narrator.

    b. Oskar has more money than the narrator.

    c. Oskar is at home in his world.

    d. Oskar knows more than the narrator.

7. In the paragraph beginning at line 124, the narrator expresses a "wild, painful longing for purity, goodness, and virtue." (lines 168–169) He also says that the achievement of these longings seems, for him,

    a. rewarding.

    b. unimportant.

    c. accomplished.

    d. impossible.

8. At the time he is setting down his tale, the narrator's age is

    a. eleven.

    b. thirty.

    c. forty-one.

    d. not revealed.

9. As to the emotional conflicts the narrator suffered as a child, we know

    a. the conflicts disappeared when the narrator became an adult.

b. the conflicts remained with him when the narrator became an adult.

c. as a result of his childhood conflicts, the narrator became a superior adult.

d. nothing as to what happened in the narrator's adulthood.

10. From the passage beginning at line 231 and ending at line 244 it can reasonably be guessed that the person largely responsible for the boy's problems is

a. his father.

b. his sister.

c. his mother.

d. Oskar Weber.

11. The total pattern of actions and emotions in his father's rooms is best explained by saying that included in the narrator's mixed-up and secret feelings towards his father is

a. bewilderment.

b. admiration.

c. gratitude.

d. hostility.

Literary and Language Skills

STYLE AND MOOD

This story by Hermann Hesse is about the deepest, troubled feelings of a young boy. Feelings such as these are like a vivid dream or a nightmare. They are real and powerful. But, they are also vague and mysterious and almost impossible to explain or describe directly in words so that another person could grasp them clearly. Yet this writer does succeed, somehow, in making the innermost emotional life of the boy very real and close to the reader. He does not achieve this success by direct explanation or description. He does so by communicating a *mood* through his style of writing. He chooses his words so as to create in the reader an emotional state similar to that of the boy. Look at these excerpts from the story.

> "controlled by some outside power and heavy with fate."

> "Other acts ... cast long shadows over all the days of our lives."

> "But the hall and somber duskiness always came first."

> "something of punishment and guilty conscience."

> "one of those days when fate lurks in the corners."

These examples of the writer's style all contribute to the dominant mood of the story. They all contribute to an expression of a mood of darkness and despair, of powerlessness and helplessness, of fear and guilt, of nameless dread. They are slow and heavy in sound, rhythm, and movement. There are no facts; nothing much happens. They serve to bring the reader down into the shadowy, shapeless, fearful inner emotional life of the boy.

Exercise A

The examples which have been given and described above are typical of the style in which the tale of the boy is told. Find and list at least five more examples of such phrases and sentences.

Exercise B

The mood of this story is established through the frequent use of sentences and phrases of the type you listed in Exercise A. In addition, the reader is bombarded with individual words that help create the mood of darkness and despair, fear and helplessness. For example, the fifth paragraph of the story includes the following words: *guilty, dreams, suffering, dreary, lifeless, discouraging, helplessness, despair, small, powerless, senseless, loathsome.* Find and list at least 20 other similar words from the story.

Exercise C

Try a creative exercise in the use of words to establish mood in a story. Suppose you wanted to write a story to establish a mood opposite to the one of this story. What are some words with which you might bombard the mind of the reader?

Here are five to start you off: *sunshine*, *delightful*, *reward*, *lively*, *smiling*. Can you add 20 of your own?

Vocabulary in Context

A. Carefully examine each word in its context; then decide which definition is most appropriate.

1. **presumed** (line 36)
    a. actual
    b. predicted
    c. taken for granted
    d. false

2. **insipid** (line 43)
    a. healthful; welcome
    b. poisonous; harmful
    c. flavorless; dull
    d. filling

3. **impervious** (line 84)
    a. invisible
    b. undamageable; impenetrable
    c. enjoying
    d. helpless; defenseless

4. **ardent** (line 136)
    a. intensely enthusiastic
    b. tough
    c. dishonored
    d. seriously doubting

5. **vacillation** (line 190)
   a. hesitation
   b. cure
   c. choice
   d. rest

B. Match meaning and sentence context by writing the word which most suitably fills the blank in each sentence. (Note that two words, 6 and 7, from the previous lesson are included for review.)

1. **presumed**	6. **fanatical**
2. **insipid**	7. **esteem**
3. **impervious**	
4. **ardent**	
5. **vacillation**	

a. The restaurant had a good reputation, but the food we had was ___?___.

b. Once milk was held in the highest ___?___ as a practically perfect food, but now its fat content has caused it to be downgraded on the scale of nutritional value.

c. The company produced a glass so strong that it was ___?___ even to the force of a bullet.

d. Under the law, an accused person is ___?___ to be innocent until he is proven guilty.

e. Some people can make a decision and act swiftly while others are given to delay and ___?___.

f. The ___?___ admiration that Americans have for Thomas Jefferson is expressed in the beautiful memorial to him on the banks of the Potomac.

g. She was a ___?___ housekeeper and practically drove her family crazy with her constant straightening out and dusting.

286

REΛDINC 20

Until he was ten, each November he would watch the wagon containing the dogs and the bedding and food and guns and his father and Tennie's Jim, the Negro, and Sam Fathers, the Indian, son of a slave woman and a Chickasaw chief, depart on the road to town, to Jefferson, where Major 5 de Spain and the others would join them. To the boy, at seven and eight and nine, they were not going into the Big Bottom to hunt bear and deer, but to keep yearly rendezvous with the bear which they did not even intend to kill. Two weeks later they would return, with no trophy, no head and 10 skin. He had not expected it. He had not even been afraid it would be in the wagon. He believed that even after he was ten and his father would let him go too, for those two November weeks, he would merely make another one, along with his father and Major de Spain and General Compson and 15 the others, the dogs which feared to bay it and the rifles and shotguns which failed even to bleed it, in the yearly pageant of the old bear's furious immortality.

Then he heard the dogs. It was in the second week of his first time in the camp. He stood with Sam Fathers against a 20 big oak beside the faint crossing where they had stood each dawn for nine days now, hearing the dogs. He had heard them once before, one morning last week—a murmur, sourceless, echoing through the wet woods, swelling presently into separate voices which he could recognize and call by name. 25 He had raised and cocked the gun as Sam told him and stood

Excerpt from "The Bear." Copyright 1942 and renewed 1970 by Estelle Faulkner and Jill Faulkner Summers. Reprinted from GO DOWN, MOSES, by William Faulkner, by permission of Random House, Inc.

motionless again while the uproar, the invisible course, swept up and past and faded; it seemed to him that he could actually see the deer, the buck, blond, smoke-colored, elongated with speed, fleeing, vanishing, the woods, the gray solitude, still ringing even when the cries of the dogs had died away.

"Now let the hammers down," Sam said.

"You knew they were not coming here too," he said.

"Yes," Sam said. "I want you to learn how to do when you didn't shoot. It's after the chance for the bear or the deer has done already come and gone that men and dogs get killed."

"Anyway," he said, "it was just a deer."

Then on the tenth morning he heard the dogs again. And he readied the too-long, too-heavy gun as Sam had taught him, before Sam even spoke. But this time it was no deer, no ringing chorus of dogs running strong on a free scent, but a moiling yapping an octave too high, with something more than indecision and even abjectness in it, not even moving very fast, taking a long time to pass completely out of hearing, leaving even then somewhere in the air that echo, thin, slightly hysterical, abject, almost grieving, with no sense of a fleeing, unseen, smoke-colored, grass-eating shape ahead of it, and Sam who had taught him first of all to cock the gun and take position where he could see everywhere and then never move again, had himself moved up beside him; he could hear Sam breathing at his shoulder and he could see the arched curve of the old man's inhaling nostrils.

"Hah," Sam said. "Not even running. Walking."

"Old Ben!" the boy said. "But up here!" he cried. "Way up here!"

"He do it every year," Sam said. "Once. Maybe to see who in camp this time, if he can shoot or not. Whether we got the dog yet that can bay and hold him. He'll take them to the river, then he'll send them back home. We may as well go back, too; see how they look when they come back to camp."

When they reached the camp the hounds were already there, ten of them crouching back under the kitchen, the boy and Sam squatting to peer back into the obscurity where they huddled, quiet, the eyes luminous, glowing at them and vanishing, and no sound, only that effluvium of something more than dog, stronger than dog and not just animal, just beast, because still there had been nothing in front of that abject and almost painful yapping save the solitude, the wilderness, so that when the eleventh hound came in at noon and with all the others watching—even old Uncle Ash, who called himself first a cook—Sam daubed the tattered ear and the raked shoulder with turpentine and axle grease, to the boy it was still no living creature, but the wilderness which, leaning for the moment down, had patted lightly once the hound's temerity.

"Just like a man," Sam said. "Just like folks. Put off as long as she could having to be brave, knowing all the time that sooner or later she would have to be brave once to keep on living with herself, and knowing all the time beforehand what was going to happen to her when she done it."

That afternoon, himself on the one-eyed wagon mule which did not mind the smell of blood nor, as they told him, of bear, and with Sam on the other one, they rode for more than three hours through the rapid, shortening winter day. They followed no path, no trail even that he could see; almost at once they were in a country which he had never seen before. Then he knew why Sam had made him ride the mule which would not spook. The sound one stopped short and tried to whirl and bolt even as Sam got down, blowing its breath, jerking and wrenching at the rein while Sam held it, coaxing it forward with his voice, since he could not risk tying it, drawing it forward while the boy got down from the marred one.

Then, standing beside Sam in the gloom of the dying afternoon, he looked down at the rotted overturned log, gutted and scored with claw marks and, in the wet earth beside it,

the print of the enormous warped two-toed foot. He knew
100 now what he had smelled when he peered under the kitchen
where the dogs huddled. He realized for the first time that
the bear which had run in his listening and loomed in his
dreams since before he could remember to the contrary, and
which, therefore, must have existed in the listening and
105 dreams of his father and Major de Spain and even old General
Compson, too, before they began to remember in their turn,
was a mortal animal, and that if they had departed for the
camp each November without any actual hope of bringing its
trophy back, it was not because it could not be slain, but
110 because so far they had no actual hope to.

"Tomorrow," he said.

"We'll try tomorrow," Sam said. "We ain't got the dog
yet."

"We've got eleven. They ran him this morning."

115 "It won't need but one," Sam said. "He ain't here. Maybe
he ain't nowhere. The only other way will be for him to run
by accident over somebody that has a gun."

"That wouldn't be me," the boy said. "It will be Walter or
Major or—"

120 "It might," Sam said. "You watch close in the morning.
Because he's smart. That's how come he has lived this long.
If he gets hemmed up and has to pick out somebody to run
over, he will pick out you."

"How?" the boy said. "How will he know—" He ceased.
125 "You mean he already knows me, that I ain't never been
here before, ain't had time to find out yet whether I—" He
ceased again, looking at Sam, the old man whose face revealed
nothing until it smiled. He said humbly, not even amazed,
"It was me he was watching. I don't reckon he did need to
130 come but once."

The next morning they left the camp three hours before
daylight. They rode this time because it was too far to walk,
even the dogs in the wagon; again the first gray light found
him in a place which he had never seen before, where Sam

290

had placed him and told him to stay and then departed. With 135
the gun which was too big for him, which did not even belong
to him, but to Major de Spain, and which he had fired only
once—at a stump on the first day, to learn the recoil and how
to reload it—he stood against a gum tree beside a little bayou
whose black still water crept without movement out of a 140
canebrake and crossed a small clearing and into cane again,
where, invisible, a bird—the big woodpecker called Lord-to-
God by Negroes—clattered at a dead limb.

It was a stand like any other, dissimilar only in incidentals
to the one where he had stood each morning for ten days; a 145
territory new to him, yet no less familiar than that other one
which, after almost two weeks, he had come to believe he
knew a little—the same solitude, the same loneliness through
which human beings had merely passed without altering it,
leaving no mark, no scar, which looked exactly as it must 150
have looked when the first ancestor of Sam Fathers' Chickasaw predecessors crept into it and looked about, club or
stone ax or bone arrow drawn and poised; different only because, squatting at the edge of the kitchen, he smelled the
hounds huddled and cringing beneath it and saw the raked 155
ear and shoulder of the one who, Sam said, had had to be
brave once in order to live with herself, and saw yesterday in
the earth beside the gutted log the print of the living foot.

He heard no dogs at all. He never did hear them. He only
heard the drumming of the woodpecker stop short off and 160
knew that the bear was looking at him. He never saw it. He
did not know whether it was in front of him or behind him.
He did not move, holding the useless gun, which he had not
even had warning to cock and which even now he did not
cock, tasting in his saliva that taint as of brass which he knew 165
now because he had smelled it when he peered under the
kitchen at the huddled dogs.

Then it was gone. As abruptly as it had ceased, the woodpecker's dry, monotonous clatter set up again, and after a
while he even believed he could hear the dogs—a murmur, 170

scarce a sound even, which he had probably been hearing for some time before he even remarked it, drifting into hearing and then out again, dying away. They came nowhere near him. If it was a bear they ran, it was another bear. It was
175 Sam himself who came out of the cane and crossed the bayou, followed by the injured bitch of yesterday. She was almost at heel, like a bird dog, making no sound. She came and crouched against his leg, trembling, staring off into the cane.

180   "I didn't see him," he said. "I didn't, Sam!"

    "I know it," Sam said. "He done the looking. You didn't hear him neither, did you?"

    "No," the boy said. "I—"

    "He's smart," Sam said. "Too smart." He looked down at
185 the hound, trembling faintly and steadily against the boy's knee. From the raked shoulder a few drops of fresh blood oozed and clung. "Too big. We ain't got the dog yet. But maybe someday. Maybe not next time. But someday."

    So I must see him, he thought. *I must look at him*. Other-
190 wise, it seemed to him that it would go on like this forever, as it had gone on with his father and Major de Spain, who was older than his father, and even with old General Compson, who had been old enough to be a brigade commander in 1865. Otherwise, it would go on so forever, next time and
195 next time, after and after and after. It seemed to him that he could see the two of them, himself and the bear, shadowy in the limbo from which time emerged, becoming time; the old bear absolved of mortality and himself partaking, sharing a little of it, enough of it. And he knew now what he had
200 smelled in the huddled dogs and tasted in his saliva. He recognized fear. *So I will have to see him*, he thought, with-out dread or even hope. *I will have to look at him*.

Reading Comprehension

The exercises that follow are based on the passage you have just read. Each exercise consists of an incomplete statement followed by four choices. Select the choice that best completes the statement. Go back to the passage for rereading to whatever extent is necessary to help you choose your answer.

1. "... shotguns which failed even to bleed it ..." (line 17)
   Here the word "bleed" is used to mean
   a. kill.
   b. frighten.
   c. wound.
   d. entrap.

2. "... the yearly pageant of the old bear's furious immortality." (lines 17–18) These words are used to suggest
   a. the boy's early impression of the nature of the annual November hunting expedition.
   b. that the bear is supernatural and immortal.
   c. that the adults worshiped the bear as though he were a primitive god.
   d. the boy's eagerness for the time when he would be old enough to join the others.

3. The action of the story begins with Sam Fathers teaching the boy an important hunting lesson. The purpose of the lesson is to
   a. prevent the accidental killing during the hunt of another hunter or one of the dogs.
   b. show the boy that a hunter sometimes thinks he sees the hunted animal when none is there.
   c. teach the boy he must shoot fast.
   d. practice the cocking and uncocking of the firing mechanism.

4. The name of the "immortal" bear is
   a. Old Ben.
   b. Ash.
   c. Two-toe.
   d. not given.

5. In the remarks beginning, "He do it every year" (line 57), Sam is referring to
   a. the hound.
   b. the boy's father.
   c. himself.
   d. the bear.

6. In his remarks beginning, "Just like a man" (line 78), Sam is referring to
   a. the eleventh hound.
   b. the bear.
   c. Uncle Ash.
   d. the wilderness.

7. The boy first realizes that the bear is a mortal animal when he
   a. smells the huddling hounds.
   b. sees the bear's footprint.
   c. sees Sam's mule "spook."
   d. is ten.

8. "How?" the boy said. "How will he know—" (line 124) From Sam, the boy learns in surprising answer to this question that
   a. no one has actually ever seen the bear.
   b. the boy's father has been watching him closely.
   c. Walter and Major don't carry a gun.
   d. the bear has been stalking *him*.

9. Waiting in his stand against a gum tree, the boy first becomes aware that the bear is looking at him because
   a. he smells the bear, "tasting in his saliva that taint of brass."
   b. he sees the bear.
   c. he hears the dogs.

d. he realizes that the woodpecker has stopped drumming.

10. In the last paragraph, the boy expresses the feeling that if he is to succeed in the quest after the bear, where his father, the Major, and the General have failed, he must
    a. face the bear without dread or hope.
    b. outwit the bear.
    c. go on forever like the others.
    d. learn to shoot straight and fast.

Literary and Language Skills

SYMBOLISM

The deepest and strongest emotions and thoughts are often complicated and vague. It is hard to pin them down in words that describe or explain. Instead, we often use *symbols* to express and represent deep and strong emotions and thoughts.

Some symbols are common and well-known objects. For example, the flag of a country is a symbol used to express and represent the patriotic feelings of the citizens. Sometimes the word rather than the object itself is used. For example, "light" is commonly used as a symbol of knowledge or of goodness. Some other well-known symbols of these types are: the dove for peace, green for jealousy, snow for purity.

Symbols are sometimes used by the writer of fiction to express deep and complicated feelings or themes. Such symbols are original, created by the writer to fit his particular purpose. The reader who wants to get the most out of a story will need to recognize and understand a writer's use of symbols. Two examples of symbolism in fiction will help you.

The Call of the Wild is a famous novel by Jack London which you may have read. It is the story of a big, strong dog named Buck who is stolen from his master's home and sent to the northern wilderness of the Yukon, where such dogs were needed to pull sleds. At one level, the story of Buck is simply an action-packed adventure story. At another level, the story has deeper symbolic meaning. In the wilderness, in order to survive, Buck sheds the ways of civilization and falls back on the deep and primitive instincts that form his inner makeup. Jack London uses Buck as a symbol for man. Man, too, says London, is basically a creature of powerful primitive instincts and his primitive, savage nature has been only lightly covered by the thin layer of civilized learning. This symbolism is strongly suggested by passages in the story such as the following, in which Buck dreams of a primitive caveman of prehistoric days—the ancestor of modern man.

Best of all, perhaps, he loved to lie near the fire, hind legs crouched under him, fore legs stretched out in front, head raised, and eyes blinking dreamily at the flames. Sometimes he thought of Judge Miller's big house in the sun-kissed Santa Clara Valley, and of the cement swimming-tank, and Ysabel, the Mexican hairless, and Toots, the Japanese pug; but oftener he remembered the man in the red sweater, the death of Curly, the great fight with Spitz, and the good things he had eaten or would like to eat. He was not homesick. The Sunland was very dim and distant, and such memories had no power over him. Far more potent were the memories of his heredity that gave things he had never seen before a seeming familiarity; the instincts (which were but the memories of his ancestors become habits) which had lapsed in later days, and still later, in him, quickened and became alive again.

Sometimes as he crouched there, blinking dreamily at the flames, it seemed that the flames were of another fire, and that as he crouched by this other fire he saw another and different man from the half-breed cook before him. This other man was shorter of leg and longer of arm, with muscles that were stringy and knotty rather than rounded and swelling. The hair of this man was long and matted, and his head slanted back under it from the eyes. He uttered strange sounds, and seemed very much afraid of the darkness, into which he peered continually, clutching in his hand, which hung midway between knee and foot, a stick with a heavy stone made fast to the end. He was all but naked, a ragged and fire-scorched skin hanging part way down his back, but on his body there was much hair. In some places, across the chest and shoulders and down the outside of the arms and thighs, it was matted into almost a thick fur. He did not stand erect, but with trunk inclined forward from the hips, on legs that bent at the knees. About his body there was a peculiar springiness, or resiliency, almost catlike, and a quick alertness as of one who lived in perpetual fear of things seen and unseen.

At other times this hairy man squatted by the fire with head between his legs and slept. On such occasions his elbows were on his knees, his hands clasped above his head as though to shed rain by the hairy arms. And beyond that fire, in the circling darkness, Buck could see many gleaming coals, two by two, always two by two, which he knew to be the eyes of great beasts of prey. And he could hear the crashing of their bodies through the undergrowth, and the noises they made in the night. And dreaming there by the Yukon bank, with lazy eyes blinking at the fire, these sounds and sights of another world would make the hair to rise along his back and stand on end across his shoulders and up his neck, till he whimpered low and suppressedly, or growled softly . . .

Another famous novel is *The Red Badge of Courage* by Stephen Crane. This Civil War novel begins with a scene on the day before a great battle. That night the new recruits of the Northern army look across the river on the other side of which is camped the enemy whom they will battle the next day. Crane writes:

> ". . . one could see across it the red eyelike gleam of hostile campfires set in the low brows of distant hills."

In this description, the enemy camp is seen to appear like a monster with gleaming red eyes set in low brows. This monster has symbolic meaning. It represents the dread and fear in the minds of the young inexperienced soldiers as they anticipate the terrible events of the battle they will soon be in. Throughout this story, Crane uses symbols of this kind to express the innermost, unspoken feelings of the soldiers.

Exercise A

How does a reader recognize symbolism in a story? If an ordinary thing or object is treated in an unusual way or given unusual characteristics, it may be intended by the writer to have special meaning as a symbol. Consider Old Ben, the bear, in William Faulkner's story. Is Old Ben merely a bear, or is he a symbol of some larger meaning? Old Ben is unusual in several ways. An example is the annual November expedition by the adults to hunt him, an expedition that is never successful, so that the young boy thinks it is only some kind of pageant or ceremony that the adults perform. What other examples can you give of ways in which Old Ben is unusual?

Exercise B

If Old Ben has a number of unusual characteristics, then it is likely that Faulkner intended him to be not only a bear, but also a symbol of larger meaning. Often the writer will support and clarify the meaning of a symbol by discussing directly the symbolic meaning. Find a passage in the story in which Faulkner seems to be directly discussing Old Ben's meaning as a symbol.

Exercise C

Writers use symbols to express meanings which are hard to pin down in ordinary descriptions and explanations. It is up to the reader to put into words for himself the meaning of a symbol in a story. Keep in mind your answers to Exercises A and B. How would you explain the symbolic meaning of Old Ben?

SENTENCE STYLE

Every fine writer has his own unique sentence style. That sentence style is one of the important means by which the writer's work is given freshness and force. William Faulkner, who is one of the great American writers of this century, has an unusual and strong sentence style. He packs a great many powerful words into one sentence. Learning a little bit about how his sentences are composed will help you to appreciate his writing and will help you in your own composition of sentences.

Exercise D

Here is a typical long, strong Faulkner sentence.

> "Until he was ten, each November he would watch the wagon containing the dogs and the bedding and food and guns and his father and Tennie's Jim, the Negro, and Sam Fathers, the Indian, son of a slave woman and a Chickasaw chief, depart on the road to town, to Jefferson, where Major de Spain and the others would join them."

A notable element of the style of this sentence is the inclusion of a long and interesting list of *words in series*. Write the nouns that make up this list. Include only the main nouns and omit all modifying words or phrases. (Hint: every item in your list will be a single word, except one—the name of a person. Another hint: each noun in your list will be the object of the verbal *containing*. Still another: there are seven nouns in the series.)

Exercise E

In the same sentence, Faulkner also uses *words and phrases in apposition* as an element in his sentence style. Two of the nouns you listed in answer to Exercise D are followed by words in apposition. What are the two appositional words or phrases? Elsewhere in the sentence, one prepositional phrase is used in apposition to another. What are the two phrases?

Exercise F

Can you compose sentences modeled after Faulkner's in the use of *words in a series* and *words or phrases in apposition?* Here are two examples modeled after Faulkner's style for you to examine.

1. Among the hordes that sought their way to the beach late that hot afternoon were mothers with infants, teenagers, the local high-school population, men with night-shift jobs, elderly people, the retired who no longer worked or had families, vacationers, dwellers in the depths of the city, dwellers in the near-by suburbs, the usual daily trade, the surfers, snorkelers, and sun-worshipers.

2. Most sought relief in the surf, the cooling, tangy, foaming, briny, ever-moving waters, swimming, floating, splashing, diving, plunging out of sight of the sun, standing still waist-deep, sitting at water's edge where frothy bubbles laved their legs.

Now write two or three sentences of your own modeled after Faulkner in the use of words in series and words or phrases in apposition.

Vocabulary in Context

A. Carefully examine each word in its context; then decide which definition is most appropriate.

1. **rendezvous** (line 8)
   a. lengthy talks
   b. death
   c. appointed meeting
   d. quarreling

2. **elongated** (line 29)
   a. withered
   b. unseen
   c. stretched out
   d. worn out

3. **abject** (line 47)
   a. downcast
   b. protecting
   c. peaceful
   d. resting

4. **limbo** (line 197)
   a. a game of chance
   b. giant hand
   c. hourglass
   d. place of forgetfulness

5. **partaking** (line 198)
   a. voting
   b. placing
   c. panting
   d. sharing

B. Match meaning and sentence context by writing the word which most suitably fills the blank in each sentence. (Note that two words, 6 and 7, from the previous lesson are included for review.)

301

1. rendezvous
2. elongated
3. abject
4. limbo
5. partaking
6. impervious
7. ardent

a. He was so exhausted that he fell into a deep and dreamless ___?___ as soon as he lay down.

b. As the comet came closer to the sun, its tail became more and more ___?___ behind it.

c. The conspirators arranged a secret, midnight ___?___.

d. The beaches are filled with ___?___ lovers of the sun, eagerly roasting their skins to well-done.

e. Pasteur's confidence in his germ theory of disease made him ___?___ to the puny attacks of his opponents.

f. The hungry family joined in ___?___ of the delicious-looking turkey.

g. The injured quarterback limped off the field, aching in body and ___?___ in spirit.

GROWING
(Unit Four)

Vocabulary in Context

WORD LIST

1. abject	14. florid
2. ardent	15. impervious
3. bigots	16. insipid
4. burly	17. limbo
5. conciliate	18. luminous
6. deft	19. partaking
7. degraded	20. presumed
8. deluded	21. rendezvous
9. disposition	22. tantalizing
10. elongated	23. vacillation
11. esteem	24. vulnerable
12. excursion	25. wariness
13. fanatical	

Exercise A—SYNONYMS

The three words in each group below appear together in Roget's Thesaurus because they are synonyms or are closely related in meaning. Select the list word which you feel also can be added to each group as a synonym or as a word closely related in meaning.

1. shamed, disgraced, humiliated
2. shining, aglow, resplendent
3. watchfulness, prudence, caution
4. skilled, accomplished, competent
5. tendency, temperament, inclination
6. honor, respect, reverence
7. uncertainty, hesitation, indecision
8. tasteless, flat, drab
9. gaudy, ornate, colorful
10. sharing, cooperating, participating

Exercise B—CONTEXTS

A number of pairs of these list words are related in meaning. In some cases there is a similarity in the meanings. In other cases there is a degree of oppositeness. Look at each pair below. Which pairs are similar in meaning? Which are more nearly opposite in meaning? In which is there little or no relationship in meaning? (Note: forms of the words have been changed when necessary so that all pairs are in the same form.) (Helpful hint: 3 of the pairs are similar in meaning, 5 of the pairs are more nearly opposite in meaning, 2 of the pairs have little or no relationship in meaning.)

1. degraded—esteemed
2. ardent—insipid
3. luminous—presumed
4. abject—degraded
5. rendezvous—elongation
6. fanatical—bigoted
7. tantalizing—conciliating
8. impervious—vulnerable
9. wariness—vacillation
10. florid—insipid

Exercise C—MORE CONTEXTS

Following each list word below are the names of three famous people or events of history. Which historical name is best matched with the list word?

1. **degraded**
   Benedict Arnold   Daniel Boone   King Alfred

2. **burly**
   Charles Lindbergh   Cassius   Winston Churchill

3. **vacillation**
   Alexander the Great   Neville Chamberlain   Napoleon

4. **bigots**
   Fabian Society   Abolitionists   Ku Klux Klan

5. **fanatical**
   Thomas Jefferson   Robespierre   Queen Elizabeth

6. **esteem**
   Florence Nightingale   Andrew Johnson   King Louis XIV

7. **conciliate**
   General Custer   Henry Clay   Hitler

8. **rendezvous**
   Yalta   Appalachia   Canary Islands

9. **limbo**
   Los Angeles   Paris   Devil's Island

10. **deft**
    Czar Nicholas   Thomas Edison   President Harding

Exercise D—ANALOGIES

Decide what the relationship is between the pair of words given first. From the four choices, select the pair of words that comes closest to expressing the same relationship as the given pair.

1. degraded : benefactor
   a. traitor : disgraced
   b. traitor : patriot
   c. honored : evildoer
   d. employee : promoted

2. presumed : proved
   a. theory : fact
   b. unknown : known
   c. light : darkness
   d. come : gone

3. rendezvous : lovers
   a. meeting : parting
   b. plot : conspiracy
   c. session : court
   d. talk : secret

4. vulnerable : fort
   a. gun : tank
   b. leaking : dam
   c. opening : closing
   d. attack : defense

5. wariness : opponent
   a. cat : mouse
   b. cat : dog
   c. war : peace
   d. trust : ally

Literary and Language Skills

Exercise E—OVERVIEW

Through your work in this book you have learned about many literary and language skills. Your understanding of these will add greatly to your power as a reader and writer. This exercise will review and reinforce your understanding of such elements as: allusions; quotations; incongruity and humor; verbal imagery through sense appeal; the power of suggestion; appreciating the setting; understanding characterization; similes and metaphors; sentence composition and style; and symbolism.

Below are sentences or short passages taken from the works of fine writers. First read each passage, then answer the questions that follow it.

> Not from her did the young ones get those water-clear eyes. Her eyes were black and shrewd and searching, a band of hair showed black streaked with gray, her seamed

dry face was brown as seasoned bark, and she walked in her rubber boots with the stride of a man.

—*Holiday*, Katherine Ann Porter

1. Use the power of suggestion and decide the relationship between the woman being described and "the young ones."

2. In the same way decide where the young ones *did* get those water-clear eyes.

3. What trait is suggested by the description of the woman's walk?

4. What simile supports the same suggestion?

5. What colors are painted into this description? How do they affect the characterization of the woman?

6. " . . . she walked in her rubber boots with the stride of a man." What are the two prepositional phrases?

7. By changing the position of prepositional phrases, give two different ways in which the above statement could be composed.

The voices that he knew so well, the common words, the quiet of the classroom when the voices paused and the silence was filled by the sound of softly browsing cattle as the other boys munched their lunches tranquilly, lulled his aching soul.

—*A Portait of the Artist as a Young Man*, James Joyce

8. Give the three words used in a series as subject of the verb "lulled."

9. Give two examples of sense-appealing imagery (sound).

10. Give three words from the sentence that help to contribute to a mood of peacefulness and harmony.

11. What are the two parts of this sentence connected by *and?*

12. Which phrase helps to picture the *setting* surrounding the schoolhouse?

13. Name at least one sight your imagination can add to the setting through the power of suggestion.

> It was as if everything were looking at me with such matter-of-factness and such untroubled conscience, the town and the church tower, the fields and the path, the flowering grass and the butterflies, and as if everything pretty and pleasurable, everything that usually gave me delight, were now alien and under an evil spell.
>
> —*Klingsor's Last Summer*, Hermann Hesse

14. Complete the series of nouns that begins with the word "town."

15. This series is used in apposition with one pronoun. What is the pronoun?

16. Which words in the sentence summarize the mood that should be created by the series of nouns?

17. Which words state the contradictory inner mood of the speaker?

18. Through the power of suggestion, what conclusion can you come to about the speaker?

> Walking to the taffrail, I was in time to make out, on the very edge of a darkness thrown by a towering black mass like the very gateway of Erebus—yes, I was in time to catch an evanescent glimpse of my white hat left behind to mark the spot where the sharer of my cabin and of my thoughts, as though he were my second self, had lowered himself into the water to take his punishment: a free man, a proud swimmer striking out for a new destiny.
>
> —*The Secret Sharer*, Joseph Conrad

19. What is the setting here? Which words suggest that setting to you?

20. Which phrase appears to be an allusion to mythology? What is your guess as to its meaning?

21. Several words and phrases suggest a symbolic meaning. What are they?

22. What meaning of the word "evanescent" is suggested to you by its context in the sentence?

23. What is the most vivid sight image in the sentence?

24. What two prepositional phrases are connected by *and* to create an interesting and thought-provoking meaning?

25. What kind of phrase does the sentence begin with?

26. Bearing in mind all the information you get from this sentence, what is your guess as to what the "towering black mass" is?

The Montana sunset lay between two mountains like a gigantic bruise from which dark arteries spread themselves over a poisoned sky.
—*A Diamond as Big as the Ritz*, F. Scott Fitzgerald

27. What literary device is illustrated by the words "like a gigantic bruise"?

28. How do the words "dark arteries" and "poisoned" fit into the meaning? What is the whole picture created?

29. What strong (and serious, not humorous) incongruity is contained in this sentence? What meaning is suggested?

30. Rewrite the sentence so that it contains a metaphor.

In the morning the train was near Paris, and after the American lady had come out from the washroom, looking very wholesome and middle-aged and American in spite of not having slept, and had taken the cloth off the birdcage and hung the cage in the sun, she went back to the restaurant car for breakfast.

—*A Canary for One*, Ernest Hemingway

31. What is the setting here?

32. What element of humorous incongruity does the sentence contain?

33. Which adjective also seems incongruous and suggests that the author may be treating the character with mocking humor?

34. What is the name of the two sentence parts that the first *and* connects?

35. With what other verbs is the verb "had come" connected by the conjunction *and*?

Themes for Growing

FOR THINKING

A few years ago a psychologist wrote a book called *Games People Play*. The book was a popular best-seller for a long time. Many examples of the "games" people "play" occur in the passages you have read in this book. What "games" does Herbie Bookbinder "play" when he first meets Lucille Glass? What "games" does Cress Delahanty "play"? Bottles Barton? The narrator in *When You Run Away*? From other passages, select three or four other examples of your own of game-playing.

FOR DISCUSSION

What is the real meaning of "The Games People Play"? What explanations are there for this game-playing? Why may young people in their growing years be noticeably given to game-playing?

FOR WRITING

Select a person you know who you feel does a lot of game-playing. (You can use yourself if you wish.) First, tell something about the person generally. Then tell about the person's game-playing. Finally, explain what you feel about the person's game-playing.

INDEX TO LITERARY AND LANGUAGE SKILLS